INTRODUCING THE SOCIO
OF FOOD & EATING

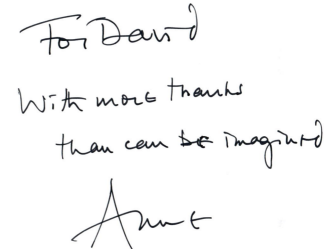

For David

With more thanks
than can be imagined

Also available from Bloomsbury

THE FOOD AND FOLKLORE READER
Lucy Long

FOOD STUDIES
Willa Zhen

THE HANDBOOK OF FOOD RESEARCH
edited by Anne Murcott, Warren Belasco & Peter Jackson

THE SOCIOLOGY OF FOOD
Jean-Pierre Poulain

WHY FOOD MATTERS
Melissa Caldwell

INTRODUCING THE SOCIOLOGY OF FOOD & EATING

Anne Murcott

BLOOMSBURY ACADEMIC

LONDON • NEW YORK • OXFORD • NEW DELHI • SYDNEY

BLOOMSBURY ACADEMIC
Bloomsbury Publishing Plc
50 Bedford Square, London, WC1B 3DP, UK
1385 Broadway, New York, NY 10018, USA

BLOOMSBURY, BLOOMSBURY ACADEMIC and the Diana logo are trademarks
of Bloomsbury Publishing Plc

First published in Great Britain 2019

A catalogue record for this book is available from the British Library.

A catalog record for this book is available from the Library of Congress.

ISBN: HB: 978-1-3500-2202-7
       PB: 978-1-3500-2201-0
       ePDF: 978-1-3500-2203-4
       ePub: 978-1-3500-2204-1

Typeset by RefineCatch Limited, Bungay, Suffolk
Printed and bound in Great Britain

To find out more about our authors and books visit www.bloomsbury.com
and sign up for our newsletters.

In memory of my father

Simmon Latutin G.C. (1916–1944)

CONTENTS

PREFACE

Nothing remotely like the phrase 'the sociology of food and eating' could be found when I edited a small collection of specially commissioned essays using it as the title (Murcott 1983a). Thereafter my work covers a wide range of topics – conceptions of meals (1982) GM foodstuffs (1999a, 2001) changes in taste during pregnancy (1988b) food as national identity (1996) the history of UK food and nutrition policy (1994, 1999b) women's ideas of 'good' food (1993) the elusiveness of 'eating' (2013b) etc. – developing ethnographic investigations, textual studies, and devising symbolic interactionist analyses.

Three decades later it has become a cliché to observe how greatly and rapidly the field has expanded (Murcott 2013a). The broader backdrop is, of course, the huge rise in personal, public, practical and policy, never mind celebrity and commercial interest in what and how people eat, in who has too much and who has too little. An ability to pick an informed way through this deluge of discussion and debate is needed as a sound basis for helping assess the rights and wrongs of it all. My purpose is, however, not to give advice about what to do, but to contribute to providing that firm basis. For the expansion of research has not been matched by a sufficiently steady improvement in quality. There is a tendency to rely far too heavily on reproducing what undeniably thoughtful journalists and food writers have to offer in place of well-grounded sociological appraisal. Furthermore, grand generalizations are too readily based on the self-referential preoccupations about food and eating of those in wealthy countries, with too little heed to comparison historically or geographically. These and more limitations find their way into textbooks. As a result, undergraduate students in particular are not being as well served as they deserve.

It would be very foolish to think that this book could remedy every ill detectable in existing contributions. And this is not the place for critiques of poor-quality contributions. Instead the book tries to exemplify what is good, distinctively sociological (or similar) work. Evidence lies at the heart of the discipline, requiring concomitant attention to the manner in which a topic is conceptualized for investigation, the way good-quality appropriate evidence is amassed and the manner in which it is to be interpreted. These are encapsulated in this book's talking of 'sociological thinking'.

It would be equally foolish to imagine this book could be comprehensive in its coverage of relevant topics or in the range of sociological approaches and theoretical perspectives represented. The scope is limited to the ingestion of solid items (but on water see Wilk 2006, on alcoholic accompaniments to meals see Zubaida 2014). Omitted completely is consideration of items other than sources of nourishment that go into the mouth, from chewing gum (Redclift 2004), drugs of all kinds, stimulants such as caffeine, khat, coca leaf or tobacco, from charcoal- coal- or earth-eating (geophagia) or other 'unorthodox' items (McClancy, Henry and Macbeth 2007). Equally there is no space to discuss the culturally and historically moveable lines between the categories of foods, drink or medicines (Adelman and Haushofer 2018). Social aspects of conditions such as eating disorders or other diet-related medical conditions (e.g. diabetes or food allergy) are also excluded, as is analysis of the social and political aspects of obesity (Guthman 2011, Monaghan 2008).

The main pedagogic intent of this book concerns identifying and conveying what is peculiarly sociological – perspectives shared with its close relatives of anthropology, cultural geography and social history. These are distinct from the increasing clamour of various popular, policy and practitioner voices commenting on food, also different from more distant disciplinary contributions. This is not to claim superiority of the sociological over other disciplines. Neither is it to debunk or decry commentaries from other quarters, even though it strongly advocates scientific scepticism. Rather, it aims to illuminate something different from them, something that also has a value when trying to understand what is going on, along with stressing the importance of a stronger, evidenced, basis for effective action.

The book is introductory in two ways. It presents the sociology of food and eating to readers who have not met it before. It also aims to introduces the discipline of sociology via discussions of research on food and eating. Either way, no previous familiarity with the discipline (or indeed with any of the social sciences) is assumed. But it is not just to serve undergraduates. It is also to stand as an introduction for graduate students turning to the study of food and society for the first time, and indeed, for those known to academic publishers as 'interested general readers'. The text keeps technical vocabulary to a minimum and explains significant terms when they are introduced.

Above all, in placing evidence at the centre, this book seeks to make sociological thinking clearer, more explicit and based on something more secure – more scholarly even – than has always been sufficiently obvious in the enormous expansion of the field. Furthermore, it attempts to contribute to the much-needed improvement in quality by introducing research procedures – design, method, occasionally ethics – wherever feasible. The book does not rely on reciting 'findings' but emphasises concentrating on what sociological thinking might look like in the search for good quality evidence which lies at its heart.

****

A word is needed about the reproduction on the cover of 'Breakfast', a 1955 painting by Alfred Janes.[1] Incidentally my reasons for choosing to reproduce the work are unlikely to have crossed the artist's mind, for many of the pieces Janes made during the 1950s deal with his preoccupation at the time with the way hands and faces come together. Ordinarily I am vehemently opposed to sociology book covers carrying illustrations of people, let alone sociology books on food that are decorated with gorgeous displays of fruit or nineteenth-century grocers' shop fronts, shopping trolleys/carts or cheery picnics. For newcomers to sociology are often taken aback that the discipline can be so intensely abstract and I can see no reason for a cover to mislead them further. In addition to admiring the painting, I have a particular reason for making an exception here, which is where Chapter One starts.

ACKNOWLEDGEMENTS

This book nearly did not get written, and once begun almost did not get finished. Just as I started, 18 months of major construction work (still continuing as I write) began immediately next door with no advance notice, becoming so unbearably disruptive as to make work impossible. That this book has appeared is thanks to the many good friends who, in addition to family, kindly offered space to work: Alan Berrill, Andrew George, Jane Hill, Colin Hutchens, Hilly Janes, Virginia Low, Gerry McMullan, David McVicar, Jeanette Page, Sara Shepherd, Sarah Weir and most particularly those who, for extended periods, generously housed me, my laptop, piles of books and mounds of papers: Hilary Rose and Steven Rose; Lindy Sharpe and Ian Jack; Chris Thompson and Dorothy Thompson; Anne Pyburn and Rick Wilk.

Over the last few years, four people, both long standing colleagues and firm friends, have become even more important. Indeed, this book owes its very existence to Hugh Campbell. Until he suggested I ought to write it, nothing of the kind had crossed my mind. Thereafter, he and David Evans encouraged me to pursue the suggestion in the most constructive and creative way imaginable continuing to be especially supportive, listening, reading and offering invaluable comments on drafts at every stage – and much more besides. I am particularly grateful to Hugh for the opportunity to try out early plans by running a 2016 undergraduate summer school at the University of Otago. I thank them both for generously allowing me to draw heavily on our co-authored article for a section in Chapter 9. My deep debt to them both, especially Hugh, is far greater than these thanks can convey.

Then there is Peter Jackson with whom I have collaborated on various projects. Our discussions continue to expand my thinking about food and the social sciences. He kindly read the entire first draft resulting in thoughtful and sharp-eyed observations which greatly improved subsequent revisions. As important as the other three is Lindy Sharpe who brings acumen, detailed knowledge and good friendship to our regular late afternoon conversations about food and society. She is an inestimable, companionable mainstay.

At the University of Otago I must thank David Reynolds who worked diligently as summer school tutor while finalising his MA thesis and administrative staff, Nicki Topliss and Susan Davies at CSAFE, Pam Jemmett and Helen O'Sullivan at SGSW. Friends and colleagues who always make my visits to Dunedin most congenial include Helen Leach, Henrik Moller, Fiona Stirling and, above all, Marion Familton who is forever especially good and supportive company. I am grateful for the summer school students' good humour, candour (horrified on discovering that, unimaginably, many in 1950s Britain had no fridge) and willingness patiently to tolerate an English professor who needed explanations about Dunedin student foodways.

I must also thank others (too many for all to be named) for their conversations and comments over many years. Professor Emerita Virginia Olesen (UCSF), now in her nineties, must be mentioned first. Without her enthusiastic response in 1976 to the very early work, my research on food may well have come to nothing. I have been fortunate to remain in touch with her ever since. Vying for first mention is the late Professor Emeritus Michael Banton, another nonagenarian, whose courses on social theory and social class I attended as an undergraduate at the University of Edinburgh. This book in particular has benefited from our many conversations about how sociological work should be done and the text has been improved by his discerning eye. Roger Dickinson, Katie Graf, Lizzie Hull, Jakob Klein, James Staples and Sami Zubaida generously provided timely comments on early drafts of various sections. Other colleagues/friends whose conversations are always thought-provoking include: Sue Aldworth, Helen Atkinson, Andy Balmer, Jane Barrett, Rosie Blau, Lissa Caldwell, John Coveney, Robert Dingwall, Joy Dobbs, Jukka Gronow, Bente Halkier, Louise Hide, Lotte Holm, Ian Jack, Unni Kjærnes, Johanna Mäkelä, Jone L. Pierce, Krishnendu Ray, Polly Russell, José Sobral, Patrick Wallis, Alan Warde, Stefan Wahlen, Helena Webb, Harry West, Rick Wilk and especially the late, much missed, Sid Mintz. I am also grateful to Georgiana Parvan, Shola Radford and Susan Moore. Anonymous reviewers offered insightful comments.

Library staff are far too infrequently thanked, and there are many in various university, national and public libraries worldwide without whose patient help, throughout my career, my work would have been far slower and much harder. Charlotte Davey flexibly accepted employment to my timetable to help complete the references. I am extremely grateful for her conscientious work and good company. Colleagues at Bloomsbury have provided support and advice throughout; I am grateful to Miriam Cantwell, Jennifer Schmidt, Molly Beck and Lucy Carroll. And I thank production staff, especially Merv Honeywood, Paula Devine (who worked at weekends) and Caroline Maxwell, for reorganizing their own timetables to fit the work of copy-editing, proof correction and indexing round my hospital schedule for radiotherapy.

For the book's cover, I am particularly grateful to Hilly Janes and Ross Janes, together with the National Library of Wales, for kind permission to use a reproduction of 'Breakfast' by their late father, Alfred Janes.

A huge thank you is due to younger generations of family and close friends for keeping me attached to the digital, online and electronic world, and helping reorganize the older one of books/ paper. My elder son, Toby Murcott provides IT support with enviable patience, unflappably coming to the rescue at extremely short notice. He also provides lucid explanations that help me avoid mistakes in basic biology, chemistry and physics. My younger son Dominic Murcott is inspired in his creative management of the other hardware and software. He also invaluably proffers very shrewd all-round advice. Of the generation down, Taran Driver repeatedly helped move books around as did Al Pozniak, who also kept me going during especially intensive periods of writing with regular Sunday evening invitations when he was cooking supper for his family. His sister, Suzi Pozniak interspersed preparing for her GCSE exams with conscientious (paid) help typing sections of the list of references and sorting offprints.

Acknowledgements

In addition to thanking my sons, I am also grateful to my daughters-in-law Karen Murcott and Sian Murcott. Along with all the grandchildren (even the youngest is now old enough to volunteer to make lunch for me when I am writing) they have, in their different ways, helped and supported more than any mother and grandmother has a right to expect and could ever wish for.

Naturally I remain responsible for all errors and omissions.

CHAPTER 1
INTRODUCTION: SOCIOLOGY, FOOD AND EATING

Look at the illustration on the front cover of this book. Part of a painting called 'Breakfast' by Alfred Janes, it freezes a moment of a family's weekday morning in 1950s Britain. It powerfully conveys a sense simultaneously of the social relationships between those portrayed and of each one's relationships to the production and consumption of the food at home. Turn the book over and look at the thumbnail picture which shows the whole painting. There can be seen that it is the woman – wearing an apron to cover her dress while getting breakfast for everyone else – who is the only adult of the three not at the table. The man in his collar and tie sits there, eating the last of his breakfast, momentarily looking up from the newspaper, almost ready to go out to work. She is the 'homemaker' cooking breakfast for everyone; he is the 'breadwinner', earning the living for them all. She is kissing goodbye to the youngest boy off to school. The oldest son, adult now, also in collar and tie, sits at the table alongside his father draining his coffee cup – the next generation preparing to follow in his father's breadwinner footsteps.

The painting has the quality of a still from a film, temporarily suspending movement. Despite the static portrayal of mobility, the very *nature* of the things (their materiality) is powerfully conveyed – the hasty gulping down the last of the coffee no longer too hot to drink, the smell of the poised forkful of food – coupled with the temporality indicated in the swiftness of the kiss goodbye and the way the middle of the three boys is already half way out of the door. Everything signals a sense of routine, of an ordinary, familiarly rushed weekday morning in which eating, domestic food provisioning and people's relationships to one another are intimately intertwined – usual, mundane, taken for granted.

Now think of another, very well-known painting, called 'Freedom from want' by Norman Rockwell, the twentieth-century American artist. Made in 1942 a few years before Janes', its title echoes Franklin D Roosevelt's Four Freedoms. It depicts a middle-aged man in a black suit, collar and tie, standing at the top of the dinner table. His position signals that he is head of the family, the breadwinner. He is beaming at the enormous turkey a smiling woman, with hair as grey as his, is placing on the table in front of him, carving knife and fork alongside ready for him to share it out. Nine others, of three different generations, faces alight with anticipation, are shown seated along each side of the table which is beautifully laid with white cloth, dishes, plates and glasses of water. Once again, the woman is wearing an apron over her dress, signalling that she is responsible for the cooking. She is shown in the very act of serving everyone else.

Social conventions placing men as family breadwinners and women as the homemakers/cooks may (or may not) have changed in the US, Britain and elsewhere since the 1950s. But whatever the prevailing conventions of a particular historical period or a certain region might be, what people eat, what the food signifies and who is expected to undertake the provisioning, are intricately tied in to the way society is organized – often represented in paintings, photographs or fiction. It is these types of social arrangements, social institutions, symbolic significances and the associated materialities that *Introducing the Sociology of Food and Eating* addresses. All these and more are to come, but for now, 'to begin at the beginning'.[1]

Background basics

Food is a fundamental requirement of life. As a result, searching for something to eat is a basic human preoccupation. For most of human history that search has taken place in the shadow of famine and starvation with the threat of hunger a normal feature of daily life. An individual cannot survive much beyond three weeks without food – and only three days without any water. But a whole society is shaken if too many of its population has to go without food. Rising prices, low wages or empty shelves in grocery stores risk civil disorder; hunger goads people to take to the streets. In 1916, 'housewives' on Manhattan's Lower East Side riot in protest against high food prices (Turner 2014). In nineteenth-century England soup kitchens repeatedly reappear to dampen down civil unrest whenever economic depression and high unemployment threaten 'to disturb the social fabric' (Burnett 2014: 31). A 2011 paper from researchers at the New England Complex Systems Institute shows that violent protests in both North Africa and the Middle East that year (and riots in 2008) coincide with high peaks in global food prices.[2] And as recently as January 2018, Reuters reports widespread looting and violence in Venezuelan towns and cities in the face of 'runaway inflation', adding that shopkeepers are defending their premises 'with sticks, knives, machetes, and firearms'.[3]

Only for about a century have even less well-off people, especially those in wealthy and more industrialized nations, been able to assume an easily accessible super-abundance of foodstuffs – a new normality for them. It means that it is extremely unlikely that either anyone involved in the production of this book or any of its readers have known hunger – not the hunger anticipating supper after a full day's revising for exams, or the appetite worked up after a long hike in the countryside, but real hunger that gnaws at the guts, last thing at night, still there first thing in the morning, day after day after day. Perhaps family stories of real hunger are still current. Some reading this book, living in, say, Boston, Massachusetts, may be descended from an Irish arrival who in the years between 1846–1850 flees the potato famine. Fabled as land of abundant food, America acts as a magnet for nineteenth-century migrants where 'they would not be stalked by hunger as in the old country' (Turner 2014: 11). Another reader might be descended from someone, perhaps in Seattle, who knows of, if not took part in, the Hunger Marches of the Great Depression of the early 1930s. Other readers, perhaps living somewhere in Europe, may be descendants of people who survived the starvation of the 1944–1945. 'Hunger Winter' during the German occupation of The Netherlands.[4] More recently, survivors of the 1959–1961 Great Famine in China when millions starved to death, contribute to a study documenting that terrible experience (Xun 2012), while, today, right now, there may be still other readers who have moved elsewhere to live, leaving behind relatives enduring shortages, struggling to find food in war-torn areas of the Middle East or Africa or family acquaintances reduced to dependence on food aid in refugee camps. The shadow of hunger is not lifted everywhere, or for all time.

Newer trends

What is much more recent is that hunger co-exists with that new normality of full supermarket shelves in rich countries – and for the wealthier in poor countries – where being able to find more than enough food can, unthinkingly, be taken for granted. An indicator of this is that the wealthier and more industrialized a nation, the smaller the percentage of household income is spent on food. The smallest percentage is in the US, the largest in Nigeria. On average the amount spent on food in the US is twice that spent in Nigeria. As significant, are the great within-country differences in both rich and poor nations, e.g. for the US 'over the past 25 years, the poorest 20% of households ... spent between 28.8% and 42.6% on food, compared with 6.5% to 9.2% spent by the wealthiest 20% of households.'[5] Moreover, this relation is dynamic as illustrated by the nineteenth-century economist Ernst Engel's proposal: the proportion of income spent on food declines as income rises. It means that, worldwide, plenty and want now stand in a novel relation to one another, historically speaking.

In the midst of plenty there appears to be a recent twist to the perennial human need to get something to eat. In rich countries, journalists, writers and commentators seem fond of saying that 'we have become obsessed by food'. They describe people being preoccupied by what they eat, whether it is becoming increasingly anxious, citing the increasing numbers of people reporting food allergies, some who worry about another food scare, others concerned about contaminants or additives in food, and those following weight-reducing diets.[6]

Journalists too point to their own, extensive mass-media coverage of food-related topics: an obesity 'epidemic'; McDonald's opening new branches round the world; an outbreak of norovirus responsible for closing a chain of Mexican restaurants; restaurant owners taking the tips diners leave for the waiters; foraging recipes from Finland; the promotion of '7-a-day' (official Australian government advice about the daily number of portions of fruit and vegetables to be eaten for good health, six in Denmark, five in the UK); the spread of food banks in rich countries as far apart as New Zealand, Germany and the US; predictions of food fashions for the forthcoming year including coconut flour, cactus water and the 'veggan' diet (vegan with eggs); the headline '15 Dead, 5 Hurt in Stampede for Food Aid in Morocco' – readers can probably add many more to this already long list.

Starting to think sociologically

This book's point of departure, chapter by chapter, is a selection of rich countries' 'obsessions' to introduce what sociologists have to say about food, society and the perennial human preoccupation with getting something to eat. In it, sociological thinking about food and eating in society is presented as an alternative to and different from such conventional wisdoms on these matters. For present purposes, conventional wisdoms are taken to mean widely held, rather general beliefs – those statements and occasional puzzlements people express when seeking to make sense of things they know, read about or talk over with one another during their daily lives. They take the form of statements of a kind sometimes described as received wisdom, common sense views, assumptions or explanations. These are often plausible, widespread as well as familiar – and can be found incorporated into mass-media discussions of food and eating, newspapers, magazine, online and elsewhere (e.g. at dietitians' conferences, among marketers developing a new advertising campaign) right through to the companionable chatter between friends in a café. By contrast, one of the defining characteristics of any science is its dedication to adding to the sum total of knowledge that is relevant no matter where or when. In sociology, this requires minor intellectual gymnastics, for researchers obviously live in a segment of the world to which such ordinary language belongs, at the same time as standing apart to investigate that world as dispassionately as can be managed. So, one of this book's aims is to encourage the scepticism integral to *any* academic discipline that accepts nothing at face value.

Thorough understandings require systematic evidence – something for which conventional wisdom has little need. Like any other science, sociology entails research that builds on pre-existing bodies of knowledge, is conducted according to carefully developed procedures, with results double-checked by experts. In order to understand – and improve – myriad aspects of food and society, then, sociological thinking is essential and strenuous efforts are needed to do it as well as possible.

This book introduces a set of perspectives which is not as widely known as the conventional wisdoms with which they are contrasted.[7] They are also probably less widely known than other social scientific contributions to the study of food and eating such as those in psychology or economics, and are certainly very different from those that place a sole emphasis on diet and nutrition, on food science and technology, or on marketing studies of 'consumer behaviour'. Sociological perspectives often lead in novel directions adopting less familiar angles. In turn, these angles reveal that social life and the place of food and eating within it is intricate and anything but neat and tidy. Some studies primarily use food as a 'lens' on aspects of social organization or of socially differentiated opportunities, providing a 'window on the political', revealing global trends or illuminating new versions of 'identity' involved in everyday eating (Watson and Caldwell 2005: 1). Other studies concentrate primarily on the food in 'food and society', its nature and transformations, the contexts of purchase or the social organization of eating. But before this chapter goes any further with such necessary preliminaries, there

Box 1 Research

Research is a word that is now widely used every day (e.g. when searching websites for flight times, new phones etc). Academic/scientific research is completely different, conducted by adopting designs and techniques established according to agreed criteria developed by specialists, refined over extended periods of time – yielding dependable, enduring results. 'Research methods' is a quick heading for a far wider range of matters than simply methods, including types of research approach, research design and techniques of data collection and analysis.

Sociological research is no different from any scientific research in that it should begin with a research question/problem formulated in the light of pre-existing evidence and relevant theories – perhaps to fill a gap in knowledge, update earlier work or investigate a new phenomenon. Resources (funding, time, staff) must also be considered. All this takes place alongside thinking through what the overall social scientific approach is to be. In the social sciences, it means asking whether the work is to depend on existing materials to conduct secondary analyses (e.g. re-analysis of an archived data-set (Bishop 2007), examining historical materials (Cochoy 2015) or collecting brand new data (Rozin *et al* 2006)). Research must also be designed (see Box 23).

Note that research is not complete until it is peer reviewed and published in scientific journals. 'Peer review' is the process of academic quality control requiring that articles submitted to journals are assessed by fellow experts in the relevant field who (usually) are not told the identity of the authors who, likewise, are 'blinded' to the identity of reviewers.

is a tale to tell. It opens with news stories reporting children's ignorance about the origins of their food.

Getting behind a headline: 'children don't even know ...'

A number of shocking statistics show a worrying number of young children have some pretty major knowledge gaps when it comes to food.

Survey finds many children do not know where food comes from.

Survey of urban teens finds alarming lack of knowledge about farming and food production.[8]

All three are headlines of news articles of 2015 and 2016 from, respectively, the UK, Australia and New Zealand. Of American children an article in the *Huffington Post* remarks 'The sad reality is that many children don't know where their food comes from'.[9] The articles report survey findings such as '41% of kids don't know that eggs come from chickens' or '3 per cent of children think bananas are made in a factory'. This last adds that not only do more than half of 'British kids not know grapes grow on vines (and) more scarily over a quarter of adults do not know how bananas are grown'.[10] This is not surprising. As is widely observed, people now have very little direct contact with agriculture, so many live in towns and cities (Jackson et al 2010, Åsebø 2007). Even in New Zealand, where agriculture is so prominent that it makes up over half of the country's total exports, reports record that 72 per cent of children 'don't know anything, or know just a little, about how food gets from farm to plate'.[11]

Such ignorance about plant or animal food sources, geographic origins or the route from 'field to fork' is presented as self-evidently deplorable, increasing the risk that children will grow up not knowing how to feed themselves healthily, unable to shop wisely, to cook properly (FSA 2016: 35). These reports explain that the ignorance results from children's living in cities giving them little or no familiarity with farms and agriculture. City children's experience of looking for food simply means opening the door of the refrigerator – and if asked, they would probably explain, as one commentator sarcastically noted, that its contents come from the grocery store.[12]

Instead of being shocked at the children's ignorance, how about pausing for a moment to turn things round and realize that their saying food comes from the fridge or the supermarket is both correct and rational. Asked how food gets in to the shop in the first place, those same children are very likely to say they do not know – and no more do many adults. Having learned the fact of life that chickens lay eggs, people do not, it seems, know much more about the source of their food. Indeed, each episode of a UK, mid-evening TV programme on food is introduced with the question 'but what do we *really* know about where it all comes from' confident that viewers will know very little indeed.[13] Informing them is turned into lively entertainment.

Informing the public can be commercially important too. It led the US Farmers & Ranchers Alliance, to commission some market research in 2011 finding that '(C)onsumers think about food production constantly, yet know very little about how food is brought to the dinner table'.[14] Commercial interest in conveying a positive image of food's origins is not new. A nineteenth-century instance is Henry Heinz's 'ambitious brand creation strategy' for marketing his ketchup, sauces and pickles (the latter bottled by uniformed women employees at his Pittsburgh factory) – with the company opening 'its manufacturing facilities to the public in the 1890s, using the tours to support its brand and advertise its reputation for quality, purity, and cleanliness' (Koehn 1999: 380).

The line of thinking that side-steps being alarmed at children's apparent ignorance prompts other questions.[15] Take just one: what would children 50 years, a century, several centuries ago know about where food comes from, especially those living in cities? What might the surroundings be like in which children grew up? What contact, if any, would they have with animal husbandry, cheese making or picking cabbages? One small clue is to be found in a handful of street names in modern English cities which is all that survives of the site of Mediaeval markets, names such as Poultry in the City of London where poulterers set out their stalls or the Shambles (meaning open air slaughterhouse) in York where butchers also display their meat for sale. Although most people live in rural areas until the mid-nineteenth century (the city of Manchester's population doubled between about 1821 and 1851) the origins of city-dwellers' food supply is easily seen right into the centre of towns and cities; animals destined for meat are driven through the street to slaughter, piggeries are widespread (Scola 1992) and even 'respectable people and tradesmen' keep pigs, while right into the early twentieth century, 'milking cows are kept crowded in yards, cellars or closed shed within cities and towns' (Smith 1979: 212) The same applies elsewhere not just in older European cities, such as Paris (Vialles 1994: 5) but also the New World, e.g. Melbourne (Trabsky 2013: 133).

In early American cities 'urban families keep or board dairy cows for a supply of fresh milk' and cattle are 'driven from ports, and later rail stations, to markets and slaughterhouses throughout the city' (Brinkley and Vitiello 2014: 113). Pacyga (2015 : 79) reproduces a postcard from his collection of a photograph showing sheep slaughter in Chicago circa 1890 noting the number of young boys among the employees. Indeed, the Chicago stockyards are significant. In his 1906 novel *The Jungle* Upton Sinclair presents an exposé of the insanitary and dangerous conditions of its meat packing industry at the time, sparing his readers little in his descriptions of its appalling sights, sounds and smells. He has visitors – including children – being shown around the packing plants 'for it is good advertisement', putting into the guide's mouth that 'the visitors did not see any more than the packers wanted them to'.[16] Based on close knowledge of the facts, Sinclair's fiction created a furore about unsafe food going on sale – far greater than his intended target of the dreadful working conditions – prompting the passage of the 1906 Food and Drugs Act to assure the safety of the food supply.

This historical sketch suggests that twenty-first-century city children's ignorance about where food comes from may perhaps be new. As long as there are pigs in the sties in the alleyways, sheep herded through city streets to market and cows housed in suburban dairies even up until the early twentieth century, children, well off or poor, are likely to have seen for themselves where meat and milk came from. The contrast with today is great; slaughterhouses are concealed, often out-of-town, to which animals are transported by lorry hidden from passers-by (in New Zealand's South Island they tend to be unmarked bearing just the name of the truck owners, recognizable only by the air-vents high up the sides and the farmyard stench that surrounds them). The stages from live animal to packs of plastic-film wrapped meat ready for supermarket shelves are rendered invisible (Vialles 1994). Meat on sale in public markets in Chicago around 1914 gave way quite quickly, with the move to packaged items in modern supermarkets under way by the 1920s (Turner 2014). That shift is probably slower in the UK. So the majority of independent butchers, who well into the 1950s would have whole sides of beef hanging, so it seemed from the vantage point of a child, from ceiling to sawdust-strewn floor, have gone out of business. One English shop of this kind that survives into the twenty-first century, hits the headlines when some complained of whole rabbits and pheasants, pigs' and deer heads on display in the shop window. Such butchers' displays in that rural area – so the report runs – have been just the same for centuries. Ironically, the basis of one of those complaints is to protect children from the sight.[17]

For now, this is where the tale ends. Do children in nineteenth-century New York, Melbourne or Manchester know more about where food comes from than their counterparts today? It is impossible to know. What is certain is that the modern, global food system entails more food being produced in ways that are more hidden, in more factories whose addresses are unknown, whose interiors are more out of sight and whose operations are more subject to commercial secrecy than ever before.

The food system – and its critics

To suggest that twenty-first-century children's ignorance might be new is to overstate the case. Those nineteenth- and early twentieth-century children may know about the cows in the dairy along the street or the pig sties dotted around the city. But they are probably oblivious to the origins of Heinz Tomato Ketchup (first on sale in the 1870s) or Lea and Perrins Worcestershire sauce (on the market from the early 1800s) sold in the small shop on the corner.

Even if some of today's children's ignorance is new, however, it is also true that what there is to know about food's origins has become far more complex. Agriculture is heavily industrialized from which many more people are ever more distant. Today the number of people employed in agriculture continues to decline – in the wealthier nations at least.[18] In 1900 over 60 per cent of the North American population are farm dwellers, but today that number is closer to 2 per cent (Jaffe and Gertler 2006: 144). By 2014, the United Nations is able to report that more than half the world's population lives in urban areas.[19]

Furthermore, more and more food is moved around the world so that what people eat is very far removed from where the food comes from and, if only for that reason, makes the origins hard to see. For the 'food chains' running from 'farm to fork' are not just multiple – different for different items – they do not just stretch for longer and longer distances, but they can also double back on themselves, forming a complicated food system. Ingredients coming from one region may be incorporated into a manufactured product in another, but then reimported to the region of origin. As the geographer Bill Pritchard declares: the 'field of food chains research is fundamentally dynamic, on account of the fact that chains themselves are in continual processes of reorganisation and restructuring' (2013: 176).

Box 2 The food system

The food system is 'the complex of institutions and organizations that define, regulate, and shape the organization of agriculture and food from field to table' (Allen and Sachs 2007).

Labels on the packs are ready reminders of the global nature of markets in food. The sociologist Lawrence Busch records his swift walk through the local supermarket in East Lansing, a university town but not a major cosmopolitan city. He is able to find

> fresh clementines from Spain, fresh peaches and grapes from Chile, fresh tomatoes from Holland still on the vine, fresh starfruit from an unknown source, dried apricots from Turkey, kiwis from New Zealand, canned hearts of palm from Brazil, canned sardines from Norway, canned tuna from Mexico, coffee from at least ten nations and a host of other food products from far away.
>
> *2004: 163*

The extent and complexity of the worldwide movement of food is less easily seen. It involves the work of more and more people in more and more organizations and agencies, largely *between* the primary producers and the shops, cafés etc. Starting with the farmers, the link runs via international corporations selling seeds; manufacturers of agricultural machinery; 'layers' of buyers/suppliers, importers and distributors, in lengthening chains (Ponte 2009: 98); transnational food-processing companies; auditing agencies; commodity traders, merchants and distributors, right through to retailers – small shops and supermarkets as well as cafés, restaurants and burger bars – and back again. Complicating things still further, there is a second, closely connected list, that cuts across the first, consisting of regulatory institutions, such as the US Food and Drug Administration (FDA), scientific advisory bodies such as the European Food Safety Authority (EFSA), politicians, civil servants, food company lobbyists and non-governmental organizations (NGOs) engaged in intricate trade agreements on behalf of national governments.

For wealthy nations' economies, the most numerous are those at each end of the chains – the primary producers/farmers and the consumers, people who need to eat. But in the middle are fewer and fewer giant multi-national corporations processing, manufacturing and distributing food. In his introductory textbook to the sociology of food and agriculture, Michael Carolan talks of the demographics of the food system as 'an hourglass'. He illustrates this for the US showing that there are some 2.2 million farms at the top of the hourglass, as few as approximately 25,000 food processors and manufacturers along with approximately 145,000 food wholesalers and retailers in the middle, providing for over 300 million consumers at the base (2016: 38). Food production is big business and a significant element of an economy. In 2015, US agriculture, food and associated industries represent $992 billion (5.5 per cent of GDP), creating 11 per cent of employment in 2015.[20] In the UK, the food/drink industry is the biggest manufacturing sector, with the whole 2017 food sector (excluding Northern Ireland) employing 3.4 million people.[21]

Globalized food systems

The interconnections of the food system are now multiple and its scale is global. But there is nothing new about foods being moved around the globe. Trading in spices is evident throughout recorded history: webs of spice routes criss-cross the globe with

China as both exporter and importer, centuries before spices are transported to Mediaeval Europe along what Europeans call 'the Silk Road' (Keay 2006). Sugar cane is introduced by Arabs expanding westward into Europe, reaching Venice by 996 (Mintz 1985). The geopolitical implications of the European quest for spices need no repetition. The tiny ships of fifteenth-century European explorers to the Americas return with turkeys, squash, potatoes and tomatoes. Later, crudely but aptly stated, the 'circular' trade between Africa, Europe and the Caribbean is established with the infamous enslavement of Africans to work in the plantations of the New World whose output of sugar is transported to England to keep the nineteenth-century factory workers going so that they can produce more cheap goods destined, among other places, for Africa. Later, towards the end of that century it is possibly more surprising to discover that 'large quantities of liquid eggs (are) imported from China' to London in the 1890s (adulterated with boracic acid to preserve them for longer) (Oddy 2007: 99).

It is easy for those living in North America or Europe to forget about routes connecting nations elsewhere. China, for instance, imports chicken pieces from Brazil (Klein 2017 personal communication). But there can be two sides to such international trade. Mintz summarizes two stories, positive and negative. Americans do not eat chicken feet. But instead of being converted into animal feed, the 250,000 pairs, resulting from the weekly volume through a chicken processing plant in the American South, are used by local people in Hong Kong whence they are shipped, to be converted into 'a delicious, indeed famed, dim sum' (2008: 133). But unwanted 'trash' food in one country does not always become a healthful delicacy elsewhere. Americans do not eat turkey tails either. These are exported to some poorer nations of the global south, where there is little that can be done with them but to grill 'the packages of fat' and put salt on them – an example where healthy local foods are replaced by inferior imported foodstuffs (2008: 135). Other problems travel worldwide too. A 'food scandal' in 2017 originating in The Netherlands spreads to such an extent that contaminated eggs are identified not just in other European countries but as distant as Hong Kong.[22] It is not only that the eggs are widely exported it is also that this information is available to journalists almost instantaneously in an agri-food system that is global and the news of it globalized.

Indeed, what is widely regarded as new is that the pace of moving foods round the world has accelerated and the complexity involved has intensified (Bryant, Bush and Wilk 2013). These are distinctive features associated with what has come to be called globalization, a term used to refer often rather approximately to the acceleration over the last few decades of increasingly dense and speedy worldwide connectedness over time and place. As the globalized food system's complexity has become more intense, so correspondingly its opacity has increased. Perhaps, then, it is not surprising that a study of Danish people's food shopping and eating habits refers to the 'inscrutabilities of the food market' (Holm 2003: 139) or that the authors of an English study declared that people's selection of food 'is at the same time both intensely personal, bound up with individual tastes and household experiences of domesticity, and thoroughly public, an important aspect of citizenship nationally and, indeed, globally. Food purchase, use and consumption bring together the private and the public, the local and the global' (Cook, Crang and Thorpe 1998:162).

One of the consequences is that '(I)n many ways the global food chain demands more trust and knowledge on the part of the consumer, though the knowledge is of a different kind from the past when 'we lived next door to "*Old MacDonald*" and perhaps also produced a substantial part of our food ourselves' (Andersen and Larsen 2015: 293). Tracing those chains through the food system requires knowledge, effort and dedication making it hard not only for children but also their elders to know where their food comes from.

Critics of the food system

The food system attracts many commentators (Murcott 2013a). Two of the fiercest critics, possibly the best known, are American investigative journalists. Eric Schlosser published *Fast Food Nation* in 2001, Michael Pollan *The Omnivore's Dilemma* in 2006. Their books are excoriating exposés of the US system of food provision. Both are compellingly written, between them covering low standards of animal husbandry, inferior working conditions and poor rates of pay to employees in the fields, processing plants and fast food restaurants. Both highlight the reliance on fossil fuels for production and transportation and/or the increasingly destructive environmental consequences of the whole system; even free-range chicken and organic lettuce are shown not to be as innocent as their certification suggests. And both point to disastrous consequences, nutritionally with rising rates of obesity and lack of food safety.

Well before their publication, the Italian food and wine writer Carlo Petrini founded 'Slow Food' – initially a response to the opening of McDonald's in Rome in 1986. Sharing much with Schlosser and Pollan, Petrini's philosophy 'seeks a rediscovery of authentic culinary traditions and the pleasures of the table, in addition to the conservation of the world's quality food and wine heritage …' working to 'improve the world's agriculture and food supply'.[23] Note, incidentally, that there are even earlier precursors. The historian Harvey Levenstein devotes a whole chapter to what he calls 'the politics of food' in which he traces some of the US 'public's disenchantment with the food supply' back to the 1950s, adding wryly that the giant corporations turn out to be 'adept at co-opting their critics' (1993: 178–194).

Critics of the critics

Sociological thinking treats Pollan's and others' critical commentaries very seriously. *Good* sociological thinking, however, does not take them at face value. It regards them not as secondary (i.e. authoritative) sources but as primary sources (i.e. data to be analysed). Good sociological thinking approaches them as the investigative journalism they are and, however excellent examples of the genre they may be, focuses on that genre to recollect there is probably an agenda and that the conventions for the search for evidence and 'fact-checking' are different from those for the sciences. This is not to say that some sociologists may not share the agenda, just as any other scientist might. But that does not – indeed *should* not – eclipse the sociological, the scientific, task of appraisal, including asking all kinds of additional questions. The necessary scepticism is well illustrated by the historian Rachel Laudan's measured scrutiny of the origins, philosophy and activities of Slow Food, pointing to historical evidence that demonstrates the 'authentic' and venerable culinary traditions Slow Food deems should be rediscovered are mostly very recent inventions (2016).

Similarly, the geographer Julie Guthman provides a systematic dissection of dichotomies such as slow food/fast food, thin/fat and thence 'good'/'bad' eaters. Attention to detailed evidence shows how facile they are. And, she adds, they de-politicize, concealing the pre-existing economic and social privilege of those who can champion the slow, remain thin and pride themselves on their virtuous eating. Good sociological thinking does not miss her observations that organic production

> depends on the same systems of marginalized labour as does fast food. Or that organic salad mix led the way in convenience packaging, and is often grown out of place and out of season. Or that fast food serves women who work outside the home who are then blamed for depending on it to manage family and work. Or that slow food presumes a tremendous amount of unpaid feminized labour.
>
> *2003: 55–6*

In effect, Laudan and Guthman are saying that the food system is extremely complex, so do not look for solutions to its problems by thinking only about what tastes good, or by looking through rose-tinted spectacles that allow nostalgia to replace checking the history or attending to evidence.

So far, this chapter shows that what begins with a handful of news reports about children's ignorance of food's origins rapidly leads straight to a focus on the worldwide food system – the complex, interlinked economic, political, social and technological organization of food provision in the twenty-first century. The route from one to the other is rapidly presented here in much compressed form but considered a little further at the end of each chapter to come. Mostly those chapters concentrate on the bulk of the literature in the sociology of food and eating, leaving discussion of the food system to lie shadowy in the background – as does the literature. Following suit, this book does much the same until Chapter 11 on the politics of food which comes a little closer to the food system via thinking about food shopping and how far people are free to choose. Shopping is the connection that virtually everyone who eats has with the food system (i.e. the point where production and consumption meet). That, however, is some way ahead. In the meantime, necessary preliminaries continue.

Conceptual Orientations to the Sociology of Food and Eating

The sociology presented in this book is not the only sociology possible. It is often easier to describe the discipline as a loose federation of different perspectives rather than anything uniform and unitary. It can also be hard to identify a boundary between the intellectual outlook of sociology and neighbouring social sciences – notably social/ cultural anthropology, human/cultural geography, social history and the interdisciplinary field of agri-food studies. Sociology does not have a monopoly on the type of thinking presented in this book. The kind introduced here is, however, a sound basis for going on to get to know other sociologies as well as for moving outwards to discover more of neighbouring social sciences.

This chapter now turns to lay some foundations on which the coming chapters can rest. First a section introduces the sociological approach that colours the whole book, inspired by C. Wright Mills *The Sociological Imagination* and sets out what is meant by 'sociological thinking'. The next section draws on anthropological as well as sociological basics showing that food is not simply 'something to eat' but is culturally identified; not everything edible, safe and nutritious is defined as food (and some distinctly unsafe items are – think of the much prized Japanese *fugu*, the pufferfish whose poison is lethal).

Box 3 Culture

Culture is a word with many different usages, both every-day and academic. It means getting used to checking one or other meaning from the disciplinary context, who is using it and for what purposes (Williams 1983). This also means getting used to the absence of definitions. It is common for sociologists, anthropologists, geographers and historians to refer to 'culture' or use adjectives such as 'socio-cultural' without defining them.

One use refers to the 'high' arts (e.g. literature, sculpture, opera or theatre). Someone who is knowledgeable about them and has appropriate aesthetic appreciation of their import is said to be 'cultured' or to display 'cultivated' taste. This is the usage picked up in parallel distinctions among self-styled 'foodies' to signal their superior skills of sophisticated dining, in good eating and the finer points of cuisine (Johnston and Bauman 2015). This meaning of culture is evaluative, where the next usage is not.

A second usage is not evaluative. It runs across technical and scholarly usages in the humanities and social sciences. Within that there is some variation. Sociologists Giddens and Sutton offer a working definition of culture: '(T)he way of life, including knowledge, customs, norms, laws and beliefs, which characterizes a particular society or social group' (2014: 135). Confining the concept to the symbolic realm is also found among cultural anthropologists (and their UK counterparts, social anthropologists) e.g. '(A) society's culture consists of whatever it is one has to know or believe in order to operate in a manner acceptable to its members' (Goodenough cited in Glasser 1988: 4).

To others, however, such definitions omit a centrally important element, artefacts and the material world of things made by people – an emphasis this book adopts. Note that, for some social scientists, culture is thought of as the opposite of nature – although 'new materialist' approaches explicitly seek to evade this distinction, arguing against reliance on binary categorization.

Then follows a section consisting of thumbnail sketches of six significant intellectual conceptual approaches in the sociology of food and eating. This is to equip readers with summaries of the major, fundamental sociological attitudes that continue to support twenty-first-century work in the field, even when authors do not reference them. The chapter ends with a guide to the way the book is organized.

Sociological thinking

Sociological thinking has already been contrasted with conventional wisdom as the approach to understanding social aspects of food and eating introduced in this book. But sociological thinking goes far beyond its capability for dissecting categories that are usually just taken-for-granted. Sociological thinking concentrates less on individuals, more on relationships between individuals. Sociological thinking entails the often-surprising discovery that those relationships display regular features repeatedly discoverable in completely unrelated parts of the world, yet also noticing differences as well as similarities. Sociological thinking analyses the socially created institutions and organizations whose existence extends beyond individual human lifespans. Sociological thinking involves the idea of social structures, whose elements, unlike the walls and floors of a building or the cells of the gut under a microscope, are invisible, but which become apparent, socially stratified in differential opportunities occurring in an ordered pattern, or in systematic (mal)distributions of power, authority and influence.

In the process, sociological thinking is closely attentive to the persistence of, as well as shifts in, social structures over long periods of time, not just months or years, but decades

---

Box 4 Social stratification

Although varying cross-culturally and historically, all known societies exhibit a division of labour based, at its simplest, on age and sex/gender. This is a society-wide feature, not the result of individual differences. Typically, divisions of labour are intertwined with some form of social stratification, a system of hierarchically ranked identifiable social groups associated with differential distributions of wealth, status, influence and/or power. A distinction is sometimes drawn between membership of group based on (a) ascribed characteristics (e.g. age, caste or skin colour) considered fixed or at least only marginally alterable by human intervention and (b) achieved characteristics (e.g. educational level whose acquisition entails a combination of individual effort and the presence/absence of social structural opportunities). Social stratification systems are not necessarily fixed. In caste-based societies – India is the most widely known – whole castes may move up or down the hierarchy. In class-based societies, mobility is typically individual (within one lifetime or between parent and child) between classes, upward or downward, while any changes in the overall system are much slower.

and centuries. Sociological thinking analyses practices and processes which arise in myriad social interactions between people, which, in turn re-create and perpetuate themselves as bases for future interaction while remaining amenable to change as time passes. Most particularly, sociological thinking does not take place detached from the world, but attends closely to evidence, its amassing, its quality and its analysis.

The inspiration of *The Sociological Imagination*

Many such facets are evident in *The Sociological Imagination* by the sociologist C. Wright Mills. He begins with an observation that remains relevant, pointing out that long-term historical changes may also mean changes for the course individuals' lives take (i.e. their biography). 'When a society is industrialised a peasant becomes a worker, a feudal lord is liquidated or becomes a businessman' (Mills 1959:3). He could have added: people no longer easily see first-hand where their food comes from, they can only indirectly know the ingredients and recipes of processed foods via the minuscule print on their labels. He was, however, writing in the late 1950s when the global food system had yet to develop into its current, especially complex version and, in parallel, had yet to receive as much public discussion and commentary as there is now, when the sociology of food had not become a distinct field of enquiry.

Mills continues: 'Neither the life of an individual' (biography) 'nor the history of a society can be understood without understanding both' (1959:3). Sociology is to concentrate, he says, on the intersection of biography, history and social structure. It needs a certain 'quality of mind ... what may be called the sociological imagination' (1959: 5). This quality of mind makes it possible to grasp the links between difficulties of somebody's personal life – what he calls 'the personal troubles of milieu' – with the wider problems peculiar to the larger historical circumstances of the time, 'the public issues of social structure' (1959: 8) (see Box 4). The same applies to eating in nineteenth-century America, observes the historian Katherine Turner: food is 'a private matter with public implications'. She adds that it is not just that poorly fed men turn to drink or that poorly fed children become poorly educated delinquents, it is also that '(U)nclean food and food business could cause disease' (2014: 19).

Food poisoning is a good example of a problem that is both private and public. Acute foodborne disease can range from a 24-hour episode to extremely serious, occasionally fatal illness. The US Centers for Disease Control and Prevention (CDC) estimates it causes 3,000 American deaths annually; the UK Food Standards Agency (FSA) assesses deaths in the UK of around 500.[24] The World Health Organization (WHO) estimates it affects almost 1 in 10 annually worldwide. About 48 million people suffer food poisoning annually in the US and a million in the UK (FSA 2011) – respectively the WHO regions with the second lowest and lowest burden of such disease globally.

Food poisoning is undeniably a personal trouble, even if a bout is short-lived it is unpleasant and debilitating. But it is also a public issue if only because in total it is expensive. Some sufferers will need medical attention – which, along with associated health services, must be paid for. Canada reports approximately 11,600 hospitalizations of a total of about 4 million (1 in 8) cases. Many sufferers will be out of action even if only for a day, unable to meet their usual obligations – whether these be swinging by the grocery store to pick up the shopping on the way home from college or running a nation's largest power station. But the scale of foodborne disease multiplies to millions of working days lost, results in US $152 billion per year in healthcare, along with workplace and other economic losses. Food poisoning and governments' interests in working to reduce its incidence is just one of the ways the private and the public are interlinked as aspects of food and society.

What is food, sociologically speaking?

Only a moment's reflection on eating elsewhere, whether at a restaurant that serves food from a distant continent or travelling to somewhere else, provides a familiar reminder of the seemingly infinite variety in the ways food is prepared. It is not only styles of cooking – the cuisine – but the ingredients themselves that are varied, so much so that in some circumstances, what is food for one social group is very firmly not food for another.

Box 5 'Food culture'

'Food culture' is an expression used in both popular and academic discussions of food and society. But this book only uses it when quoting others. What follows explains why.

Popular discussions (e.g. by journalists, food writers and critics) use the word evaluatively (Driver 1983: 181–2). Typical is a 2003 newspaper article (whose headline opens ch 5) by food writer Matthew Fort, mentioning 'food culture' several times (e.g. despite the rise of farmers' markets, there is little evidence of an 'active food culture'; although Britain's 'food culture' is not quite as 'dire' as it was; while others successfully 'protect(ing) their indigenous food cultures' with Italians good at 'preserv(ing)' theirs). Others use the expression 'food culture' in like fashion, especially those promoting the tourist industry. They mean something that is valued, can be aspired to, is capable of either improvement or deterioration and can be assessed by those in the know.

A wholly different meaning of 'food culture' is non-evaluative, parallel to the use of the analytic concept 'culture' across the social sciences (see Box 3). A distinct version of this is found among Norwegian researchers, extending to other Nordic researchers (Bergflødt, Amilien and Skuland 2012). Their definition is inclusive: '(N)ordic food culture consists of the sum of food knowledge and food experience in the Nordic countries in their respective contexts. Not only does it include the norms, values, beliefs, habits, and actual foods and dishes, but also the entire food system, from production to consumption' (2012, see also Fumey, Jackson and Raffard 2016). Extending the meaning to the whole food system in this way unavoidably includes elements beyond national borders to the extent that the food system of the Nordic countries cannot be separated from the global food system. Two observations arise. Does such extreme inclusivity limit the utility of the term? The expression surfaces astonishingly *in*frequently even in the Nordic literature in question, despite the prominence authors accord it.

Mostly, the use of 'food culture' in social scientific research on food is loose and vague – sometimes so vague that it only appears in an article's title never to be referred to again. At other times, the use is such that the meaning of a passage is not changed at all by the word's complete removal. Persisting in such casual usage is hard to defend. If some term is needed – and it is not always obvious that it is – there already are others. 'Foodways' is an example of an older expression initiated and still used by American folklorists such as Lucy Long seeking to emphasize that food is 'more than just "stuff we eat"'. She uses it to refer to the 'network of activities, habits and conceptualizations surrounding food and eating' (2015:192). 'Culinary culture' is another, defined in Mennell, Murcott and van Otterloo as 'a shorthand term for the ensemble of attitudes and tastes people bring to cooking and eating' (1992:20). Granted, Bergflødt, Amilien and Skuland think of 'food culture' as more encompassing than 'culinary culture'.

In the end, however, the use of the expression seems to make no difference. It is possible that its persistent, hazy use has been adopted by those new to the study of food and society, unfamiliar perhaps with the existing literature, or maybe borrowed by analogy with similar usages developed in the neighbouring interdisciplinary field of cultural studies. But introducing a new term (never mind leaving it undefined) is arguably a slack way of proceeding. It is preferable to check that there is no pre-existing perfectly serviceable expression that can continue to be used and thus avoid any confusion with the evaluative use. Come to that it may even be better to pause and consider whether there is any need for such a term at all – as in this book.

This surfaces now and then in groups' rude names for each other – 'in Ethiopia, the Amhara and other cereal cultivators of the north refer disparagingly to their Cushitic counterparts of the southern highlands as "*ensete*[25] eaters' (Fischler 1988: 275), Kraut (American/English name for German) or Dog People (Baschilambua Lange name for those of the Western Lange in the Congo). What counts as food also changes over time. When newly introduced to seventeenth-century Europe, tomatoes are initially regarded with suspicion; nowadays, for many in Canada, Wales or New Zealand, offal (liver, kidney, tripe etc) is most definitely inedible. So powerful can be the idea that offal is 'not food' that it can provoke physiologically detectable manifestations of disgust, such as nausea.

The point is that the human species is simultaneously selective and omnivorous (Fischler 1980). People are capable of eating anything that will fit in their mouths; '(H)umans will swallow almost anything that does not swallow them first' (Farb and

Armelagos 1980: 165). But that does not mean people are indiscriminate in what they will eat any more than it is simply that one individual likes some things more than another. It is that for whole social groups, there are culturally identifiable classifications dividing items into food and non-food. Anthropologists make such observations well before sociologists take an interest in the topic. Among the Bemba in 1930s Africa, Audrey Richards notes:

> I have watched natives eating the roasted grain of four or five maize cobs under my very eyes, only to hear them shouting to their fellows later "(A)las, we are dying of hunger. We have not had a bite to eat all day ..." To the Bemba, "millet porridge is not only necessary", but is the only constituent of the "diet which actually ranks as food".
>
> *1939: 47*

Eating is undeniably a biological necessity, but the practical definition of food is unavoidably social and cultural.

This distinction between food and non-food is the basic instance. It can extend to notions of a meal to become synonymous with food. Soma reports that '*kalau belum makan nasi, rasanya belum makan*' is a common saying in Indonesia meaning that without rice it feels as if you have not eaten (2017). The distinction can also extend to alignment with what sociologists in a much-neglected US study conducted in Southern Illinois observe, namely, some foods and certain dishes assume 'stereotyped imagery' representing the contrasting social status of groups in the area. '(B)lood pudding is a general symbol of revulsion and contempt for "them Germans in the Hills"; the eating of muskrats has come to symbolize the animal-like habits of Negroes; fish itself symbolizes the low status of "river rats," although in this case the food is actually eaten by those who use it opprobriously' (Bennet 1942: 655–6).

Analytic attention extends to more nuanced distinctions such as occasions for eating – everyday/special, banquets/picnics. A 'meal' may be a notion that is found cross-culturally, but the menu deemed proper for certain occasions can differ dramatically: compare Christmas menus such as ham or roast beef in the US, England's and New Zealand's roast turkey, Denmark's and Norway's roast pork, and Romania's cartabos (pork sausage) and salata biof (mayonnaise-covered chicken, root vegetable, gherkin and pickled pepper salad). Meals may be more or less structured (see Chapter 2). Cultural classification extends to people themselves, old or young, male or female, healthy or sick. Following a long line of similar reports (Mennell, Murcott and van Otterloo 1992) is Danish work recording the way that men consider meat a necessity for them, unlike women "(M)y husband wants meat on the table every day. 'Real men need meat', he says" (Holm and Møhl 2000). It is not only the categorization of types of food deemed appropriate for whatever the occasion is to be or whoever is to eat it, classifications of courses, even recipes are involved, as may be the number of different dishes, the crockery to be used for serving, the style of eating and the implements to be used – chopsticks, flatbread, forks for a banquet, fingers for a picnic.

Classifications of eating certain items can go even further as exemplified by a sociological study of an unexpected and rapid increase in the number of dog-meat restaurants in a Vietnamese town (dog meat is only eaten at specialist restaurants catering for men, usually middle-class, symbolizing masculinity, potency and strength) (Avieli 2011). In a region where such food is not typical, with only a couple of discreet establishments advertising in 2004, it suddenly has dozens around the town announcing dog on their menus. Local people's explanation for this abrupt popularity of dog meat – in any case a controversial culinary custom for some – involves attributing it to 'the North', the nation's ideological and political centre. Doing so conveys a strong political sense; eating dog meat is defined 'as a public manifestation of one's political inclination toward the North, while the rejection of dog meat expressed a negative attitude toward the regime' (2011: 69). In this case eating a certain food is classified not only as masculine and middle class but also counted as an expression of ideology and allegiance to a centre of power.

More variations still are found. For instance, it might be expected that McDonalds would be thought of as the same wherever, worldwide, it opens its doors. After all, its menu is intended to be standard, reassuringly predictable so that customers spotting its Golden Arches anywhere in the world can know what they will find. But as Watson and his colleagues show, McDonalds' means different things to different people in one or other country in East Asia – foreign/exotic vs foreign/suspect etc (2006).

How edible items are categorized extends in other directions. As soon as taxes or tariffs are levied on some things but not others, then determining how an object on sale is to be classified becomes very important. In the European Union, cakes and biscuits belong to separate categories for the purposes of value added tax (VAT), a sales tax.[26] Challenges occasionally surface in the mass media.[27] More prosaically, the intricacies of the classifications involved are such that one food producers' association has provided a guide for its members.[28] Export similarly illuminates contrasting social definitions of items as food. The US Department of Agriculture (USDA) prohibits the human consumption of sheep's lights (lungs), a key ingredient in haggis, that symbol of Scotland. McSween's, the Edinburgh-based haggis producer, reformulates the recipe using lamb's hearts instead.[29] In turn, the US produces beef reared without hormones for the European market where their use is banned.

Organized attempts deliberately to change classifications are not confined to arguments with tax authorities, and are often evident in applications to regulatory authorities to permit items to go on sale.[30] The history of introducing margarine as an alternative to butter require people be persuaded to find the novelty acceptable (Ball and Lilly 1982). Today an instance attempting to persuade people to eat insects in parts of the world such as North America or Europe where there is little or no tradition of eating them is inspired by the need to feed a rapidly increasing world population (van Huis et al, 2013). In London, a small start-up company also dedicated to promoting insect eating acknowledges the need to shift the cultural classification of insects as inedible to edible, changing people's taste both literally and metaphorically (Stock et al, 2016).

Examples such as those just provided tend to emphasize the attribution of meaning via the human capacity to impute meaning expressed in words. But for Emma Roe, things

> become food through how they are *handled* by humans, not by how they are described and named. Attending to what people say about foodstuff is only half of the story about how things become food; the second half is what people *do* with the material foodstuff.

> *2006: 105, emphases added*

Her discussion adopts a 'relational materialist' approach which shifts thinking across the social sciences to by-pass a long-standing contrast between 'nature' and 'society'. Instead of assuming the former is subordinated to the latter, they are equalized (Goodman 2001). In this way, the actual stuff of things is foregrounded to concentrate on the manner in which their very substance makes a difference when things and people are, often literally, in touch. Food is no exception. It is also an intriguing example, because on eating, the food becomes the person which, in supporting his/her survival, transforms the person who eats it. Indeed, the very act of eating thereby defines a substance as food. Whether it does someone any good, makes them ill or even kills them, starkly underlines the point.

In sum, then, it is an empirical observation that the meaning of food is not fixed but varies historically and socio-culturally. How sociologists conceptualize it is a theme running through the work of some of the key contributions to the field, to be considered next.

Six classic approaches

This section provides the briefest of memos for each of six important approaches to topics in food and society. For convenience they are presented as associated with six eminent scholarly forebears whose work (despite often being ignored) includes provocative statements of some of the enduring basic intellectual approaches, compelling insights and concepts on which sociological thinking about food and eating currently draws.

'The meal'
Georg Simmel (1858–1918) German sociologist

Simmel's essay, 'The Sociology of the Meal' first appears in a 1910 newspaper. It remains inaccessible to all unable to read German until 1994 when Michael Symons translates it into English and provides a commentary (1994). Simmel points to an inescapable irony about eating. Although eating is common to everyone, it is also supremely individual. Several can see or hear the same thing, but 'what the individual eats, no one else can eat under any circumstances' (1994: 346). Everyone has this individuality in common. Simmel jumps from there to place the meal at the centre of the social relationships involved in eating, going on to a detailed discussion of the rules governing behaviour at meals, especially the prohibitions. Just one of his illustrations is 'the Cambridge Guild of the eleventh century decrees a severe penalty for anyone who eats and drinks with the murderer of a fellow member' (1994: 346). So, rules about who is considered a suitable group member are intimately associated with rules about who may eat with whom.

Food's symbolic significance
Claude Lévi-Strauss (1908–2009) French anthropologist

Highly influential in the 1960s, Lévi-Strauss's work is rapidly translated into English. Interested in the tension between nature and culture in social life, he declares that if food is going to be good to eat (*bonnes à manger*) it must also be 'good to think' (*bonnes à penser*). He thus picks out a human tendency to attach symbolic significance to phenomena, including the capacity (varying cross-culturally) to allocate items into food/ non-food categories. So, human activity can make food serve as a medium of communication and thereby allows it to be analysed as such. All these come together in his 'culinary triangle' showing that cooking and rotting (two transformations of foodstuffs from a raw state) can be mapped on to a dimension of nature vs culture demonstrating transformations from the former to the latter (Lévi-Strauss 1966). Critics are sceptical of details of his contribution, but the importance in subsequent research of attention to the symbolic significance attributed to food cannot be overstated.

The structure of meals
Mary Douglas (1921–2007) English social anthropologist

Like Simmel, Douglas is interested in rules surrounding meals and like Lévi-Strauss she also develops analyses of them with reference to some kind of code that allows meanings to be deciphered. In particular, she recognizes rules governing the patterning of meals making it possible to analyse them as if they have a structure. What is culturally defined as a meal has patterns, different courses repeat similar patterns, as do weekday/ weekend menus, feasts and routine occasions (Douglas 1972). Based on an in-depth study undertaken by Michael Nicod, her MSc student who lodged for a month at a time in four working-class households in different English cities, Douglas developed her analysis demonstrating the repeating patterns of a succession of 'correspondences' of the meal system (e.g. a first and second course share a structure of 'staple, centre and dressing' but differ with the first as savoury with potato, meat or fish (vegetables) and gravy while the second is sweet composed of cereal (eg pastry), fruit and custard or cream (Douglas and Nicod 1974)).

Industrial food
Jack Goody (1919–2015) British social anthropologist

Goody's *Cooking, Cuisine and Class* is devoted to understanding how an *haute cuisine* of very high social classes develops in some societies but not others (1982). His work is singled out here, less for that investigation and more for his inclusion not only of cross-cultural comparison and attention to history, but also for his discussion of what he summarizes as 'industrial food'. Granting that 'lark's tongues are not promising ingredients for a mass cuisine' and that 'canned food is not always the best basis for a gourmet meal' he attributes to industrial food an enormous improvement in 'quantity, quality and variety (of) the diet of the urban working populations of the western world' (1982: 154). He goes further, referring to 'the world system' whose trends he regards as radical, reducing differences 'within and between socio-cultural systems', a homogenizing effect which is creeping round the world. While not evaluating the consequences, he starts to point out factors that need studying, such as the consequences of differential spending power within and between nations. One small but telling addition is needed. Almost alone at the time his book is published, Goody includes attention to stages of production from fields, manufacture, storage, transport to household eating. But – and this is the significance – he does not end with cooking and serving but includes clearing up and disposal as the final stage. Despite being undeservedly infrequently cited, the book introduces many topics and debates to emerge as part of the later development of the sociology of food and agri-food studies as distinct fields of study.

'Practices', distinction and social class differences in food and eating
Pierre Bourdieu (1930–2002) French sociologist

Bourdieu's work waits only a few years to be translated into English. Credited (with others) for the development of theories of 'practice', his contribution is based on his 1950s anthropological research in Algeria that reveals myriad categorizations of food (e.g. winter/summer, male/female). What he means by 'practice' is somewhat elusive but may be summarized as typically referring to everyday actions/activities that are regular and repeated, of which members of a social group/culture may remain half-conscious but will readily recognize, for there are generally agreed criteria about right or wrong versions (1977 [1972]). His other major work to include analyses of food and eating is *Distinction* (1984 [1979]) showing the correspondence between social class and taste in art, music (and more) as well as food. He illuminates his case by noting class variation not only in the foods themselves but also in ways they are prepared and served – displays of larger amounts being working class, more 'refined' portions being middle class, working class eating is more relaxed, whereas the middle class are 'concerned to eat with all due form' (1984: 196).

Material context prior to the symbolic and 'supplier induced demand'
Sidney Mintz (1922–2015) American anthropologist

Mintz' eminently readable 1985 *Sweetness and Power* asks how sugar moves from being a cure for plague in Mediaeval Europe, later a hugely expensive luxury in Elizabethan England (Elizabeth 1 is reputed to have had black, decayed teeth due to her fondness of it) to essential source of calories for the nineteenth-century urban labouring classes working in the factories of Britain's industrial revolution, eventually to arrive in the twentieth century as a commonplace of everyone's diet. The work covers the iniquities of the trade in slaves from Africa to the plantations of the Caribbean (where Mintz did fieldwork among sugar cane workers) in detailing the politics and economics of centuries' growth in sugar production and global consumption. His question necessarily recognizes the symbolic significance of a foodstuff. But going beyond Douglas or Lévi-Strauss he anchors his analysis by insisting that the material circumstances must be included. The exercise of power and economic interests involved that underlie the meanings of sugar must be understood to make sense of the shifts symbolically. Yes, rituals, meanings of meals or ingredients need to be deciphered, but it is essential to 'decode(s) the process of codification, and not merely the code itself' (Mintz: 1985: 14). Meaning is consequent upon political and economic activity studied over time and, where necessary, globally. Study of economic activity requires attention to supply and to demand. But it is vital, Mintz says, not to forget ways in which the two are linked, notably as 'supplier induced demand' reflecting the vested interest that suppliers have in stimulating demand for their products.

Two implications of the 'classics'

The preceding paragraphs on contributions associated with six major scholars are no more than headlines about their work (for fuller introductory discussions, Murcott 1988a, Murcott 2013a). Two implications need noting. One stresses the importance of realizing that meaning does not inhere in foods or in the organization of eating, but is attributed to each, socio-culturally. This remains the case, despite contemporary fashions to write as if the foods themselves do something independently of the social attribution of symbolic significance and that, by and of themselves they change people's lives as if they are motivated in the same way that people are. Personifying it to say that 'sugar changes the world' can be a catchy slogan, but it risks eliding the political, economic, social and cultural forces which Mintz shows must be analysed to understand how changes come about.

This is not to say that the non-human world has no consequences in social life – quite the contrary. Food's materiality (i.e. that it consists of matter) has direct and indirect effects. That it is organic (as opposed to inorganic) means it decays. Human beings are also composed of matter – they are simultaneously organic (like food) and also social. For them, eating putrid food may have the consequences as already discussed above – consequences which go well beyond any one individual with food poisoning. Indirect effects of food's materiality are evident in the huge modern system consisting of machinery, objects, personnel, engineering processes, transport and more, that is dedicated to keeping food fresh (Freidberg 2009). More than that, now well established and rapidly expanding intellectual developments that are sometimes brought together under a heading of 'new materialism', approach human and non-human relationships to evade not only the contrast between the two but also to side-step any idea that one is privileged over the other – as indicated earlier. Instead, the analytic focus is on the relationship between them to highlight 'assemblages' of both things and human beings that in some fashion are in contact with one another. For instance, Fox et al. provide a materialist analysis of obesity, illustrating among other things an unexpected contrast in the before-and-after assemblage of people who start classified as overweight or obese, but who then make great efforts at weight reduction. Fox et al. observe that it might be imagined that the two would be mirror images of each other – a large number of foodstuffs, arrays of enticements to eat, many snacks about the place before vs the removal of all those after weight reduction regimes are introduced. This is not so, they argue, for the 'after' assemblage comprises all the same things as the 'before' but with the *addition* of accoutrements, things and ideas to do with slimming (2018).

The second implication of the 'classics' is a reminder not to remain inside a sort of bubble by looking only at studies of wealthy countries undertaken by researchers who by-pass work from poorer nations or from other time periods. Too often, no doubt unthinkingly and by default, researchers generalize from their own era, their own locality and first-hand experience, risking presenting misleading conclusions or relying on unexamined assumptions. One of the latter is the manner in which far too often researchers proclaim and celebrate the pleasure of eating as if it is universally enjoyable. Return to Simmel, for instance, to recollect his focus on prohibitions. Here is a reminder that sharing, enjoyment in eating or enjoyment in others' company is only one aspect of eating meals together. That some are included may commonly mean there are others who are excluded.

Return to Simmel too to remember his pointing out the irony that though everyone eats, no-one can, literally, share eating a mouthful with anyone else. So there is the shadow of another aspect of eating – scarcity, or worse, a complete lack of food. The anthropologist Colin Turnbull reports how the Ik, a slowly starving group in East Africa facing dire shortage, eat solo (1972). The historian Zhou Xun's study of survivors' recollections of the famine in Mao's China records people hiding food even from members of their own family, lying to them as well as stealing (2012). Any impulse to share looks as if it is eclipsed by the direst of hunger. Even when able to secure some food, hungry people may still shun eating with others: impoverished 'squeegee' Canadian street kids (so-called because they dodge the traffic to clean car windscreens/ windshields in the hope of earning a handful of coins) dislike eating free meals alongside others in canteens for the homeless – dirty places, dirty people they explain (Dachner and Tarasuk 2002). Even when there is sufficient, the meaning of eating does not always entail pleasure. Among the Tallensi in the 1930s, '(E)ating is a serious business; there is no conversation at meal-times, and as soon as a group has finished they disperse' (Fortes and Fortes 1936: 271). The anthropologist Clifford Geertz reports that for the Balinese eating is anything but a pleasure:

> The Balinese revulsion against any behavior regarded as animal-like can hardly be overstressed. Babies are not allowed to crawl for that reason . . . Not only defecation but eating is regarded as a disgusting, almost obscene activity, to be conducted hurriedly and privately, because of its association with animality.
>
> *1973: 419–20*

The book's organization and ways of reading it

Most of the book (Chapters 2 to 10) is organized along the lines of the tale of children's ignorance told at the start of this chapter. Each chapter begins (and is titled by) an instance of conventional wisdom, then introduced by a handful of media headlines about one or other aspect of the way people eat etc. Each ends with a box summarizing selected key points. Sociological thinking differs from conventional, everyday wisdom in that, as systematically and rigorously as possible it *investigates* topics rather than taking their understanding for granted. Concepts and theorizing covered are those typical of the study of food and society (e.g. commensality or food regimes) along with those of enduring sociological significance such as class, gender, age, ethnicity, power, identity (Giddens and Sutton 2014)

As an introduction, this book is open-ended, less concerned to tell readers what topics to think about, much more to foreground *how* to think about them. A key aim of the book is to underline the importance of academic research evidence, and of attention to its nature and quality. That means paying attention to the way the research evidence is acquired (Boxes 1, 9, 11, 12, 14, 18, 21, 23, 27) and two chapters go into considerable details about methods (e.g. Chapters 2 and 8). This is, of course, not to claim that sociology is alone in stressing the significance of evidence – quite the contrary. Sociology is among many disciplines which similarly underline the centrality of evidence, the manner in which it is collected and the assessment of whether it is appropriate/good enough for the purpose to which it is put.

The book cannot be comprehensive simply because the field is now too big. The variety of topics covered is also limited by the range and volume of existing research (Murcott, Belasco and Jackson 2013). Any book which must have recourse to the sociological research literature is shaped, to some extent, by what has/has not been studied. As far as possible, references have been selected that are easily accessible, with a deliberate bias towards items readily locatable in university libraries and/or open access available via online search engines such as Google Scholar.

The book also does one more thing. It introduces a thin thread which gradually leads the discussion from *eating* to thinking about the *food system* of which eating is a part, to make the path revealed by that thread clearer. This chapter's earlier tale of children's knowledge about the origins of food is a compressed version of it. In general, the literature on eating contains myriad references to industrially produced, processed and distributed food, but infrequently draws attention to it let alone embarks on analytic consideration. That thread continues through the chapters, surfacing in a brief summary section at the end of each, culminating in a more concentrated discussion of the food system in the penultimate chapter. In so doing, this book attempts no more than to draw attention to the links, making them more noticeable. The thread's starting point, for the topics of Chapters 2 to 10, is everyone's first-hand experience of 'food and society', eating at home, eating out, cooking, dealing with packaging and waste food etc. Attending to the place of food in the everyday world, the book incorporates glimpses of the world beyond which enters daily life via the mass media, if only to serve as a springboard for those chapters.

Box 6 The mass media

The mass media is represented via quotations opening Chapters 2 to 10. News and other kinds of more specialist coverage of myriad topics, including those to do with food, feature somewhere in everyone's daily life, directly or indirectly e.g. cropping up in conversation among friends or in many ways via social media.[1] There are two reasons for selecting apt quotations from the mass media rather than novels, reports or leaflets distributed in supermarkets. They are likely to be most familiar to most of this book's readers and the sources for all quotations used are openly accessible online. Note that they are selected in this book to illustrate specific points, but none represent the range of mass media coverage of the topic in question.

The quotations are also selective in other ways which have to do with the nature of the mass media (conventionally characterized). Many are headlines. The relationship between a newspaper or magazine headline to the article beneath it reflects a division of work and responsibilities among those putting the whole thing together. Journalists will provide their copy (i.e. the text of their article). Others will edit – and sometime cut – the copy, and still other staff will write the headline.

The way one or other newspaper, online news site, or other website presents a topic reflects at least two things. One is the 'angle' that newspaper or site is dedicated to presenting (e.g. support for a political party, developing an agenda for a pressure group, or representing the concerns of a specific social group such as parents). The other is that the paper or site must survive. Its funding may be based on sales, on subscriptions, on grants from an interested sector of industry, on advertising or a combination of these. It may operate as a business or a not-for-profit organization. Whichever it is, readers – or those quoting from it – cannot automatically assume the content is innocent of whatever the imperatives are for its survival, unless demonstrably free of them. (Devereux 2013, Markham 2017)

---

[1] Social media is wholly bypassed in this book despite its extent, for unlike older mass media, they are not necessarily permanent or readily accessible.

Arriving at Chapter 11 the thread is taken in different directions, makes power more explicit and looks more closely at the food system's nexus between eating and provisioning.

The book concludes with a short chapter recapitulating stepping from 'conventional wisdom' to 'sociological thinking' via sets of questions, enabling readers to develop their own fluency in making the move for themselves.

There are other ways to read this book. Readers whose main interest is to find results of sociological study about food and eating, will find examples throughout. Readers who wish to learn what is distinctive about sociological thinking, will find it is the main feature that runs prominently throughout, the presentation of which is the book's central purpose. If readers wish to study sociological work more closely, whether pursuing a course in sociology of food and eating, the book provides detail of selected elements of the discipline and associated matters in occasional boxes alongside the main text. A substantial list of references giving the source of the evidence drawn upon throughout will readily lead an interested reader into the heart of sociological and allied work on food and society.

Everyone's involvement in the food system

This first chapter makes one further point, returning to the global food system to reflect on another, this time subjective, aspect of it. Everyone, the book's readers, editors and author, are all in some way caught up in that system over and above their own daily experience of eating (or not eating) even if not actively thinking about it all the time. The precise nature of that experience will vary in terms of biography, social structure and history, but it will also vary from place to place. The food system may be global, but within it there are myriad variations that are local. The topics presented in the following chapters reflect geographic and cross-cultural variation as far as is feasible. But any book, no matter what its subject, is inclined to be coloured by the place and times in which it is written. Readers know about where they live, thus able to provide their own local shading, brightened, it is hoped, by a deeper sociological understanding. In addition to such limitations of place, there are also the limitations of the nature of sociological work on food and eating itself. The field is most fully developed in Europe and North America (where, globally speaking, hunger is probably least prevalent) with much published in or translated into English thus risking Anglophone and other biases in what follows, despite every effort to limit them.

The point, however, highlights an additional purpose of this book. This is to present readers with fresh ways of reflecting on their own personal experience of food and eating along with their own attitude to the food system. Readers might ponder on any changes in their own lives that may have taken place over, say, the last five or even ten years as a matter of personal biography (e.g. moving to a new city, becoming a parent), historical events (e.g. a change in food prices) or some social structural shift linking personal circumstances to public issues. One of the book's aims is to provide readers with the intellectual 'tools' for re-considering, should they wish, any of their own 'obsessions' or conventional wisdoms about food in a newly informed light.

Box 7 Chapter One – Selected Key Points

1. Sociological thinking contributes to further understanding about food and society by providing perspectives that differ from, contrast or even conflict with 'conventional wisdoms'.
2. Sociological thinking is presented as studying food and society via conjunctions between 'public issues' and 'private troubles' at the intersection of biography, history and social structure

3. The modern, global food system's complexity contributes to difficulties in knowing foods' origins.

4. Critics of the food system e.g. Michael Pollan, Eric Schlosser and Carlo Petrini (Slow Food) are themselves criticized for (a) ignoring history and (b) overlooking the way their campaigns continue to assume unpaid kitchen work for women and low paid work in fields/restaurants/cafés for disadvantaged social groups/migrants.

5. What food is does not inhere in an item but is defined socially and culturally by meanings attributed to it.

6. Concise expositions of six 'classic' contributions to sociological research about food and society provide key reference points.

CHAPTER 2
FOOD AT HOME: 'THE FAMILY MEAL IN DECLINE?'

For many families, the weeks between Thanksgiving and New Year are about the only time they get together for meals. The rest of the year, eating is largely a matter of self-service.[1]

Ten per cent of families never have a family meal together in the week.[2]

The traditional family meal is becoming a thing of the past, with more than a third of Aussies eating most of their at-home meals on the sofa while watching TV.[3]

Families drift apart if they don't eat together. Sixty per cent of families don't eat together on Sundays. One in four don't even have a dining table. Top chef Aldo Zilli is horrified.[4]

Only a casual eye needs to be kept on the mass media coverage of food topics to discover how frequently the idea encapsulated in the quotations above appears. A suggestion that 'the family meal' is dying out is greeted with disapproval and alarm, as if lamenting its passing. The assumption that family dinners are a 'good thing' appears deeply engrained; the idea of a family meal is more than a mere notion, it also expresses an ideal, something which ought to happen i.e. is strongly normative. To get a sense of just how powerful the idea can be, try rewriting the second headline quoted above to run something like:

'At last! Ten per cent of families have got rid of family meals completely.'

Would this not be unthinkable? Certainly, it has not been possible so far to locate a news report greeting the matter as the successful abolition of something out-dated. Those that come close turn out to reinforce the value of family meals by claiming they can still be found and/or are 'staging a comeback'.[5]

Prompted by these headlines, this chapter leads in several directions. First it examines the 'public issue' that proclaims that family meals are good for everyone, especially for the health and welfare of children and adolescents. In the process it critically scrutinizes the involvement of (public health) research. Second, it briefly considers its 'private trouble' counterpart introducing sociological research which reports that a good many people think family meals are special and valuable, particularly for their own children, but find it hard to achieve. Then the main parts of the chapter concentrate on what sociologists have said about the claim that family meals are disappearing, in the process introducing questions about the social

Box 8 Sex and gender

It is important for academic purposes to make a conceptual distinction between the realm of the biological and that of the social, even though the two are intertwined and both contribute to behaviour. Such a distinction lies at the heart of understanding all kinds of observable differences between men's and women's place in society. This resolves into reserving the term 'sex' for biological (i.e. reproductive/anatomical) differences between males and females. 'Gender', on the other hand, refers to the socio-cultural realm, differences in what counts as masculine or feminine, learned psychological predispositions, a personal sense of identity and the social roles a man or a woman is expected to occupy (Oakley 1972). Gender and associated notions of masculinity and femininity vary cross-culturally and historically in the way that sex, the biology, does not. This basic distinction between sex and gender is, however, currently the subject of debate, with academics taking into account developments such as the capacity for human alteration of the body – by surgery, medication, tattooing, piercing etc – or a person's identification as gender neutral.

It is common to find that 'gender' is used as a synonym for studies concentrating on the typically disadvantaged social positions of women, rather than reserving the term to refer to socio-culturally defined relationships between men and women. For non-technical, everyday usages, the word 'gender' has widely replaced the word 'sex' (e.g. for form-filling, answering surveys, or in everyday expressions such as 'gender pay gap').

organization of everyday eating, showing that the terms people use to refer to the way they eat need careful study. The chapter moves on to consider social structure, demonstrating the significance of gender as a basic dimension of social stratification for eating at home, before turning to deal with definitions of terms and, finally, discussing the value of the concept 'commensality' in understanding fundamental social features of meals.

The discussion illustrates the way that the study of food and eating may serve as a lens on societal features. As the anthropologist Richard Wilk observes: '(F)amily meals represent an unusual nexus of local and national politics, of family and individual power, and the forces of ideologies and practices of gender, age, and cultural identity' (2010: 434).

Family meals as a public issue

'America's drug problem is not going to be solved in court rooms, legislative hearing rooms or classrooms, by judges, politicians or teachers. It will be solved in living rooms and dining rooms and across kitchen tables – by parents and families.' So declares the Chairman and President of The National Center on Addiction and Substance Abuse (CASA) introducing its 2005 report *The Importance of Family Dinners.*[6] His view of the virtues of family meals is widespread, one that is almost as ubiquitous as quotations lamenting their decline. The CASA report states family meals avert a long list of risky behaviours among teenagers, using illegal drugs, tobacco or under-age alcohol. Other public health/nutrition studies also claim they prevent other difficulties like unhealthy eating, obesity, poor school performance and that they also avoid psychiatric distress such as depression (eg Eisenberg et al 2004, Neumark-Sztainer et al 2010, Videon and Manning 2003).

The annual CASA studies stand out. They date from the mid-1990s and are self-published on a website without going through the quality checks of peer review (see Box 1). Reports such as '(F)requent family dining is associated with lower rates of teen smoking, drinking, illegal drug use and prescription drug abuse' are typical (CASA 2007: ii). Perhaps because the CASA reports are freely available they are cited by parenting websites with the gist summarized in the journalist Miriam Weinstein's 2005 book she dramatically entitles *The Surprising Power of Family Meals: How Eating Together Makes Us Smarter, Stronger, Healthier and Happier.*[7] CASA's work is influential in making the significance of family meals a public (and public health) issue.

Yet there are very serious criticisms to be levelled at their studies. Several concern technical and methodological limitations basic to many sciences, not just to sociology. These include inconsistencies in the way different studies define family meals or recording body size based on respondents' own reports of assessments rather than on researchers' taking independent measurements (Utter 2011). Unqualified reliance on telephone interviews in the study of addictions is also unwise (Greenfield, Midanik and Rogers 2000). Gravest of all is a shortcoming that lies at the very heart of the claim that family meals prevent problems. It revolves around an elementary – though all too frequent – set of mistakes in the interpretation of statistical findings.

Methodological limitations of CASA reports

Table 2.1 shows a correlation, statistical association, between the infrequency of family meals and frequency of problems. Note that the strength of the correlation is not given.

Table 2.1 Per cent teens who have used alcohol, tobacco, marijuana, other illegal drugs or abused prescription drugs (2007) (by frequency of family dinners per week)

	5 to 7 dinners	*0 to 2 dinners*
Alcohol	30	47
Tobacco	10	26
Marijuana	8	25
Other Illegal	2	7
Prescription	2	7

Source: CASA 2007: 5.

This, however, is what the preventive power of family dinners celebrated by the Chairman and President of CASA is based on. It is a shaky foundation. First there is the elementary mistake in interpreting correlation as cause. Just because two variables are shown to be connected does not mean any more than that. No conclusion can be drawn that a change in one is the result of a change in the other. Nothing more can be said other than that the variables are associated.

Related to this error is the failure to control for other factors to see whether any account for *both* the lower frequency of family meals *and* the health problems being measured. Strong disapproval of smoking and talking about values over a meal may *both* be features of social groups enjoying higher incomes. Heavier tobacco use and difficulties in scheduling eating together may *both* be features of social groups where adults are employed on shift- and night work and/or in groups where employment is uncertain and wages are either low or non-existent. Both these could explain the associations shown in the table, yet have nothing to do with any effects of family meals.

Yet the CASA studies do not seem even to measure factors such as levels of education or income, degrees of social disadvantage or other measures of social class, without which it is impossible to determine whether family meals have an independent effect on teenage behaviour. While perhaps the CASA studies are a florid example of the shortcomings of this literature more generally, deficiencies are none the less starting to be identified by sociologists (Musick and Meier 2012, Meier and Musick 2014) as well as social policy analysts (Skafida 2013) and public health researchers (Miller, Waldfogel and Wen-Jui 2012, Martin-Biggers et al 2014).

Criticisms of bias in research

Important criticisms like these begin to refine the research. Others develop different objections. The US anthropologist Richard Wilk (2010) provides a strongly argued way of tackling such work. He talks of family meal as powerful 'icon', beginning his discussion with the contrast between what people think is good – the normative – and what actually happens – the performative. He roundly criticizes fellow anthropologists for emphasizing only one aspect of the social functions of arrangements for eating together, the one that promotes 'togetherness', symbolizing shared membership of a group. He notes that the evidence from societies other than those of the US or Europe or 'the West' shows people less likely to eat with their spouses and/or children and more likely to eat with others of their own age, or gender. His point is that when the evidence is side-lined and 'what should be' is conflated with 'what is' i.e. by assuming family meals are normal, any departure stops being considered as just another pattern, it becomes abnormal, deviant, some sort of social problem.

Moreover, Wilk argues that this assumption is made by the privileged, professional classes, whose own middle-class values are unwittingly being incorporated into the assumptions that the family meal is the norm thus casting it as normative. In effect, Wilk insists that the way studies of links between family meals and teenage problems etc are framed, is itself middle class. It thus risks distorting the case by going beyond the nutritional or other science, turning difference into something deemed lacking. Wilk is very clear about his own position: family meals are

> worth studying in themselves, but that means being able to account for the moral rhetoric which has obscured real meals behind a rosy set of ideals, and paying close attention to negative emotions and behaviors at the dinner table without stigmatizing them or labelling them as deviant. The positive and negative sides of family meals are not just moral opposites; they are part of the same phenomenon and should not be divided up. (My) stance is in itself a political one, in that it counters the use of a normative 'happy family meal' as a rhetorical tool for punishing those who lack the means or desire to conform to the cultural mores of a dominant class.
>
> *2010: 435*

Given that the *idea* of a family meal overemphasizes togetherness and devalues its opposite, he argues that together they add up to punitive middle-class 'moralizing' of any who, for whatever reason, do not match it. And this, he insists, cannot be ignored when studying family meals.

Other critics develop a different line of thinking, providing historical data to propose that the anxiety is merely a 'moral panic', for, they argue, the current anxiety about the demise of family meals is unfounded since the past against which they are claimed to be declining never happened (Jackson 2009). In so saying such critics follow journalists who frequently use the expression to describe an overreaction to a supposed problem. Note that in turn, journalists borrow it from the British sociologist Stanley Cohen who originally invented it to analyse public reaction to competing gangs of young people whose 'anti-social' activities one holiday weekend in 1965 hit the headlines (1972) but in the process, have converted its meaning from the original. The relevance of 'moral panic' to the study of a public issue about fears family meals are disappearing is neither unequivocal nor confirmed (Murcott 2012). More significant is that the way family meals emerge as a private trouble do not mirror its framing as a public concern.

Family meals as private troubles

Time after time, sociological research records that 'eating together as a family' is an ideal to which many people are strongly committed. It is valued as a means of teaching children table manners (Warde 2016), found among the middle aged as a way of recreating possibly rose-tinted recollection of their own childhood (Kyle 1999) and reported among rural dwellers in Australia as representing family cohesion and sociality (Lupton, 2000). Work in the US by DeVault (1991) in the UK, Charles and Kerr (1988) in Australia, Coveney (2000) in Norway, Bugge and Almås (2006) in France, Gatley (2016) repeatedly reports people's cherishing the very thought of the family assembling round the table to eat, talk and exchange news. Whatever the particular impetus, this work testifies to the manner in which such occasions are valued and 'togetherness' prized.

It is, however, essential to recognize that this evidence refers to the *idea* of family meals, identifiable by asking people questions in an interview rather than observing them at the table. This is different from identifying any private troubles of family meals. Difficulties arise in the daily realities of what happens at family mealtimes, detecting which require different and often more difficult investigative approaches. Few have followed Sally Wiggins' lead in conducting Conversation Analytic (CA) research (intensely detailed dissection of videoed talk and action) to analyse the intricacy of the social interaction involved in how eating is linked to talking about the food during the meal. For instance, it illuminates the more-or-less successful bargaining between small children and parents' injunctions to 'eat up, it's good for you' (Wiggins 2004, Laurier and Wiggins 2011).

More readily studied are people's reports of their arrangements for family meals. The anthropologist Len Mars draws on an eclectic collection of texts (including fiction) about Jewish mealtimes to show that harmony and conflict co-exist – togetherness may be valued, but competition or subtly barbed comparisons are also relished. In any case, not everyone thinks of family meals as desirable all the time. Parents on low incomes reportedly long to eat peacefully together escaping children's noise and demands – stopped only by the knowledge that eating as a family is cheaper, not least in switching on the stove once only (Dobson 1994). Teenagers say that eating together appeals less to them than to their parents (Brannen et al 1994).

If the family meal is not always harmonious it can also be hard to organize. Schedules do not always fit with other valued family activities – one child has basketball practice, another after-school club, a parent has to work late. Secondary analysis of the UK's 'National Diet and Nutrition Survey' reports that additional factors affecting whether families are able to eat together during the week do not just include parents' employment schedules, but also childrens' ages, childcare regimes and difficulties in coordinating food preferences and tastes (Brannen, O'Connell and Mooney 2013). Yet 'eating together as a family' survives. An especially valuable comparative study is a pair of social surveys, 15 years apart, of changes or otherwise in people's reports of their day to day eating in four Nordic countries (Gronow and Holm forthcoming).

Box 9 The social survey

The survey is a type of quantitative research design, not a method. It is used in many different sciences (e.g. ethology or botany) to assess the size of a population of animals or plants. The social survey designed in the same way, meeting parallel criteria, is adopted by social scientists or public health researchers and in applied enquiries such as opinion polling or market research. It is used to study the distribution of, and correlation between, features of interest among human populations (e.g. age and preference for numbers of ice-cream flavours). Unlike a census which, by definition, includes the whole population, surveys draw a sample from it. The type of sample deemed to give the most dependably robust results – in the UK at least – is the random probability sample whereby every member of the population has an equal chance of being included. Market research purposes may be better served by using the quicker and less labour-intensive quota sampling – selecting cases according to some characteristic such as age or area of residence until a pre-determined quota in each category is reached. Various methods can be used for social surveys' data collection. Most common are questionnaires, either completed by respondents themselves – distributed by post (now infrequent), by e-mail, or handed out (e.g. in a classroom or at a meeting)—or with the questions posed by trained interviewers.

Despite public expressions of disquiet lest family meals are disappearing, the authors find no evidence for their demise in that part of the world.

The family meal – three histories

In this section, the significance of evidence is pursued further through three different histories. The first is the history of sociological research on family meals and it shows a shift. From the 1970s to the 2000s, social scientists can be found who uncritically reproduce unsupported assertions repeating the conventional wisdom that people no longer eat together (summarized in Murcott 2012). But some 20 years ago a more questioning stance starts to emerge (Murcott 1997), furthered by noticing cross-national contrasts underlying different studies. In Britain, for instance, research starts to expose a fear of 'moral decline' or lest the institution of the family is becoming unstable (Warde 2016: 60). In France, by contrast, the problem is framed more in terms of loss of structured meals as a social institution, an anxiety about adverse consequences for culinary traditions or the sociable pleasures of eating (Poulain 2002). The explanation offered points to increasing emphasis on the individual that, coupled with the ideology of 'consumer choice' (Chapter 11), replaces collective conventions (Warde 2012).

The second two histories involve additional lines of thought about family meals, although both need to be evidenced to continue side-stepping accepting received wisdom at face value. The first of these additional histories arises in the call for dependable evidence for the claimed decline, including specification of the type of data that are needed. Self-evidently, statements about the supposed disappearance of family meals are couched in historical terms: 'once there were many, now there are fewer' is the gist. Many of the reports of decline cited in the mass media are prompted by the publication of market research surveys (for examples see Murcott 1997).

Box 10 Sociological research and market research

Investigations of social activities are not only conducted in universities or research institutes, but also by commercial companies. Market research, in particular – especially about food purchases, cooking and eating – may well deal with similar topics to sociological research. But there are critical differences between the two – which is not to say that one or other type is superior or that there are not well/badly conducted examples of either.

As its name indicates, market research is geared to investigating economic activities associated with a market for goods and services. Opinion polling is a closely associated type of work. Typically, such investigation is conducted by specialist independent businesses serving commercial clients such as businesses, mass media corporations, also government departments, political parties, NGOs etc. By contrast, sociological research is largely undertaken in academic and allied settings (e.g. independent scientific research institutes) and is geared as much to furthering knowledge as to having some practical impact. Although it may well have additional purposes, a prime rationale of academic research is understanding and furthering knowledge, in contrast to prime purposes of market and allied research which are to support sales, policy making, campaigning etc. The economics of each setting means that market and allied research can typically be completed more quickly than academic, university based research.

Market research is typically provided for a single business client which buys the investigation and to whom the results may be confidential, at least for the period when they are deemed commercially sensitive (i.e. risking providing information advantageous to competitors). Results are infrequently made widely available. Versions or summaries that are not commercially sensitive may be published – typically available at a price affordable only by businesses, not individual academic researchers or even university libraries. Quality control is a matter of satisfaction by clients, expressed via their readiness to return to the same research company.

Quality control in scientific research is completely different. Scientific research is not complete until results are published, primarily in scientific journals. Above all, articles first have to pass the scrutiny of other scientists (commonly at least two or three) to be published (i.e. peer reviewed) (see Box 1). Sociological research is peer reviewed. Market research is not.

Market and academic researchers occasionally hold unfavourable stereotypical views of one another – views to be set aside when recollecting that market research can range from very 'quick and dirty' to being expertly carried out according to academic research criteria with as wide a range in standards across academic research. Publication in academic journals does not always guarantee suitably conducted research.

Such surveys – whether market or academic research – are often referred to as 'snapshots' since they record phenomena at a particular date. Reports that one in five people surveyed never have a family meal can say nothing about whether that represents an increase or decrease. The conclusion that they are declining is not to be found in the data, but in the way they are greeted by commentators. To demonstrate a decline (or otherwise), trend data are needed i.e. data provided by studies designed to show changes over a period of time. Although recently remedied by the pair of Nordic surveys (1997 and 2012) already mentioned, the difficulty is finding data for earlier periods with which to make comparisons. Why would anyone think of collecting them in, say, the 1950s, the 1920s or even in 1900, let alone raise the funds to do so?

A handful of researchers have been most ingenious in getting around the difficulty of the lack of evidence. Several have looked for existing statistics assembled for other purposes and reanalysed them specifically to test whether family meals are disappearing – not just in single 'Western' nations (Mestdag and Vandeweyer 2005) but also compared cross-nationally (Warde et al 2007). They report reductions in time spent preparing and eating meals, record variation between nations, yet still find that eating together is the most likely way families spend time with each other (especially those with dependent children) despite increased time pressures making coordination harder. But, they add, the data need to be interpreted in the light of other broader social changes (e.g. alterations in the composition of households) especially increases in the proportion of the population living alone who, by definition, have no other co-residents with whom to eat.

The geographer Peter Jackson is just as resourceful but instead of looking for existing survey or statistical data, he returned to detailed interviews recorded in the early 1970s. Collected by the oral historian Paul Thompson they consist of more than 400 life histories of those born at the turn of the nineteenth and twentieth centuries.

Re-analysing them, Jackson and his colleagues find that recollections of life in the 1910s show, as now, that:

Box 11 Oral history

Oral history is a relatively young branch of history (Perks and Thomson 2016). It breaks with the discipline's long-standing reliance on documentary evidence by capitalizing on living memory. Oral historians primarily proceed by talking to older people about what they have personally experienced in their own lives, together with capturing memories of major events etc through which they lived. In effect, people are invited to reminisce to a researcher who audio- or video-records their conversation. In this respect, its methods overlaps with those used by sociologists, among others, notably interviews. Archived oral histories are beginning to be re-analysed by sociologists.

family meal-times and domestic routines were highly contingent on other practices, mainly taking place outside the home. The "family meal" may have been venerated by some families as a (middle-class) ideal. But the ideal was rarely attained in practice. Where "family meals" did take place among our Edwardian families, it usually occurred on weekdays at mid-day and on Sundays, a pattern that was largely dictated by the demands of paid employment outside the home.

Jackson et al 2009: 145

As they point out, equal investigative rigour is required today to establish good evidence before 'the ideological assertion of a general decline in the "family meal" is accepted as fact' (Jackson et al 2009: 145).

A third history is also needed. This one is of the very idea of the family meal itself as valuable (Murcott 1997). The similarities between the Edwardians' reminiscences of family meals being an ideal that was hard to put into practice and interviewees in recent studies are striking: other commitments get in the way. By now, the following extract from a research report will sound familiar:

Meal-time as family reunion time was taken for granted a generation ago; . . . there is arising a conscious effort to 'save meal-times, at least, for the family'. As one mother expressed it . . . 'Even if we have only a little time at home together, we want to make the most of that little. In our family we always try to have Sunday breakfast and dinner together at least' . . . 'I ate only seven meals at home all last week and three of those were on Sunday' said one father.

Lynd and Lynd 1929: 153–4

Familiar, it may be, but the report is almost 90 years old. It comes from a sociological 'classic', the study of Muncie, a small town in Indiana, to which the authors, Robert Lynd and Helen Lynd gave the pseudonym Middletown. Their data recording a 'conscious effort to "save meal-times . . . for the family"' were collected between January 1924 and June 1925 and place the previous generation's reputed family reunions at the dinner table in the final decade of the *nineteenth* century. In other words, they date the existence of an established anxiety about the decline of the family meal, in at least one small American town, to not so long after the end of the First World War.

Putting these three histories together reveals little support for the *actual* decline of family meals, much more evidence of *fears* for their imminent demise. So saying, raises the question as to how and why these fears persist. One suggestion is that harking back to a probably non-existent perfect time of togetherness at family meals represents a 'myth to live by'. These comprise stories people tell 'in order to explain who they are, where they have come from, and why they live as they do. Whether or not they are "true" in any historical or scientific sense, such stories have consequences in the real world'. They shape our beliefs, and so influence our actions (Cameron 2007: 4). This line of thinking returns to the way that an ideal – a political ideology as Wilk trenchantly puts it – creeps in to colour discussions which are ostensibly free of them. The people 'most likely to express anxiety about the possible disappearance of families eating together are those whose own social origins are the source of an allegiance to middle-class values and the middle-class valuation of family meals' (Murcott 1997: 44). Simone Cinotto's historical work underlines the way that the 'proper family mealtime' originates among the Victorian middle class. Although achieving normative dominance thereafter (continuing to hit the headlines today) he observes that 'with the partial exception of the 1950s, only a minority of American families could ever live by it' (2006: 17).

Having unearthed the ideological elements of discussions of the (supposed) demise of family meals, the remainder of this chapter is devoted to two broader sociological considerations. One deals with meals and gender (a fundamental feature of social structure) and the other focuses more intently on terminology and the meanings of 'meals', 'family' and 'family meals'.

Family meals and gender

As already noted, sociologists repeatedly report that interviewees value the 'togetherness' of family meals with some continuing to interpret meals as 'essential for the unity of the family' (Mäkelä 2000: 11). But family unity does not necessarily mean social homogeneity or equality at home, whether at the table or in the kitchen. Social structural features, wider forms of social stratification are refracted through the family and household. The most notable is gender closely followed by age/different generations, with class as the context. Keep Norman Rockwell's painting and the cover of this book in mind (see Chapter 1), then read on.

These features are extremely well illustrated by little-known ethnographic research conducted decades ago in a small Scottish village (Littlejohn 1963). The domestic organization of food and eating forms only a very small part of his multiple-method study of many aspects of life in the village community.

Box 12 Ethnography and participant observation

Ethnography and participant observation are sometimes used synonymously. Both emphasize generating data about life as it is lived, naturally occurring rather than derived from arrangements such as interviews for a social survey, specially 'set up' for the purposes of the investigation. As its name implies, participant observation entails the researcher's observing by taking part in people's daily lives in their usual 'habitat' over time. The primary means of recording is the fieldwork diary, augmented by photographs, video to produce a daily, very detailed, account of observations, initial interpretations, notes for further work etc. Originating in anthropological research in societies or among social groups usually wholly unfamiliar to the researcher, participant observation entails identifying the setting/ group and then joining to become a temporary member of it. Participant observation starts with watching what does and does not happen and listening to what is said, thereafter extending to asking questions – commonly informally – and more like the usual everyday talk between people than even an unstructured interview. Anthropological and a good deal of sociological participant observation requires sustaining the fieldwork over months and years rather than hours or days. Analysis requires moving beyond merely reproducing fieldnotes to produce an original interpretation of what has been observed (Hammersley and Atkinson 2007, Atkinson 2017).

Of the period, a routine feature of everyday life is 'tea', the late afternoon meal at home, when all family members assemble, no matter which social class. Gender differences are prominent. Littlejohn notes, however, that male dominance is especially clear in working-class households, whereas in the upper-middle men do dominate, but defer to women in domestic matters. Both styles are manifest in what he calls the 'ceremony surrounding meals, particularly tea' (1963: 127).

In the highest-ranking class, everyone sits down at the table together, including the woman of the house. At her side are the teapot, milk jug, sugar bowl and all the cups. Everyone waits for her to invite them to begin eating and it is very bad manners for a visitor to help themselves to any food on the table. Members of the family are also to wait for the woman to invite them to eat. If they want something they have to ask for it, adding 'please'. 'The food itself is so arranged as to facilitate the woman's presiding over the meal – bread is cut thin, often made into minute sandwiches, scones are small, and large cakes are put on the table uncut, so that if anyone wants a piece of cake he or she can only have it after the housewife (sic) has specially cut one for them. She pours the tea for each person, enquiring whether they wish milk and sugar duly adding both to the cup accordingly before handing it down the table to them' (1963: 128).

Table arrangements in the lowest ranking class are very different. Tea starts with everyone except the woman sitting at the table. She walks round the table pouring tea into the empty cups she has earlier set beside each place. Only then does she sit down. Everyone only gets tea in their cup. The milk and sugar are in the centre of the table and each person simply reaches out his hand for them and adds whatever they wish to their cup. The food is in the centre of the table too and each person again reaches out a hand, takes what they want without reference to the wife or anyone else. If some plate of food is beyond arm's reach, a person takes their knife and stabs the desired item on the serving plate to bring it onto their own plate. Again, the food is arranged specifically to fit into this pattern of activity. '(B)read is cut thick and is never made into sandwiches, scones are large, and cakes are put on the table already cut into pieces.' If anyone wants more tea, they 'simply pass their cup to the housewife (sic) *without using any words*. Often, however, she rises and brings the teapot' as soon as she sees an empty cup (1963: 129, emphasis added).

Littlejohn's months of very detailed participant observation show how the ordinary daily arrangements for a late afternoon/early evening meal reveal that in the upper-middle classes, the wife has control over the food. Everyone, he says, 'gets food by virtue of her kindness'. By contrast, the working-class wife 'has no control over the food but instead performs a servant-like role during the meal' (1963: 128, 129).

The purpose of quoting his work at length here is not to suggest that these patterns still exist in exactly the same way half a century later (suitable evidence is lacking) but to illustrate how the workings of gender and of class can be made evident in the most mundane of domestic events using methods of repeated close scrutiny and carefully itemized commonplace practices. Research like Littlejohn's can be taken together with many other findings about gendered divisions of domestic labour and associated arrangements across the generations, including the changing emphasis as to whether children are mouths to feed, hands to help or both.

Other household types

It is, however, still the case that there is insufficient good quality research that focuses systematically and comparatively across different household types. So more detailed work on class variations in different regions remains to be developed; historically, Turner notes that the late-nineteenth/early twentieth-century reality of US working-class life meant that family life and the employment sphere was not readily separable, so cooking was not always entirely relegated to women, given their need to take paid work (2014). Similarly, more attention is needed to different stages of the life course or varying household composition as well as variations by gender, hetero-/same- sex households, despite decades' old calls for it (Murcott 1986). A notable exception to the last is the sociologist Christopher Carrington's study of the everyday life of members of 52 households he refers to as 'lesbigay' (lesbians, bisexuals or gay men) (1999). Methodologically, his study is a commendable advance on those which rely solely on a single qualitative interview with only one household member. His work comes far closer to the all-round detail of participant observation by augmenting such interviews with 'weeklong time periods when I would dwell with the families I was studying'[8] or 'tag along with them while they conducted their domestic affairs' (1999: 23). Coupled with his own biography, gay son of a single mother, which he indicates leads to a heightened sensitivity to domestic labour, his is one of the more nuanced discussions of the subtleties of food provisioning.

There are, however, sustained features revealed in what research there is. Set against the background of OECD social indicators confirming that in 29 economies women undertake more unpaid work than men[9] social surveys and sociological research consistently report that women typically remain responsible for 'foodwork' – a new-ish expression to encompass what earlier is referred to as 'domestic food provision' describing all the tasks necessary before and after food is put on the table. It is still women in the US, across Europe etc (Charles & Kerr 1988, deVault 1991, Julier 2013, Lupton 2000, Warde et al 2007) who are responsible for the organization of cooking facilities, overseeing shopping/ensuring the acquisition of appropriate supplies, and maintaining the smooth running not just of eating arrangements but of the (heterosexual) household overall. It is not that men, or dependent children (or other household members) do not cook (Murcott 1983d). They do. But the generalization holds that theirs is generally a different position vis-à-vis routine, daily food provision and they typically do not take overall responsibility for the management of everything from acquisition of foodstuffs through to disposal of leftovers. This pattern is most marked in households with dependent children, but it can persist after they have left home (Mason 1987).

In effect, this discussion raises the question as to what the words 'cook' and 'cooking' mean, although it is noticeable that the researchers cited thus far typically do not ever discuss the matter (but see Short 2006). The terms can either be pre-defined by researchers against which empirical investigations are set, or the social definition can be the focus of the research (as in Murcott 1983d). The activity is also the subject of intense commercial focus as the food writer Laura Shapiro shows when in the early 1950s the US industry sought to redefine cooking as part of their major efforts to promote 'packaged-food cuisine' (2004: 60).

In addition, a sustained theme in the literature on domestic meals revolves around the gendered differences in the amounts and types of food different family members eat. Widely reported for more than 100 years, women in poverty-stricken households stint themselves or even go completely without food so that the men – on whose wages all depend – are given the lion's share of meagre rations to keep up their strength to work (Mennell, Murcott and van Otterloo 1992). Such calamitous arrangements are echoed in patterns of far better-off households. And it is of a piece with observations made elsewhere, e.g. in 1930s Ghana (then the Gold Coast) when a woman has completed cooking, she 'takes much trouble in arranging her husband's portion in neat slices (but) she is less fastidious about the other portions' (Fortes and Fortes 1936: 270). It remains evident in 1980s Chicago (DeVault 1991) and the north of England (Charles and Kerr 1988) with men also receiving better things to eat than everyone else.

Widely uncovered, such privileges accorded to men are echoed in menu choices. When studies do not simply collect reports of 'who does what task' but also reveal how men and women think about those tasks, it starts to become evident that being responsible for them does not necessarily confer autonomy in decision making. Regularly doing the shopping or cooking most of the food, does not mean also having the freedom to decide what is bought or which dishes are prepared. Indeed, the research rather strongly suggests that all those tasks undertaken by women are as a service to the remaining family members no matter which social class, with some studies reporting that the performance of this task is considered to be the counterpart to men's going out to work to provide the family's financial support (e.g. Murcott 1983b). The extent to which wives' incomes are considered supplementary or necessary to support the household varies historically. Moreover, a greater commitment to sharing home making among younger couples is likely to be changing such patterns (as a study of 22 middle-class partners in Scotland suggests, Kemmer et al 1998) though as yet there is still insufficient evidence to be sure how widespread it is (but see O'Connell and Brannen 2016). Further shifts are suggested in Australian research reporting that child-centred attitudes result in even quite young children having an influence on menus (Dixon and Banwell 2004).

Pleasing husbands and children by providing foods they particularly like is found over several decades on dispersed continents. In the first half of the twentieth century 'male immigrants, in particular, were reluctant to change their eating habits, mothers often found themselves cooking two separate meals, with Italian dishes for their husbands and "American" ones for their children' (Poe 2001:142). In Los Angeles County (California) Beck notes the same pattern in other studies, finding that '(F)amilies in our study often served extra dishes to please individual family members who did not like the rest of the meal' (Beck 2007). In South Wales, women report being unable to venture new recipes or 'experiment', accepting it as normal that they defer to their husband's (less adventurous) tastes (Murcott 1983b) while far more recently a UK study finds that cooking more than one menu is a means of diffusing mealtime tension (Thompson et al 2016). Similarly, Haldis Haukanes' research among Czech families confirms that menus are carefully adapted to individual wants. It is not the shared meal which binds a family together, she says, but food's 'flow – the constant stream of food distributed to individual family members thanks to the woman's intensive activity. The family as a collective "we", therefore, largely depends on the woman's readiness to perform her role as expected' (2007, para 32).

Gender is not the only social structural dimension that is evident in domestic life. Carrington, for instance, illustrates the manner in which food provisioning in lesbigay households reflect both class (middle vs working class tastes in ingredients, dishes and cuisines) and ethnic identity (loyalty to shops in an 'ethnic' area of the city, despite higher than supermarket prices) (1999). In sum, then, the work remains lop-sided insofar as there is no systematic overall picture of the range of household types. What there is illustrates how domestic food provision is powerfully gendered.

Families/households, meals and family meals

The discussion so far has almost completely side-stepped the question of what anyone means by a 'family meal' or how it is to be identified, and, come to that, what either 'family' or 'meal' are to mean. So, this section tackles such terminology, not, however to arrive at authoritative definitions, but to help think through the literature discussed in this and later chapters.

Families/households

The swiftest answer to the question 'what is a family' is that it is hugely variable. Who counts as family, who is entitled to inherit names and property, who is responsible for the upbringing of children (socialization) and care of dependents and who, as of right, can be turned to in times of need or old age, varies very widely across different cultures and over different historical periods. Under which roof people live and with which family members (if any) or others is also variable. Adding to the complication, where people eat (as opposed to where they sleep) and with which family members they eat, never mind who is responsible for providing the food or cooking can cross-cut all of these variations.

Everyday usage tends to elide the notions of 'family' and 'household' such that a common-sense understanding of 'family' amounts to 'parents and their children living together in the same home'. That understanding extends to the unspoken assumption that those children's grandparents may now live at a different address, even if once one of their parents had been the child at that other address – and so on. In practice, there are many variants such as people married for a second or third time, with children spending half a week in turn at separate addresses with each biological parent who in turn is now living with their new spouse. A newer variant, in several countries (e.g. in the US or Sweden) is the number of people living on their own is increasing, newer still is the number of those in their twenties returning to live with their parents.[10]

Sometimes, it is essential to be able to sort out detailed distinctions between 'family' and 'household'. The former is about who is related to whom, with a further distinction between 'kin' – those related by blood (or adoption) – and 'affines', those related by marriage (or equivalent). So, siblings are kin to one another where their mother and father are, by definition, in an affinal relationship to one another. Household is about living arrangements, where people sleep, shelter, store belongings etc. While American, Singaporean or French households may mostly consist only of one couple and their children, there are variations – additions such as an elderly grandparent or among the wealthier, a live-in maid – even in nations where family and household are typically the same. In other parts of the world, living arrangements can be far more varied.

Conducting a census in any country is one important occasion when such distinctions are needed. The definition of household for the purposes of conducting the U.K. Census in 2011 focuses on food and eating: '(O)ne person living alone; or a group of people (not necessarily related) living at the same address who share cooking facilities and share a living room or sitting room or dining area' (ONS 2014: 3). But making the distinction is also essential in worldwide study of 'who eats with whom'. It is not just that men and women may eat separately; Tallensi males and females in pre-Second World War northern Ghana only eat together in special circumstances – women cook, and the organization of the work of supplying food, whether subsistence farming or at the local market, is also strongly gendered (Fortes and Fortes 1936) The way kin is reckoned may also determine where or with whom a child, woman or man eats or who cooks and for whom and whether they eat together – all elements of social life of a complexity that might baffle those accustomed to the simpler patterns of much of the global north (e.g. Feldman-Savelsberg 1995, Carsten 1995, Hutchinson 1992, Janowski and Kerlogue 2007).

Meals

The word 'meal' can, colloquially, refer to both the occasion and the food. Introducing her study of American meals Alice Julier asks '(W)hat counts as a meal? Does it need to be cooked in the home? Include rice? Can it be cold? How much can come from cardboard boxes?' (2013: 3). Names for occasions for eating are not necessarily uniform even in a single nation, reflecting fine-grained distinctions to do with time of day, the pattern of eating throughout the day, the presence or absence of others, degrees of formality, where it is eaten, the extent to which all or any elements are industrially processed and still more (Murcott 2013). Daily patterns change: for instance, the reduction in Vienna from five to three meals over the twentieth century is associated with industrialization and the organization of work (Rotenberg 1981). New words are introduced; marketers are apparently responsible for the word 'grazing' to refer to eating small things at irregular but frequent intervals, sometimes near-continuously, and for creating a verb out of 'snack'.

A distinction needs to be made between researchers' own understandings and their definitions of meals or other named/unnamed occasions for eating compared to what their research participants mean. When undertaking social surveys and other types of quantitative study, researchers must decide in advance of collecting data how to operationalize what they are after i.e. specify what is to qualify as an instance to count it. But there are no good reasons to suppose that researchers' own ideas of what counts as a meal correspond to others' or indeed can capture variations among others' – quite the opposite, for researchers are, by definition, located in a particular social structural position, if nothing else by virtue of their university level education. Thus, their understandings may be atypical. Making the distinction between researchers' and respondents' understandings is helped by suspending judgement, adopting, for instance, the term 'food event' (which) is an occasion when food is eaten no matter what research participants do or do not call it. Its introduction by Douglas is deliberately designed to make possible reference to an occasion without prejudice as to whether people define it as a meal or not (Douglas and Nicod 1974).

Keeping an open mind in this fashion allows the collection of data about nuanced discriminations and conceptions of arrangements for eating by paying attention to the *everyday* manner in which people refer to food events. Listening and watching for such conceptions in, a study of 30 years ago leads first to noticing that people talked, as if in inverted commas, of a 'cooked dinner' and then led on to the realization of the proprieties and social conventions surrounding its several nuanced connotations in terms of the menu, the place it is eaten, the day of the week, and more (Murcott 1982). A 'cooked dinner' is a 'proper meal' whose opposite is a 'snack' or 'fry-up'. In just the same way that what counts as food is a culturally defined sub-set of all things a particular social group recognizes as edible (see Chapter 1) so too the idea of a 'proper meal' is found cross-culturally, even if the menu varies dramatically. For instance, a proper meal in Sweden means 'potatoes, meatballs, baked Falun sausage, spaghetti and mincemeat sauce, fried fish and a salad, maybe some ice cream for dessert' (Brembeck 2005: 258).

Family meal

It will be evident by now, that the English language expression 'family meal' carries a great many shades of meaning (Murcott 2011). Whether or how 'family meal' is defined, depends on the circumstances. Any public-issue expression of anxiety lest it is declining has little need for formal definitions to make the point. Public health researchers studying links between family meals and teenage problems focus on the presence (or otherwise) of parents when adolescents eat, commonly taking at face value whatever answer respondents give, without stopping to determine the degree of uniformity (or otherwise) among responses. Fewer researchers pay attention to what is being eaten, when and where it is eaten, or the kind of occasion.[11]

As yet, sociological discussions of the matter have not developed much clarity. Several refer to family meals rather than offer clear specifications. Some adopt the same investigative strategy as public health researchers, largely leaving it to respondents' interpretations, e.g. in a study of 312 Houston families (McIntosh 2010). Others come closer, e.g. Mestag and Glorieux 2009. The Nordic studies cover operationalization in detail: specifying a multi-person household; the meal which is hot (cooked) happens at home, is eaten in the company of other family members and by all the family/household members together. Thus, family meals are those which gather the entire household together, with 'family' and 'household' used synonymously. Using this definition, the first Nordic study confirms the continued existence of family meals in the Nordic countries, some 60 per cent of all hot meals being family meals. These were more frequent among older people and among households with children. Furthermore, couples with children were more likely to have family meals than single people with children (Kjaernes, 2001). Similar patterns are reported for England (O'Connell and Brannen 2016). All the same, unexpected approximations remain in the literature. Even Warde's recent, highly sophisticated, discussion which attempts to summarize relevant elements of the proper family meal is rough and ready in conflating respondents' notions of a 'proper meal' and 'family meal' with no empirical warrant for so doing – in the process referring to a source which never once mentions the expression 'family meal' (Warde 2016: 60). At least Alice Julier carefully skirts such difficulties in her study of more than 100 New Englanders, pinpointing instead the manner in which critics such as Pollan ignore the way that cooking meals is gendered (2013: 20).

Despite being detailed, it is very hard to find sufficiently fine-grained distinctions that allow nuances to be well captured. The picture of the gendered maldistribution of power in the existing literature may or may not reflect most up-to-date circumstances, so questions still remain. How far does a family meal require the same menu for all to eat, seated, at the same table, at the same time? Or is it still a family meal if a portion of the same menu can be put on one side for a latecomer who eats solo after everyone else has finished? Or does it count if everyone eats at the same time, but all eat something different – and so on. There is also the question of the amount each person eats, when, or even whether they eat and the way this is/is not gendered. Especially important is the question as to whether a family meal must be taken at home and/or cooked by one of the family members. Does a meal at McDonalds count as a family meal or a take-away pizza with everyone watching the television? (Brembeck 2005). Far more research is needed.

Commensality

Much like the literature's variability and degrees of vagueness in what 'family meal' is to mean, the use of the important technical term 'commensality' is as vague and variable.

Derived from Latin ('com-' together, 'mensa' a table) this concept has a long history in anthropology and sociology to analyse the social organization of, and cultural conventions surrounding, eating together. It is possible to discern strong (more detailed, specified) and weak (minimal, general) definitions. A clear example of the weak version is adopted by the sociologist Jeffrey Sobal: 'eating food together ... and who someone shares the intimacy of eating with is an important dimension of the sociability of meals. Commensal partners are people chosen to share a meal' (Sobal 2000: 122). Although it has the advantage of a convenient shorthand that saves words, this use adds nothing to 'eating food together'. Some usages go a little further in studies emphasizing positive aspects of eating together e.g. the provision of a shared meal in 1980s rural Russia in return for helping with farming tasks (Rogers 2005) or recording the deliberate use of shared meals to contribute to conflict resolution (Hess 2007)).

Strong versions of the concept of commensality incorporate socio-cultural rules for the vital activities of survival: who may and may not eat with whom. Commensality is implicated in social stratification of one kind or another. Anthropologists tend to emphasize inclusion/exclusion and marking social boundaries. As Maurice Bloch observes: '(I)n all societies, sharing food is a way of establishing closeness, while, conversely, the refusal to share is one of the clearest marks of distance and enmity (Bloch 1999: 133). The 'classic' example is the Indian caste system's strict rules governing eating, food preparation etc where commensality lies at 'the root of all caste distinction' (Iversen and Raghavendra 2006: 312). Sociologists of an older generation tend to highlight commensality's implication in 'social distance' – the approval or otherwise of marriage partners, suitability or otherwise of those with whom people may properly take a meal.

Paying careful attention to the strong version of commensality is essential, for it serves as a reminder that though for many, eating together is about enjoying the food and strengthening familial bonds, this is only one, often idealized, aspect. Certainly, there are reports by women (and men) of their taking pleasure in preparing enjoyable meals for others (Murcott 1983b, Johnston and Baumann 2015). But great care is needed not to romanticize. Recognize that commensality 'is also a matter of authority, in terms of who controls the household diet, and confrontation' (Cook, Crang and Thorpe 1998: 165). Reliance on the weak version risks eclipsing even asking about, let alone documenting, the extent of disharmony, exclusion, the unequal distribution of labour or of satisfaction of preferences.

Remaining alert to the strong version also underlines the importance of attention to history and to help avoid the dangers (already discussed) of assuming that familiar patterns are long-standing. Alertness to the strong version similarly helps guard against ethnocentrism i.e. observers' assuming their way of life applies everywhere. Helen Tuomainen's study of Ghanaians living in London finds the possibility of family meals *without* company that is nonetheless aligned with kinship patterns and household structures in Ghana, helping preserve strong family and community bonds (2014).

The French sociologist Claude Grignon deserves the final 'say' on commensality, and family meals. He, too, insists on an historical perspective. Yes, he remarks, there is plenty that is positive about commensality and it may well support social integration. But, this happens because commensality first allows the limits of the group to be redrawn, its internal hierarchies to be restored and if necessary to be redefined. Thus serious study has to be prevented from confusing, as is too often the case, commensality with conviviality, which is a result of the former, even if its euphoric manifestations are easier and more pleasant to describe.

Grignon 2001: 24

His strictures are invaluable reminders not to be blinded by the ideal of family meals, no matter how highly valued. Remember that such an arrangement is historically and cross-culturally *unusual*; the 'family meal' occurs only in certain parts of the world and is only around a century-and-a-half old. Start thinking instead of understanding the variety of modes in which people eat together, noting those who are and are not members of the group. Ask who decides the menu? Who does the work of serving the food and clearing away afterwards? That way the sociological study of the social organization of eating will be placed on a more secure footing.

Family meals and the thread towards the food system

To round off this chapter there are a couple of things to ponder on. The first is that the various directions which have been introduced illustrate how focusing on food can serve as a lens on societal features. There is the persistence, in Wilk's vocabulary of the ideology of family meals and the consistent demonstration of the prominence of gender as a general social structural feature in the domestic organization of meals. There is also the way that the feared decline of family meals is characterized as a problem whose solution is laid at the door of those who do not conform to the values of the very people who deem it a public problem – a view not matched as a private trouble. This is a version of the sociological thinking of Howard Becker, who is less concerned with the social characteristics of 'outsiders' (those who do not conform) but much more preoccupied with 'the process by which they come to be thought of as outsiders' (Becker 1963: 10).

The second thing is to anchor this chapter toward the context of the food system. The chapter's material focuses on eating, yet it remains almost silent on the acquisition of the food. Provision and production is viewed only from the domestic kitchen – only brief reference to the social organization of shopping compared to cooking. In the various literatures on family meals, it is as if the wider market for food, let alone the even broader system of food production is irrelevant. If family meals are above all home-based meals, then this hints at the idea of home cooking, of homemade food, as being the opposite of food that is commercially manufactured. This is neatly pointed out in a pair of studies based in an academic marketing department.

Summarizing their findings, they list difference between homemade and commercially made: the former has imperfections, made by the hand of a nameable person whereas the latter is standardized and anonymous, the former 'lacks the commercial profit-making character of "market-made" which 'originate from an impersonal production system' (Moisio, Arnould and Price 2004: 367). Younger people, however, think homemade only needs someone to cook in the kitchen for those they know and care for without having to cook exclusively from raw ingredients but using industrially produced items as long as the cook is making an effort. However, for the oldest research participants, it means fresh ingredients and following a recipe (increasingly known by the colloquialism 'from scratch'). The authors note a twist and point to the 'Martha Stewart industry' and women's magazines as a source of opinions about homemade. In the UK images of the virtues of homemade are widespread. A notable example is a series of near soap-opera television commercials of a family whose meals are enhanced and whose 'togetherness' secured by the addition of an Oxo cube (dehydrated meat stock) so well known that it is the subject of widespread review and commentary.[12] The imagery of family, meals and home is used to advertise a commercially manufactured ingredient – an irony and link deserving more detailed investigation.

Box 13 Chapter 2 – Selected Key Points

1. Although the death of the family meal is widely proclaimed, insufficient suitable evidence is available to be sure.
2. Research used to claim the value of family meals in reducing adolescent alcohol, tobacco or illicit drug use is often poor and unreliable.
3. People widely value the *idea* of family meals.
4. Some researchers argue that white, middle class 'moralizing' underpins criticism of those whose economic/social circumstances make it especially hard regularly to organize such meals.
5. A gendered division of labour whereby women are responsible for provisioning and cooking as a service to men and children remains widespread
6. Weak and strong versions of the term 'commensality' occur in the literature; the strong is favoured for it incorporates attention to cultural conventions and rules for social inclusion/exclusion of those who may eat together.
7. Recognizing that family meals are cross-culturally and historically unusual helps side-step analyses which confuse enjoying mealtimes with properly designed sociological study.

CHAPTER 3
FOOD IN PUBLIC: 'WE ARE ALL EATING OUT NOWADAYS'

'Everyone you know is eating out ... restaurants are packed night after night'[1]

'Nearly two thirds of Singaporeans (61 percent) ate out more frequently in the past year than they did in the two years prior'[2]

'Kiwis are opting for cheaper eats, but dining on them more frequently than ever before, according to the latest snapshot of the New Zealand hospitality industry'[3]

These three headlines, from the USA, Singapore and New Zealand, illustrate a common refrain among those reporting the current extent of eating out. But they are far less condemnatory about this eating pattern than the headlines about family meals, just saying instead that eating out is widespread or picking out trends towards healthy eating or maybe gluten free in restaurant/café menus. Eating out is significant in that it constitutes a sufficiently large contribution to industrialized economies to make it worthwhile for governments to collect associated statistics. Those figures are, in turn, the subject of reports and newspaper articles: one dataset records that the sector represented nearly 4 per cent of total UK GDP in 2014[4] and in the US created 47,000 new jobs in January 2016.[5] But however widespread the habit, it may not be surprising to find that 'we' are not 'all' eating out nowadays, or at least not nearly as much as this chapter's title and quotations imply.

Contrasting with Chapter 2 which is primarily about eating at home, this starts by reflecting on the various interests in eating out, moves on to what sociologists have to say about the matter and then goes on to examine sociological studies of restaurants, both behind the scenes in the kitchen as well as seated at the table. Sociologists' research on such topics is often interested in what eating out says about the character of contemporary society, using food and eating as a 'lens'. This paves the way for Chapter 3 which shifts to the overarching question: 'where do people eat?' by juxtaposing 'eating out' with 'eating in'. Note that the English expression, 'eating *out*' would make little sense without its counterpart 'eating *in*'. Both are ordinary expressions of daily life in English speaking countries and are readily understood for many purposes including food prepared at home eaten away (a packed lunch to school) or food prepared commercially brought back home to eat (a take-away/take-out pizza). It is a distinction 'automatically' made in, for instance, people's believing they are less likely to get food poisoning eating at home than eating out as reported both for the UK[6] and young Bangladeshi students in Dhaka who consider street foods or shops selling local food unsafe whereas home-cooked food (together with global branded fast-food chains) is thought of as 'hygienic' (Zaman Selim & Joarder 2013).

One of the themes running throughout this chapter illustrates a version of the sociological imagination. Rather than only presenting the results of studies of eating out, the chapter reflects on the thinking involved when asking what is to count as 'eating out'. Furthermore, it deals not only with the way it is defined but also enquires about who is doing the defining, to see what light can be shed on familiar, commonsense assumptions about eating out. After a section on those interested in trends in eating out, the chapter goes on to discuss relationships between restaurants/café employees and diners, before examining other variants on eating away from home.

Different interests in patterns in eating out

Various organizations have an interest in knowing about trends in eating out. First, there is the catering industry itself (from Michelin starred restaurants and small cafés, school and hospital canteens in so far as catering here is commercial rather than domestic) which has a keen commercial interest, served by market research agencies (see Box 10). These provide information about variations between sectors. They often pay considerable attention to the patterns of eating out among young people who are a commercially important segment of the market with, potentially, a lifetime of patronage of fast-food outlets, cafés and restaurants ahead. Here one major concern is with identifying the latest fashion, ideally before it becomes widespread. That way business can capitalize on it and adapt their 'offer' (the current marketing expression) to gain competitive advantage or not to lose market share.

Second, many nations' departments of agriculture (or trade or tourism) collect such statistics, monitoring the food and drink sector of the economy. In the US and New Zealand, they report steady increases over the last three decades or so in the rate of eating food prepared outside the home and/or the proportion of household expenditure devoted to, or the proportion of total calories consumed accounted for, by eating out. Focus group data (Box 18) from Singapore's Agri-food and Veterinary Authority[7] suggest that eating out involves less wasted edible food than eating at home. By collecting data on which meals people do and do not eat at home the UK Food Standards Agency's survey puts the familiar meaning of 'eating out' in context, reporting that more than half the respondents (58%) ate breakfast *and* main evening meals at home in the seven days before the interview. Incidentally, it would perhaps not occur to some people in certain countries when talking conversationally of eating out to include breakfast. Workers in the building trade would think of breakfast in a 'caff'[8] as wholly unremarkable, while in the US, going out to a coffee shop in the morning, especially if staying in a hotel is commonplace. The rhythms of the working day are reflected in the data for eating lunch out: less than a third (30%) did so daily for the previous week and just over a third ate lunch at home twice or less. This survey also confirms that those with larger incomes are more likely to report eating out both for lunch and the main evening meal than those with smaller incomes.

Third, among academics, public health researchers are concerned with eating out because they find that the food is most likely to be higher in fat, sugar and salt and low in vegetables (the reverse of dietary advice) than meals at home (e.g. Kant and Graubard 2004; Lachat et al 2012). A survey (Box 9) of over 55,000 participants in Brazil reports, however, that eating away from home was associated with 'overweight and obesity only among men ... suggesting that women make healthier food choices when they eat out' (Bezerra and Sichieri 2009: 2037). Another carried out by public health researchers also reflects the rhythms of working life. Their analysis of ten years of data about older Americans shows that a woman's retirement from work coincides with the couple's spending less on eating out – the authors judging this not a result of a drop in income, but because women have more time to prepare meals at home (Chung et al 2007). Public health researchers are also interested in rates of eating out to limit food poisoning in circumstances where assuring safety and hygiene are at issue, e.g. among street food vendors in Lomé (Togo) and more generally in sub-Saharan Africa, where eating out in this fashion is reported to be increasing (Adjirah et al 2013). Contributions to the academic marketing/business literature, by contrast, tend to be aligned with the industry's interests (e.g. Di Vita et al 2016). A small study of eating out in South Korea contrasting hedonic (pleasurable or otherwise) and utilitarian motives (i.e. fun vs refuelling) recommends that to increase custom '(M)arketing strategies in Korea should focus on mood, various menu items, kindness of employees, reputation and image, and facilities rather than price' (Park 2004: 93).

Variation in meanings of 'eating out'

In addition to recording social structural variation in patterns of eating out via income, age and in relation to working life, what is striking about all these different sources is the variety of definitions of eating out that have been adopted. This makes it difficult for anyone wanting an overall picture or asking about differences/similarities (e.g. cross-nationally) as to do so requires being sure like is compared with like. Recognizing the diversity of definitions is also important for any attempt at registering change (e.g. done by collecting data over a period of years on the number of times people eat a two-course meal in a restaurant, a quantitative assessment). But if the classifications and definitions according to which data are collected are themselves altered over those same periods, social changes may thereby also be revealed reflected in the very decisions made by those running the investigations, even if securely capturing any changes remains difficult. Anne Lhuissier elegantly illustrates this feature in her comparison of questionnaires and associated definitions in almost 75 years of government surveys in France and in the UK. Her work draws attention to the way that the type of definition adopted reflects the purpose for which collecting the data is undertaken. Lhuissier shows that in France, the type of place, restaurant or works canteen, café or packed lunch at school, takes priority over the content of the food, whereas in the UK, 'the what' is more important than 'the where', reflecting 'resolutely nutritional' aims (Lhuissier 2014).

Sociological studies of eating out

Sociological research on eating out is still sparse.[9] Julier's work in New England ingeniously comes close, but Warde and Martens' 1995 study focusing on eating out in three English cities is probably the first of its kind anywhere (Warde and Martens 2000). This 20-year-old work reports that those with higher incomes, younger rather than older and men more than women are more likely to eat out.[10] It confirms one common sense assumption that eating out is unusual, reserved for a special occasion, a birthday, a treat, or as an interviewee put it, 'a change from the everyday' (Warde and Martens 2000: 45). But their study does not confirm another assumption about contemporary consumption: that eating out allows a person complete freedom to eat whatever they wish. It is not only that someone is constrained in what they eat by the depth of their pocket or the range of places to eat within a suitable distance. It is also that there are compromises to be made among those with whom the person will be eating, particularly in negotiations about which restaurant or café to go to. Echoing the point, Julier commendably focuses on a specific and even less frequently studied version of eating out, at another's house or other informal gatherings. One of her interviewees talks about a 'potluck' where, food allergies apart, people are expected not to fuss about something they would not necessarily choose (2013: 16).

Interested in what, if any, changes have taken place in 20 years, Warde repeats the study in 2015. The 1995 survey records that eating out is 'special'. Replicating the design and methods, the newer study reveals that eating out continues to be described as enjoyable. But distinct differences show up. In 2015, a smaller proportion than in 1995 report: dressing up to go out to eat; deciding weeks in advance; taking two or more hours over the meal; eating a three-course meal. Add their finding that fewer said they ate out most recently as a special occasion in 2015 than in 1995 (22% compared with 29% respectively) with the converse of more describing the most recent occasion as convenient/speedy in 2015 than in 1995 (26 and 19% respectively). A different overall picture starts to emerge. It is not yet known how far this is peculiar to the three English cities studied, whether there are parallel shifts in rural areas, in other UK nations or elsewhere. It is very likely in many US cities, but it seems the research has not yet been done. A 2012 study in four Nordic countries finds, however, that eating out remains occasional and is not integral to everyday eating (Lund et al 2017).

A view of the distinction between eating out and eating in is implicit in the extension to the second study by Warde and his colleagues. They selected 31 survey participants who recorded an interest in eating, entertaining and cooking for additional, semi-structured interviews (Paddock et al 2017: 2). These interviews augment the changed picture of increased emphasis on 'ordinary' eating out alongside 'special' eating out. The former are more frequent, quick/convenient occasions less likely to be planned very far in advance. In particular, the follow up interviews suggest that women may be making the most of informal places to eat out with their female friends. Unlike 1995, the restaurant has, for some, become a place where, unlike home, women have no responsibility for playing host, no ordinary domestic chores to get in the way and can

Box 14 Interviews

Interviews are occasions when a researcher converses with someone to generate data. Interviews may involve more than one researcher and/or two or more interviewees. They may be conducted 'face-to-face', by telephone or online, either via video link or e-mail. They divide into three main types: structured, semi-structured and unstructured. The first is most appropriate for quantitative research where standardization of the wording and the order of questions is of paramount importance. Interviewers have no scope for introducing lines of enquiry outside their instructions. This confines answers, typically by presenting a list of alternatives from which interviewees select. Semi-structured interviews are widely used in qualitative research. Interviewers begin with a pre-set collection of questions/topics, but invite interviewees to answer/comment in their own words in whatever direction makes best sense to them. Interviewers also have scope to introduce ad-hoc follow-up questions depending on earlier answers. Unstructured interviews are typical of work inspired by ethnography. They aim only minimally to guide the conversation. Interviewers ask very broad general questions to initiate the conversation seeking to persuade the interviewee to talk as their thoughts take them. A record of the resulting data can be made in various ways: in written form by either/both interviewer or interviewee which used pen and paper until the invention of the laptop. CAPI (Computer Assisted Personal Interviewing) is now common for structured interviewing. Audio- or video- recording is used for semi- and unstructured-interviews, also e-mail, via websites etc. Semi-structured and unstructured interview data are commonly transcribed in whole or in part to convert them to text.

Analysis of structured interview material is quantitative – converting answers into numerical form for presentation as tables, an efficient, compressed form of conveying large volumes of material. Analysis of semi-structured and unstructured interviews varies. It ranges from looking very like the analysis of structured interviews on topics which can be pre-specified, right through to the preferable development of original understandings which introduce interpretations that could not have been anticipated easily (if at all) at the outset. Data are displayed as text – whose presentation is far less space-efficient than tables. Good practice requires the inclusion of the questions/comments posed/offered by the interviewer to provide context in support of the researcher's interpretation of the material, despite its posing problems for the overall length of the write-up.

choose what they want to eat without having to cater for their families' tastes, able to relax with their female friends away from the gendered conventions for eating at home (Paddock 2017: 7).

Their recent article stresses two important features of sociological thinking. One reflects Mintz' central point (see Chapter 1) that meanings attributed to food and eating do not occur in a vacuum, but arise in a context of distinct, historically definable circumstances.

> The driving forces of change are not simply shifts in meaning. Increase in ordinary meals which are described as quick and convenient reflects the changing nature of market provision. There are more restaurants in total and greater availability of places designed for informal dining. Provision and patterns of consumption co-evolve.
>
> *Paddock et al 2017: 8*

In other words, the normalization of eating out found in the three English cities is facilitated by the growth in places making it possible. This might also mean that similar normalization may be less evident in geographic areas without the same rate of growth in cafés and restaurants.

The second important feature of sociological thinking is their observation about the new, wider currency of the idea of eating out as something usual rather than special – in turn a reminder of the intersection of biography and history. Those in their sixties in the 1995 study would have been in their forties in 1975 when 'it had been uncommon for anyone on a moderate or low income to eat out except on holiday or at midday in the working week' (Paddock 2017: 7). By 2015, their counterparts now in their sixties would, when in their forties in 1995, have had the opportunity to become used to many more places to eat out: '(A)nother twenty years of regular and normalised eating out has meant that almost everyone is familiar with the activity. The practice has matured along with a population which has more or less a life-time of experience of eating meals out on commercial premises' (Paddock et al 2017:7). This is a neat example of a conjunction between historical changes (the growth in the number of more widely affordable cafés and restaurants) and individual biographies (more people spending more of their lives where there is now a greater number of places to eat out in the three cities studied). Comparison with Caldwell's study of McDonald's in Moscow is instructive: there, what was exotic in the 1990s is considered pretty ordinary a decade later (Caldwell 2004, also Yan 2000) while Julier confirms how widespread is eating out in New England (2013).

Restaurants: workers and diners, backstage and frontstage

It is noticeable that some of the small number of sociological studies of restaurants[11] occupy a different location in the literature from that on eating out, concentrating on them as a workplace rather than on habits of eating out. Working in the catering industry involves long, 'unsocial' hours – illustrated in popular accounts such as Anthony Bourdain's *Kitchen Confidential*, historically comparatively low wages (Gabriel 1988) and working conditions that can be hot, cramped and sometimes dangerous (Fine 1996). William F Whyte's is one of the very earliest sociological studies, based on 14 months' participant observation (Box 12) and interviewing (with three colleagues) in 12 Chicago restaurants in the 1940s. It shows how pressure to serve diners promptly creates friction, even open conflict among staff. This is transmitted from waitresses to pantry workers, runners to chefs and back again. Tensions risk being further transmitted to customers thereby threatening satisfactory service precisely because the 'restaurant is a combination production and service unit. It differs from the factory, which is solely a production unit, and also from the retail store, which is solely a service unit' (Whyte 1949: 302). Similar friction is recorded in two geographically distant ethnographic studies of the late 1980s; Paules worked as a waitress at a New Jersey fast-food restaurant (1991), Crang as a waiter at a barbecue-style themed restaurant in London (Crang 1994).

'Backstage'/'frontstage'

Although his research is not dedicated to studying restaurants, Erving Goffman's observations of the workings of the dining room of a Shetland hotel in Scotland in the late 1950s provided the basis for his developing an especially widely used sociological distinction (i.e. backstage' vs 'frontstage') to understand small-scale social interaction in any situation. Kitchens are 'backstage' where the lowly social origins (a local crofting background) of the managers are on display. The dining room is 'frontstage' where the managers seek to present themselves as more middle class, as well as rather different from the waitresses whose work casts them in the role of diners' servants.

> The doors leading from the kitchen to the other parts of the hotel were a constant sore spot in the organization of work. The maids (waitresses) wanted to keep the doors open to make it easier to carry food trays back and forth, to gather information about whether guests were ready or not for the service which was to be performed for them ... (feeling) they did not have too much to lose by being observed in their own milieu by guests who glanced into the kitchen when passing the open doors. The managers, on the other hand, wanted to keep the door closed so that the middle-class role imputed to them by the guests would not be discredited by a disclosure of their crofter habits. Hardly a day passed when these doors were not angrily banged shut and angrily banged open.
>
> *Goffman 1956: 72*

The metaphor enshrined in what are now elevated to the status of disciplinary concepts does not just have wide, general sociological currency, but has also been used by Erickson in her study that proposes restaurants are 'carefully managed stages for the exchange of cash for food and service' (2007:22). Eating out is to be a pleasure which diners are expected to know how to perform – evident in studies in which the theatrical metaphor is extended. Acting in the 'right' way, individual display as a matter of identity and taste, is widely emphasized in the literature on eating out, whether in Macau cafés (e.g. Simpson 2008) gourmet food writings (Johnston and Baumann 2007) or signalling social aspirations by working in a modern 'western restaurant' in north east China (Hsu 2005).

Studies record that notably, there is a distinct social distance between staff and customers (Mars and Nicod 1984). Interviews with 41 chefs in California record their disdain for some diners (especially wealthy ones) who treat them as inferior, disliking them 'because they seemed not to see the chefs as they saw themselves' (i.e. as skilled craft workers) (Hendley 2016: 472). At the café where Crang worked, however, management required waiting staff to put on a paradoxical performance of 'being themselves', acting as being friends with the diners yet being simultaneously required to follow the prescribed form of words to greet customers, recommend drinks etc., all to conjure the desired atmosphere and assure the profitability of the business (Crang 1994). The smiling welcome required to accompany the work of waiting at table, even if it must be faked, is the same as expected in other service occupations such as receptionist, flight attendant or shop assistant, wryly, if aptly, described by the sociologist Arlie Hochschild in the sub-title of her book as the 'commercialisation of human feeling' (2003).

Performance, along with an undercurrent of a sense of excitement, the fanciful and even the exotic, is also central to both Finkelstein's books on the sociology of dining out. Eating out is, she notes, supposed to be a personally pleasing, civilized occasion when diners want to see and be seen, everything enacted in public. But, she argues, eating at a restaurant turns out to be the complete opposite. Echoing Hochschild's analysis, she observes that all concerned are playing a part, not just the staff. Certainly, restaurateurs and their employees play along, appearing to be delighted to serve, playing down the fact that they are in business; diners, too, seek to satisfy their private pleasures by eating out, overlooking the primacy of the commercial interests of the restaurant. This mismatch is concealed by each side's familiarity with the performances required, made 'all the more convincing for being unrehearsed and spontaneous' – wherein she thinks lies its incivility (Finkelstein 1989: 178). Concealment also features in her more recent book, with restaurants 'highly engineered', obscuring the commercially calculating underpinnings (2014 :viii), the frontstage atmosphere in the dining room is manufactured, geared to social display, with the realities of the kitchen, the steam and dirty plates, hidden backstage behind the scenes along with the accountants keeping an eye on the takings. Everyone must eat, but, 'in the West, the popularity of the restaurant has connected such ordinary acts to big business and redefined food as a form of consumable entertainment' (2014: 198). Performance may be common to Goffman's and Finkelstein's examinations of dining, but the former's aim is to expose and *understand* minuscule features of social interaction. Finkelstein's – or so it appears – is to expose and *evaluate* its features as unedifying.

Eating out: pleasure/discomfort

Note that Finkelstein stresses the pleasures of eating out, as if they are universal. Her concern to censure rather than document the nature of contemporary society means that both her books disregard full attention to empirical evidence, so a search for counter-examples of unpleasant instances of eating out are not even considered. Yet there are those for whom eating out is not automatically or unequivocally a pleasure. The rise of commercialization of children's birthday parties, the public display and the undercurrent of competition involved is reported to be a source of anxiety among Australian mothers (Jennings and Brace-Govan 2014) while women on holiday do not always relish eating out solo (Heimtun 2010) any more than do many others, on holiday or not.

Historically, the nineteenth century English working class, unused to eating outside their home in public, find large-scale provision for the poor in church halls an unhappy experience (Burnett 2014: 31) echoed by that in communal kitchens during World War I (Oddy 3002). In any case, eating out almost anywhere in the twenty-first century[12] is in public, involving diners putting themselves on display. Understanding the disinclination to eat out among many, including 'overweight' women requires little imagination:

> Rose: I always choose healthy meals with plenty of veg . . . it depends on if people can see me when I am eating as to whether I have a sweet.

> Ella: I don't mind having fattening food such as pastry but 1 couldn't be seen to be eating cake or fried foods such as chips.

> Val: I have vegetarian meals because they look healthier . . . I'd rather have steak or chicken etc. but they often come with chips.

> *Zdrodowski 1996: 661*

Well aware that their plates as well as their physical size are on display, these women by-pass their preferences attempting to evade unfavourable judgements from onlookers. This chimes with more general sensitivities about eating in public, especially for those whose possibly upwardly socially mobile social structural position means they are new to the activity unlike those being born into the class in which, at whatever period is in question, it is routine. There are several centuries of etiquette manuals which provide the sociologist Norbert Elias with a rich source of data in developing his theories of 'the civilizing process', a gradual shift from public control of unacceptable behaviour to self-policing and self-control (1969). Now that restaurant dining is reportedly is less formal new etiquette manuals appear.[13]

Eating out, eating in – and in between

It is important neither to be caught up in the 'moralizing' about the family meals of the previous chapter nor fascinated by the sheer variety of cafés, diners and restaurants, and food trucks that are increasingly familiar. To do so risks forgetting that there are other places where people eat. Moreover, the distinction between eating out and eating in is not clear cut. Indeed, Wessel talks of 'non place' when discussing the current fashion for providing 'culturally diverse cuisine in stylishly branded and highly equipped catering trucks' (2012: 514).

The historian John Burnett comes at that point from another direction. In both nineteenth-century New England and England, the pattern is upside down: those eating out 'more than any other class' are the people whose extreme poverty places them at the *bottom* of the social pile, a major and ironic contrast with that familiar twentieth-century assumption that eating out is for the better off. A century ago it is agricultural labourers in particular who ate out far more than the wealthy; working on the land means eating out no matter what the weather; farm work commonly requires being too far away from home to be able to return during the day, necessitating portable food (like Cornish pasties) protected in some way and filling enough to allow the labourer (often children) to keep going for a long working day.

Their poverty-stricken urban counterparts fare little better, living in cramped overcrowded Victorian housing, creating a 'common sight' of slum children sitting on the doorstep eating a bit of bread – 'not quite "eating out"', as Burnett tartly observes (204: 27). Nineteenth-century-city workers in the docks or factories, cabmen or labourers in the building trades buy their food from streetsellers, often several times a day. Indeed, the mid-nineteenth century social investigations of the journalist Henry Mayhew estimate over 40,000 London's street traders, the vast majority selling food, with 6,000 providing 'street food' ready to eat and drink there and then, heirs to the considerable variety of London's street food available since the twelfth century (Spencer 2002: 61). At the other end of the nineteenth-century social scale, are the splendid dinners for guests in their enormous new mansions or the very special occasions at Delmonico's restaurant in New York City (Levenstein 1988).

Research of the twenty-first century varies in the detail with which what is to count as eating out is specified. Burnett makes clear that his social history of eating out in England details it as 'normally understood' (2014: xiii), primarily for pleasure rather than necessity. Warde and Martens (2000: 46–47) follow the lead of their 1995 interviewees to define eating out as a sociable activity in a specific place, provided commercially, the work done by someone other than the diner, for a special occasion involving having a meal i.e. excluding snacks and breakfasts. Like Finkelstein, their concern is to use eating at restaurants as a lens, in their case, for examining the extent of individual discretion/ freedom of choice in a 'consumer society'.

By contrast, the rest of this chapter shifts squarely to consider places *between* eating out and eating in, rather than by-passing the distinction or defining it out of the way. It means switching to the broader question 'where do people eat' or perhaps even better, under what social organizational circumstances and with what consequences do (and can) people move from where they are one minute to somewhere else to eat the next (whether from one room to another, from field to the shade of a bush, home to expensive restaurant). The next chapter moves to other 'in between' places, works canteen or school dining hall.[14]

To do this, several familiar questions/variables must be thought about separately. Do people move to the food, or is it brought to them? Where do people live in relation to where they eat? Who prepares the food and where? Is the relationship between those who prepare the food and diners formal or informal, commercial or as relatives/friends? If commercial, are cooks trained and paid for their work, or might they be volunteers? Who pays for the meal? Is it the diners or is it paid for them, and if the latter, what are the arrangements, employers' subsidy, state provision or charity? Is payment monetary or in another form? Is eating fun and by choice, like the familiar assumptions about eating out, or is it something else entirely? In particular, how much autonomy do diners have over the circumstances in which they eat? Can they choose alongside whom, as well as what, they eat?

Such questions are illustrated by considering additional variants lying between clear-cut instances of eating out vs eating in. For there is an unexpectedly wide range of combinations which self-evidently blur the distinction between eating in and eating out.

Between eating out and eating in

Focusing on distinctions between eating in and eating out can, then, help answer the overall question 'where do people eat'.

Homes without a kitchen

As a rather particular instance, some may have a home, but lack a kitchen. Late nineteenth-century American utopian reformers design dwelling plans with only central kitchens so that individual women would be relieved of food preparation. Some plans require diners to move to a central dining room, in the company of both/either their family or residents of the same apartment block to take meals prepared centrally; other designs have central kitchens preparing hot meals that are then delivered to separate dwelling units (Hayden 1978). This is a pattern currently found in some facilities in the US, UK and elsewhere, for elderly people who are able to live independently, but who are less able to provision, cook and clear away for themselves. Instead, they join others each from their own small apartments (which have small, or no kitchens) in a shared dining room with the same menu usually offering some choice. Possibly far more common, however, is the reality of the very poor in wealthy nations, housed in minimal accommodation, with access either to shared, often inadequate, cooking facilities or none at all.

Tourism, holidaying

At the other end of the social scale are those engaged in what has become known as gastronomic tourism. Many tourists seek familiar food while away, but a smaller number are keen to pursue the 'art of fine food' as an element of their travels, resulting in gastronomy's being 'seen as an important source of marketable images and experiences for the tourists' (Richards 2002:11). Unlike studies by public health researchers of eating out in restaurants or of take-away food where the nutritional quality is an issue, hospitality studies' research on food, travel and leisure is widely geared to the promotion of tourism (e.g. Korea (Park 2004) Mexico (Muñoz and Wood 2009) or Togo (Adjrah 2013)) aiming to 'assist the government and tourism authorities when planning promotional activities to attract more people to visit night markets' Taiwan (Chang and Hsieh 2006: 1278).

Holidays are, in any case, a time when food and eating is reported to be out of the ordinary. A detailed anthropological study of 20 UK families' thinking about food on holiday enlarges on this notion. It reports that 'eating for pleasure' instead of 'eating as re-fuelling' signifies being on holiday – self-catering allows leisurely and thus enjoyable cooking, breaking the 'rules' of daily eating (e.g. relaxing timetables). Rule-breaking in the form of larger breakfasts than usual – especially fried – and more frequent helpings of chips/frites/French fries, are especially associated with UK holiday eating, at times generating tension between welcoming a treat and healthy eating (Williams 1997).

Once again, the concerns of nutritionists become evident. Public health researchers in the US pursue the suspicion that children gain weight at a greater rate over the long summer holidays, especially those who are already overweight, attributable to fast food and less structure to the day's eating (Branscum et al 2010). Others, however, find no weight gain between Thanksgiving and early January (Wagner et al 2012), but statistically significant evidence is reported that Americans eat more at weekends than during the week (Haines et al 2003).[15]

Whether such results are confirmed elsewhere remains to be seen. Studies typically start from the widespread notion that as a break from ordinary routines of work, holidays (and weekends) will also be marked by travel and leisure along with changes in usual eating patterns (e.g. 'treats') or, during festive seasons, dishes and meals to mark the occasion, e.g. turkey for Thanksgiving for Americans, carp at Christmas for Germans, tteokguk (rice paste soup) for Koreans at New Year. Eating as a tourist is not, however, always straightforward, especially if the cuisine as well as utensils are unfamiliar, and the quality of the kitchen hygiene unknown (Cohen and Avieli 2004).

Take-aways/take-out/carry-out

Another focus for public health concern is take-aways/take-out/carry-out and home delivery (i.e. prepared by cooks whose relation to the diner is commercial) in kitchens distant from the location it is eaten. Take-aways are typically fast-food: burgers, fried chicken, kebabs and pizza containing high levels of salt, fat and calories and lower levels of fibre than is recommended. Interest in the dietary quality of take-away food is not new. A century ago, fish and chips shops are ubiquitous in working-class areas of industrial English cities. Resorting to them attracts much criticism, deemed the result of inferior housekeeping. But, medical commentators argue, fish and chips represents a nutritionally valuable component of an otherwise deficient diet of the urban poor at the time. Today, of course, there is a wider variety of take-away food. That school children, especially of secondary school age, with more discretionary spending power than those younger, frequent take-away food shops on their journeys to and from school is of especial concern given their nutritional quality.

Simply attempting to reduce the number of such shops, however, may not satisfactorily address the nutritional problems involved. Wills et al develop a more nuanced, sociologically informed examination of the issue which they consider in its social context. They note that the relationship between students and their school contrasts with the relationship between students and commercial take-away food shops. Schools are bound by rules geared to promoting healthy eating, which cuts across what students want. Take-away shops, however, court students as customers with no nutritional constraints, thereby treating them as if they are autonomous adults – a status teenagers are keen to attain (Wills et al 2016). As a result, school food is rejected in favour of take-aways. If reducing reliance on nutritionally low-quality take-aways is to be effective, attempts are likely to need a more subtle understanding of the various social relationships involved.

Communal eating out

Where people eat take-aways is self-evidently variable – the street, school playgrounds, the sofa watching a film on Friday evenings. As variable are occasions where people 'eat out' but the food is provided on a communal basis. Julier provides a nuanced account of New England 'potlucks', impromptu, informal, sociable, communal still with defined hosts/hostesses, mostly held in public meeting places rather than a home (2013). The widespread New Zealand call of 'ladies a plate' (men are charged with bringing the alcohol) requires each to bring a plateful of food for the assembled company at community 'socials', barbecues or maybe afternoon tea for the local women's division of the Federated Farmers (Park 1991). Friends eating out at a picnic may similarly agree to share the provisioning, with the cooks drawn from the ranks of those attending, someone brings cheese sandwiches, another the salad, a third some snacks. An example of a self-catered communal eating that may have very few counterparts stands out. An ethnography of a tailgate,[16] held annually for three decades, records a dozen people cooking a pot of chilli abiding by simple rules for suitable ingredients. Instead of being shared out, pot-by-pot, however, all contributions are emptied into a *common* pot for further cooking by the organizer, who always takes some home at the end, freezing it as a 'starter' for next year's batch (Bradford and Sherry 2016).

No home at all

Thus far, this section has considered kitchenless houses, holidays and other variants of eating away from home. In this fashion, the examples discussed assume that though someone is eating out, they have a home to which to return in which they may otherwise eat. But how can someone eat out if they have nowhere to eat in? An Irish migrant to the English city of Leicester remembers life in the 1950s on first arriving aged 17 sleeping rough in a public park:

All the night ladies were there. They got to know me and they were great to me. At home, we knew nothing about prostitutes, night ladies – we knew nothing. In the middle of the night, they'd come along and they'd bring me a sandwich, they'd bring you a hot drink, a cup of tea ... might not seem like much now but it was world to me then.

Maye-Banbury Casey 2016: 12

Moving into a lodging house after six weeks, his experience illustrates the precariousness of those finding themselves without a home. This is something anyone seeking to help the impoverished in cities of wealthy nations[17] has to consider when deciding if providing food parcels is suitable or whether, without their own cooking facilities, alternatives must be found for rough sleepers, 'sofa surfers' (successive short stays in the living rooms of friends/relatives) or those housed by municipal authorities in temporary bed-and-breakfast accommodation.

As precarious is the position of longer-term homelessness. Getting enough to eat is just one of an interrelated set of daily problems to be solved. This is graphically illustrated in a detailed Canadian ethnography of 'squeegee kids', young people earning what they can by washing car windscreens/windshields. It underlines the way that getting food is an integral part of getting by on the streets, evading being denied entry to the very cheapest restaurants, banding together with two or three others to pool their resources and share 'two packages of a macaroni and cheese "dinner" mix (sold for one dollar at a nearby convenience store)' (Dachner and Tarasuk 2002: 1044). In stark contrast to eating out in restaurants for those well-off enough to do so almost unthinkingly, squeegee kids have limited choice. Some experience food poisoning after a meal from a set-menu charitable food programme and become wary. But as a 21-year-old says:

We have a choice of eating or not ... I mean there's been nights where, it looks like vomit on your plate, OK. And you're gonna eat it anyway. If you're hungry enough you're gonna eat it. I've been at that point where I was hungry enough that I didn't care what it looked like or what it tasted like you know.

Dachner and Tarasuk 2002: 1045

These examples between eating in and eating out may not affect more than a minority of the populations in wealthy nations (readers could, with little difficulty, find the published statistics of a nation of their choice roughly to calculate the proportion). They do, however, throw into sharper relief some of the assumptions and themes of thinking only in simple terms about what 'eating out' involves.

The meaning of eating out unravelled

This chapter began by noting that the claims often made about the extent of eating out vs eating in is not borne out by the evidence: it is not as all-pervasive as the headline implies. Identifying what counts as eating out is not, initially at least, considered, with the discussion relying instead on assumptions about shared understandings between researchers, authors and readers. Thereafter, highlighting the different, often contrasting interests in eating out, what counts as eating out is shown to reflect those interests – remember public health nutritionists worry about the dietary content of commercially prepared food regardless of where it is eaten. Careful scholars such as Burnett specify what they mean at the beginning, but he still sees no need to think any more about it. This chapter, however, unravels it, to end by illustrating the way that the common sense, conventional versions of what eating out denotes, do not neatly correspond to all kinds of realities, from street children's lives, to smart expensive restaurants, pizza taken home to eat, prison food and back to homelessness.

Such unravelling is not to mean abandoning thinking in terms of 'eating out'. It simply highlights reflection on the purposes to which thinking about eating out is to be put, most particularly as an example of consciously not adopting everyday terminology as if it is always adequate for the purposes of sociological analysis. It represents an instance of standing back from accepting widely held views, such as 'we all eat out now', without question. Stopping to define what is meant by eating out to someone just getting on with their life is obviously absurd: 'let's eat out tonight' serves perfectly well. But when wanting to get a sociological understanding of the variety of circumstances in which people eat, their social organization, freedoms and constraints, then it is important to realize the twentieth-century meaning of 'eating out' – enshrined in Burnett's approach and Warde and Martens' definition – is historically specific to certain (albeit numerous) social groups in particular places. In addition to arriving at that position via attention to history, the course of individual lives and to socially structured variation in opportunities just indicated, this chapter also draws attention to the extent of individual discretion in eating. For if nothing else, in underpinning the great variety in answers to the questions 'where do people eat', it provides a means of getting to grips with the socially distributed variations in how far any one person 'really' has a choice.

Eating out and the thread towards the food system

Eating in commercial premises, including just picking up a snack or cup of coffee, is one of the two most frequent ways in which everyone is in contact with the food system of provision (the other is shopping,). Although this chapter shows there is some sociological work which considers the relationship between diners and those serving them, it also illustrates how the labour of the latter is usually hidden from view. As Sachs et al observe 'consumers are shielded' from the extent to which food is provided by poorly paid often non-white staff. The less-visible areas of restaurants (like food processors and farms) are normalized. It means 'consumers do not see the faces of marginalized workers' making it 'hard to empathize and to be motivated to change inequality regimes in food work' even assuming they are aware of them (2014: 16).

The sociological work discussed also exposes the irony whereby the commercial element is to be played down. Although Finkelstein is dismayed that this is uncivilized, for many it is part of the theatre of dining out, an element in the roles each party knowingly is to play. As noted in Chapter 1, the opacity of the food system is held to lie behind many people's limited understandings of the origins of their food. Put that together with conventions downplaying awareness of the commercial nature of the restaurants/cafés and that the heat and work of their kitchens is typically behind the scenes out of sight. The result provides a different angle of the extent to which the food system is on view to the public. Do these conventions of eating out contribute to the shadowy opacity of the food system? If they do, then future work might consider how far.

Box 15 Chapter 3 – Selected Key Points

1. A distinction between the meaning of 'eating out' and 'eating in' is not clear cut. The type of definition adopted reflects the purposes for which data are collected.
2. The extent of eating out in cafés and restaurants varies internationally and historically.
3. Eating out in restaurants still represents a 'treat', reflecting social structural divisions. Recent signs of change suggest eating out is more 'normalized' and less of a special occasion.
4. Erving Goffman's conceptual distinction between 'backstage' and 'frontstage' introduced to account for social organizational differences between hotel kitchen and dining room, extends to wider sociological use.
5. Restaurant/café staff and customers alike play down their shared knowledge of the commercial element and play up the idea of dining out as special and theatrical.
6. Discussion of occasions that are a cross between eating in and eating out allows standing back more realistically to appraise the proposal that 'we all eat out nowadays'.

CHAPTER 4
FOOD IN INSTITUTIONS: 'WHY ARE HOSPITAL MEALS INADEQUATE, SCHOOL LUNCHES MEAGRE AND PRISON DIETS UNAPPETIZING?'

'Prisoners eat better food': Students hit back at Michelle Obama's school lunch program with pictures of woeful servings[1]

Public hospital food is sickening, say patients[2]

'Pupils at a South Yorkshire school are being fed fish and chips through the gates by parents who say the canteen is not providing what their children want'[3]

Prisons are feeding their inmates on less than $3.97 (New Zealand) a day[4]

Headlines such as these, and there are plenty more of the same, go right into the heart of policy, management in public and private institutions and the work of professional practitioners. Students have strong views on school lunches but so, too, do campaigners for healthier and tastier meals for them. US students complain that implementing the then First Lady's improved menus resulted in meagre unappetizing portions; the mothers of their counterparts in Yorkshire (the north of England) respond to their children's complaints about a new school meal regime, by providing alternatives (conforming less closely with dietary guidelines) they know their offspring like. Hospital patients complain and nutritionists are exercised about the poor quality of hospital meal provision. Feeding prisoners is a long-standing, delicate policy question. Though the chapter title is an overstatement (much like news headlines themselves) it points, all the same, to complaints by patients, school students and prisoners and to problems which professionals declare require solution. The question remains: why is food in institutions often poor?

Sociologists offer imaginative work which approaches such questions obliquely, shedding a different light on them. Note that so doing does not mean being indifferent to problems, quite the reverse, the motivation for undertaking research is frequently to help professionals and policy makers involved seek their resolution. The value of a sideways sociological view includes noticing that the position of the various actors involved in providing and eating school dinners, hospital meals or prison food can often put them on opposing sides.

Ethical concerns are ever-present (see Box 16) but taking sides is not centre stage in this discussion. Instead, this chapter turns to show that sociological work can help understand what may lie *behind* the reasons for complaints about poor hospital food or unpopular school dinners. It divides into two, first considering the private troubles of

Box 16 Research ethics: an illustration

Where, morally, should researchers stand in respect of a research topic? This box notes how the question might ethically be thought about for aspects of the examples discussed in this chapter.

In principle, sociologists would have difficulty deciding with whom to side: nutritionists or hospital accountants; ministers in charge of penal policy or those who committed crimes for which they are incarcerated; students wanting larger portions or practitioners and policy makers trying to reduce obesity rates. The words 'in principle' are italicized for good reason. Sociologists as citizens have their own politics and morals just like anyone else. But there is nothing intrinsic to the discipline of sociology that decides which political position or moral stance researchers are to adopt. After all, sociological understanding of illegal activities could be used to combat or to commit crime in just the same way that psychology's understandings can be used to 'brain wash' as much as resist being 'brain washed'.

Ideally, sociologists should side-step being aligned with any one position to study all sides. But at times, antagonisms are too great to be able to stand alongside sets of opponents in turn, even in the interests of understanding antipathetic viewpoints. If sociological researchers do take sides, they must proceed ethically by doing so explicitly, transparently and with eyes wide open to the implications not simply for the conduct of their research but for the consequences and impact of their work on anyone concerned when it is published.

It may be effortless, if not morally appropriate, to be outraged that a spell in hospital can leave patients malnourished and it is perhaps just as easy strongly to disapprove of someone already serving a punishment being further punished by being fed badly. In the light of repeated reports of the serious health consequences of obesity, it is less easy to work out which side to take when students complain about school meals short on food they like, while nutritionists' concern about their unbalanced diets increases.

eating meals in institutions such as schools or hospitals highlighting how this contrasts with eating on the 'outside'. Then it illustrates the social processes of making institution meals into a public issue, focusing on school meals at different historical periods in different national contexts, illuminating some of the forces that may make for unappetizing meals. In the process, the chapter continues the previous chapter's approach to eating out by addressing the very general sociological question: 'where do people eat?' Especially thought-provoking for this chapter is the developed version of that question: 'Under what social organisational circumstances and with what consequences do (and can) people move from where they are one minute to somewhere else to eat the next?' It helps highlight social institutional features and makes possible pursuing the extent to which those features allow or constrain where eating may happen.

Private troubles of hospital food, school dinners and prison meals

Hospitals, prisons and schools are very different kinds of organization and patients', prisoners' and school students' experiences of eating are not only likely to be very different, food is equally likely not to be the only, or the worst, personal 'trouble' facing them. Such institutions do, however, have features in common, inspection of which helps make sense of the way meals become a focus of attention. The notion of a 'total institution', developed by the sociologist Erving Goffman, provides a valuable intellectual framework (1961). His idea is sketched next as a prelude to examining food in such organizations that are away from home but neither 'eating in' nor 'eating out'.

Goffman's 'total institution'

Goffman developed his thinking about total institutions as a result of undertaking participant observation (see Box 12) in a US mental hospital. The notion captures key similarities between organizations which appear to have little in common except that people are housed in them, sometimes for prolonged periods. Prisons, orphanages, submarines, nurses' hostels, care homes, cruise ships, military barracks, hospitals, university halls of residence, concentration camps, deep-sea trawlers, hotels and boarding schools all 'contain' inmates who commonly spend 24 hours a day within them. Their purposes are, of course, dramatically different. An orphanage is, in principle, somewhere benign to care for children with neither home nor parents, whereas prisons are primarily designed to protect the public by depriving the offender of their freedom, thereby punishing them. Note that the difference in rationale need not prevent an orphan from feeling as if they are imprisoned or a prisoner as if they are drilled more like soldiers. Notably, total institutions share the overarching character that the complete round of daily life takes place within its confines: sleep, work, recreation, washing and, of course, eating.

A further defining characteristic is that each inmate, no matter whether or not their presence is voluntary, is treated alike, one of a batch. Inmates belong to a larger group looked after/guarded by a very different, smaller group of supervisory staff, themselves also similar to one another, if only in that they all have authority over the bigger batch, part of a hierarchical managerial organizational structure. On entering the institution, Goffman points out that inmates are literally and symbolically divested of their individual identity and take on the common identity of inmates. They are required to remove clothes belonging to the world outside (over which they have some say) and change into the institution's own uniform (over which they have none), military fatigues, hospital gowns, prisoners' coveralls. This way, inmates end up looking far more like everyone else. Simultaneously, inmates lose elements of privacy and other aspects of individuality and autonomy, where they sleep, to which parts of the institution they have access, the time they get up or the lights go out at night, including reduced or even non-existent choice of menu, of when, where or with whom they eat. In this respect, all aspects of eating in institutions are not, typically, only more limited than beyond the institution's perimeter but largely shaped by their organizational character.

Eating in a 'home away from home'

Chapter 3 suggests that the place of some meals cannot easily be classified as either 'eating in' or 'eating out'. This includes eating for those living in a home that is not theirs. Residence in all kinds of institution displays many additional features, such as whether meals are designed to be enjoyable, how eating is inseparably interwoven with other features of life 'inside' and the way the organization of eating can get caught up in attempts to resist the organization's regime.

An a-typical instance

Beginning with a strange total institution, the first illustrates the very formal dining arrangement of colleges at the English universities of Oxford and Cambridge where professors/faculty and students live, study and teach. Evening meals are occasions which are not only convivial, enjoying good food and drink, but by requiring students and teachers alike to attend, are also consciously designed to uphold college traditions thereby fostering a sense of belonging and loyalty (Di Domenico and Phillips 2009). These formal dinners are highly ritualized, with distinct conventions to be observed. As diners assemble, everyone is to stand behind their chair to wait for grace (a brief prayer in thanks for the food, often in Latin intoned aloud, either by the most senior diner alone or by the assembled company) to be said before sitting down. Or again, the decanter of port from which diners serve themselves to conclude the meal is, by convention, to be passed from diner to diner in one but not another direction round the table. These conventions are, of course, known to insiders. But they represent the risk of embarrassing mistakes for ignorant newcomers or guests. Being caught out makes highly visible the distinction between those who belong and those who do not. Similar formalities exist in the armed forces; for instance, in the UK navy, it is explained to visitors that, unlike in the other armed services, everyone remains seated for the loyal toast to the monarch that concludes a formal dinner in the officers' mess; ceiling height tends to be restricted on board ship. In these institutions, resistance to the way things are done is not at issue.

Prisons and resistance

In stark contrast, however, is food in institutions that are deliberately more austere. Even though current policies vary as to how severe the regime is to be, enjoyment is typically deemed irrelevant in prison. Both for the purposes of deterrence and considerations of social justice, nineteenth-century Belgian prison diets are not to 'be seen as "luxurious" by detainees or the outside world' (Maes et al 2017: 80). Such rationales are liable to be well recognized in the present century. Note, however, that at the end of the nineteenth century, England's Prison Commissioners recognized that extremely unattractive food posed the danger of revolt. They do not say that the diet should be enjoyable, but recommend the plainest food, albeit wholesome and in sufficient quantity to maintain health. Thereafter, however, a gradual increase in choice of menu in British prisons is recorded from the 1950s onwards (Pratt 1999).

The point is that since containment is the prime task of a prison, anything that jeopardizes order within it demands attention from the authorities. Food and eating is, then, subject to prison policies and routines along with every other aspect of life. Its provision is organized as part of running the prison and can get wrapped up in tensions between inmates and authorities that are inherent in the institution's very nature. Food's potential as a focus for disorder continues to be well recognized: a prison officer observes that food is the biggest flashpoint, adding '"If you can serve decent quality with a substantial portion, the lid'll stay on"' (Valentine and Longstaff 1998: 145).

Significance of mealtimes, lack of autonomy, resistance/adjustment

At the same time, the importance prisoners attach to food and mealtimes is widely reported in other types of institution, not least as a relief from boredom. Jaber Gubrium's ethnography of a combined nursing (for patients) and residential home (for those able to be more independent) in the US vividly captures the distinctive place of food and eating in such institutions (1975). From the inmates' point of view, time itself is marked by eating. The day is divided into three, punctuated by meals. Strikingly, many residents foreshadow the forthcoming meal, starting to think about lunch an hour beforehand, prepararing to move to the dining room where the wait for the trays to arrive can be protracted. Patients and residents routinely say they do a lot of 'sitting around' during which a 'great deal of casual talk . . . centers on dining' not just taking place during meals, but notably anticipating the next meal, and repeatedly throughout the rest of the day (1975: 172). Negative judgements abound, with black humour and sarcasm signalling hostility toward the regime (where no menus are provided in advance) with remarks like 'I wonder what poison they're going to force down our throats today?' (1975: 173). Memorably bad meals are recollected, moans greet the arrival of dishes, while the total amount of time talking about food contrasts with the great speed with which it is actually eaten. Even though inmates in Gubrium's study are elderly, frail and/or unwell, the way food figures so prominently in daily experience is echoed in other types of total institution.

Like prisoners, these patients have no choice in what, when and where to eat which for the former serves as a 'constant reminder of their distance from "home"' (Valentine and Longstaff 1998: 135). It is not just the elderly for whom having to switch to institution food means adjusting to compulsorily eating at set times; it also means living with the physiological effects of what, for many inmates, is an unusual diet – for prisoners larger breakfasts, blander dishes, poor cooking, inferior ingredients, which, coupled with less exercise, can mean weight gain, sluggishness, skin pallor, nausea etc (de Graaf and Kilty 2016). As Ugelvik observes in his study of men in an Oslo prison, food acts as a 'painful bodily manifestation of the power the institution holds over the individual' (2011: 47). Preferences are also disregarded: ready meals which are organizationally convenient to provide are disliked by inmates in a Dutch prison (Vanhouche 2015).

At times there are places within places confining people. Some prisons require inmates to eat in their cells. Others are organized so that prisoners leave their cells to eat communally – 'eating out' – but also provide 'commissary foods'[5] for sale at a tiny convenience store, which inmates with some money can take back to their cells to 'eat in' as Smoyer and Blankenship put it in their US study of 30 women ex-offenders (2014). These authors record women's complicated experience of hunger. Although the women grant that the three communal cafeteria meals a day are plentiful, its provision at set times in circumstances not of their choosing results in meals that do not sustain them until the next one. Not always having the cash to buy food that was permitted, women resorted to food that was not. Prison policy did not allow food to be taken from either the cafeteria or the kitchens where inmates worked, yet all 30 interviewees talked of the illicit movement of food from both back to their cells.

> Every participant spoke about how they traded and shared the food with each other, moving food between and within housing units and pooling resources to prepare fairly elaborate dishes using hot water and heat from hair blow dryers and radiators. These activities satiated hunger by allowing access to a greater quantity and variety of food between meals and providing women with the opportunity to gain some semblance of power by controlling when, where, and how they ate.
>
> *Smoyer and Blankenship 2014: 9*

Food becomes currency among inmates, stolen from kitchens, stockpiled, traded either for different food or other valued items like tobacco (Valentine and Longstaff 1998). Godderis (2006) records theft as a way in which inmates in a Canadian prison achieve some control over where they eat, electing to avoid communal canteens and eating stolen food in the privacy of their cells. This is one way in which eating can be used to assert individuality, representing a mode of resistance to the prison regime.

An ostensibly more congenial experience of eating in prison, a sort of adjustment to the regime, is provided in Comfort's study at San Quentin (San Francisco) or 'Papa's house' as the children of men incarcerated there call it. In an attempt to reduce the risk of their partners becoming permanently detached from home life, women relocate various everyday activities to the visitors' accommodation such that the prison becomes a 'domestic satellite' (Comfort 2002: 470). Women recounted the lengths to which they go to re-create family meals with one mother describing it for her seven-year-old son as 'just like a picnic' (2002: 480). Such a description is reminiscent of that used by Morrison in her project on food in an English primary school, describing midday eating like a large indoor picnic (Burgess and Morrison 1998) rather than anything firmly regimented.

Consider the contrast between a picnic no matter where and the ideal of an orderly lunch at home round a table: in manners, fingers instead of forks, little or altered structure to a meal with no obvious order of courses or foods conventionally served together. Here is an irony, given women's attempts at keeping the idea of family alive by taking their children to 'Papa's house' to eat.

Yet opposition to, if not outright revolt against organizational rules is an undercurrent that runs through reports of many such institutions. Even in Morrison's study, among young children only in the institution during school hours, attempts at resistance are evident. One school requires children who bring a packed lunch from home to eat in a different part of the dining hall from those taking hot meals provided by the school. But the children ignored the rule to sit with their friends, thus subverting the arrangement, providing a glimmer of autonomy (coupled with sociability) between the children, winning out over institutional efficiency (1998, Daniel and Gustfasson 2010).

Imbalance of power

Time and again, the literature on institutions makes plain the unevenness of power relationships within them (Mennell, Murcott and van Otterloo 1992: 112–15, Cohen, Krumer-Nevo and Avieli 2017). Gubrium explains that ambulant residents seek to retain a sense that they are diners, expecting the nursing staff to serve them, more like waitresses in a restaurant, despite the evident trappings of their inmate status via the staff's nursing task of distributing medication at mealtimes. Staff are resentful as a result, but tend to go along with it in the interests of a quiet life. Sick patients in the same institution are treated differently, far more like wayward children who fail to 'eat up', with the staff asserting their superior position.

Power differentials are evident across very different institutions. In stark contrast to those discussed above is the study of Irish migrants' memories of 1950s-life in lodging houses. The authors invite men, now much older, to reminisce about moving to English cities in the 1950s when still unmarried (Maye-Banbury and Casey 2016). As part of the all-in costs, men eat the evening meal where they live, a home away from home. But they are also 'inmates', not full members of the household, not allowed access to all parts of the house (rarely the kitchen) and share food/drink with the landlord/landlady by infrequent invitation only. Their generally low social status (as labourers who are also migrants) is reflected in these limits on their lives, placing them in a less-powerful position in their lodgings vis-à-vis the landlord/landlady. The grisliest parallel aligning the quality of food to institutional hierarchy, with catastrophic, often lethal, effect, is recorded where '(M)ost infamously, Nazi concentration camps distributed meals based on a strict racial hierarchy' with the best rations going to guards and camp staff while 'contaminated and spoiled foods were served to the lowest ranks of inmates' (Weinreb 2017: 79).

Much of the discussion thus far focuses on the potential for antagonism (or the grotesque example of the previous paragraph) in the case of prisons or tension in the case of other institutions. Heaven et al adopt a different stance in work directly designed to address malnutrition in hospital, including among those needing help to eat (2013).

Composed of several components, including tracing the movement of food from storeroom to patient, the study focuses on the range of tasks nursing staff are required to undertake. They uncover a high degree of inconsistency in the way the combination of tasks involved in feeding patients is carried out. They also identify illogicality. On the one hand, feeding patients unable to feed themselves (due to disability, illness or being elderly) is reported by nursing staff to be a highly skilled, time consuming task to do well. Yet this understanding co-exists with regarding the work of providing meals and helping patients eat as lower down a hierarchy where clinical procedures take precedence. The organization of food provision on a ward comes closer, then, to a hotel rather than a medical service, implicated thereby in inadequate feeding of patients facing difficulties.

These glimpses of life in total (or near total) institutions convey the complex interlinking between food and the defining features of such places. It also highlights the manner in which eating occupies so prominent a place in inmates' personal troubles of living in a 'home away from home'. Against an implicit background comparison with eating in (at home) or eating out (at a restaurant) where a greater degree of autonomy over where, when and what to eat prevails, this oblique sociological attitude to the questions of this chapter title makes it much less surprising to find meals are extremely significant to prisoners, patients and children alike and that complaints are widespread.

Making and re-making institution food as a public issue: the example of school lunches

When, where and what children eat tends to prompt special attention not least by virtue of their being regarded as 'the future' (Burnett 2013, Gullberg 2006). While this view of childhood is historically and cross-culturally variable it has prevailed for more than a century and provides a background for this section which takes school lunches as a special case of understanding institution food as a public issue. It sketches how school meals emerge as a solution to the social (and nutritional) problem of poverty and how, once invented, they appear and re-appear with the public issue revolving around their quality. That there is not a single route to either their creation or their appearance as a public concern is illustrated. The discussion of this special instance is framed by a distinctive approach to the study of social problems in the sociological tradition of symbolic interaction proposed by the American sociologist Herbert Blumer, dealt with next.

Blumer on how social problems and issues are 'made'

In 1971 Blumer took his fellow social scientists to task over the way they studied social problems, illegal and illicit activities, divorce rates, 'broken homes' and juvenile delinquency etc. to use the vocabularies of the period. Colleagues are illogical in silently assuming that these, among others, are self-evidently on the list, he writes. Instead, the vantage point needs to be shifted to ask how some human activities but not others ever get to be identified as problems in the first place. Thus, he turns the spotlight on to the processes of 'collective definition', with the reminder that a 'social problem is always a focal point for the operation of divergent and conflicting interests, intentions, and objectives. It is the interplay of these interests and objectives that constitutes the way in which a society deals with any one of its social problems' (1971: 301).

He proposes that the social processes involved can be thought of as going through five stages. To begin with, social problems are not some intrinsic social malfunction but 'the result of a process of definition in which a given condition is picked out and identified as a social problem' (1971: 301). In other words, an issue does not exist until that existence is recognized; social problems are 'made'. Unless this happens, no-one can refer to, let alone consider what to do about them until recognition gives birth to them. That, however, is not enough to initiate action. For it has, next, to be deemed respectable enough to be discussable in the mass media, organizations such as religious institutions or charities as well as among policy makers, legislators and officialdom. Initially, those aiming to identify a problem as requiring public attention must find a way of making their view legitimate, otherwise they will not be taken seriously.

Having got this far, the would-be problem needs to be moved to the next stage where it becomes a topic of 'public discussion, of controversy, of differing depictions and of diverse claims' (1971: 303). This is where proponents come up against anyone protecting pre-existing vested interests.

> Exaggerated claims and distorted depictions, subserving vested interests become commonplace. Outsiders, less involved, bring their sentiments and images to bear on their framing of the problem. Discussion, advocacy, evaluation, falsification, diversionary tactics and advancing of proposals takes place in the media of communication, in casual meetings, organized meetings, legislative chambers, and committee hearings.
>
> *1971: 303–4*

This is a critical stage. Those with vested interests, especially if they are strategically placed, well-resourced and powerful, seek to derail advocates. Unless identifying the problem survives such adverse public attention, then efforts to mobilize those with authority to deal with it may come to nothing. That still leaves two more stages: first to persuade those in charge to create an official plan of action, and second to see they assure implementation to round everything off.

As Blumer clearly notes, interests are not necessarily neatly aligned with one another. Various rationales are used for introducing school feeding. A remarkable example is the contrast across the Cold War divide (1945–1989) between East Germany (GDR) and West Germany (FRG) where communism vs capitalism is caricatured, according to historian Alice Weinreb, with the former the 'unfree' and the 'starving', the latter the 'free' and the 'satiated' (2017: 6). In the GDR the economic situation is held to require all adults be employed, a goal that 'encouraged the state to take an aggressive approach toward regulating domestic labour' reducing women's work at home by organizing feeding family members elsewhere (2017: 177). This means the energetic promotion of convenience food is part of a scientific and rational approach to domestic kitchens. Accordingly, the provision of hot meals replacing a comparatively meagre cold lunch for school children was instituted in 1950. Expected to lighten women's burden, the new policy was initially resisted as an infringement of parental rights that threatened 'the well-being of their children' (2017: 186). Complaints published in the newspapers reveal the fear that mothers' cooking would become redundant if children had eaten enough at midday to reject an evening meal. Even though uptake improved (as did children's health) 'school lunches do not sever the ties binding East German women to their kitchens' not least because school cafeterias were largely staffed by women. Despite such policy and practice, the idea of home cooking continues to be highly valued (ch 2) (2017: 188–9).

How different is the case on the other side of the Berlin Wall, where throughout the same period, 'West Germany continued to distinguish itself through its continued opposition to school lunches' (2017: 191). There the school day is shorter than in the GDR, making lunch unnecessary, a schedule said to be responsible for survey reports that some three-quarters of housewives around the mid-1960s favour 'state-sponsored school breakfasts' (2017: 191). As significant as parental rejection and, despite the rise of second-wave feminism pushing in the opposite direction, state educational institutions continuing to resist instituting lunch programmes. '(S)chool meals were conceptualized as being incompatible with the free market and consumer capitalism, which prioritized individualism and "free choice", whereas school meals deny children the opportunity to express their individual preferences, and mother's autonomy is undermined' (2017: 191). Note that this is the same conceptualization which, Morgan points out, surfaces in 1970s Britain crystallized in the form of the 1980 Education Act which changes school meals from a compulsory nationwide service to local provision on a discretionary basis (2006). Indeed, in the FRG, reliance on home-cooked lunches appears 'definitional to its identity – and to its difference from the GDR' (2017: 193) underlining the way that, though school meals are a public issue in both Germanys, the issue plays out dramatically differently in each.

Repeatedly re-making school meals as a public issue

Many countries have institutional arrangements for feeding children, providing either/both meals and, sometimes, also milk at a discount/free in schools. It might be thought that the primary, if not only, impulse behind whatever set-up is in place, is to provide a suitable amount of nutritious food for children in nurseries and schools. But in the words of the subtitle to her book on school lunches, the history of 'America's favorite welfare program' is 'surprising' (Levine 2008). It seems what makes it favourite is the involvement of interests *other* than the nutritional best interests of children.

The same illustration of Blumer's discussion is evident in the UK. John Boyd Orr, a twentieth-century Scottish medical researcher, played a significant part in making malnutrition among the poor a recognized social problem, based in part on his widely publicized research *Food Health and Income* (1936). He wrote a 1966 autobiography in which he talked of the various interests in devising school feeding schemes. Discussing producer interests, he recalled the difficulties created in the 1930s by a surplus of liquid milk diverted from butter and cheese-making. His own involvement with the arrangements for supporting prices paid to dairy farmers, led to his recommendations for solving the difficulty, proposing a government subsidy, a fifth of which be spent on 'propaganda to increase milk consumption *to get rid of the unmarketable surplus*' (Boyd Orr 1966: 112–13, emphasis added). As a result, the 'Milk in Schools Scheme' could be expanded. Only later, during the Second World War does the Minister for Food arrange that the available milk supplies be distributed based on need, prioritizing mothers and children. Certainly, both nutritionally needy children and milk producers benefit, but it demonstrates how more than an impulse to improve nutrition was involved in achieving that wartime outcome.

Chronologies of the invention of school meals further illustrate the range of interests involved. They begin in both the US and UK with the charitable 'initiative of private agencies' (Levine 2008: 33). The first in the UK, in 1864, is the Destitute Children's Dinner Society (Burnett 2004). With the introduction of compulsory education (1880) schoolteachers are faced with emaciated, hungry children, leading one headteacher and her staff to pay for pupils' food. At the same time, long standing anxiety about the population's lack of physical fitness is confirmed by the discovery that army recruiting for the South African War (1899–1902) reveals more than a third of volunteers are unfit to serve. This revelation serves as a major spur to the creation of the 1904 Inter-departmental Committee on Physical Deterioration which records witnesses' evidence about the poor diet and feeble health of schoolchidren. (Report 1904 Vol II).

Throughout the twentieth century, the invention of school meals is associated with their origins in feeding the poor, an image that has had to be shaken off at successive periods and the respectability of school meals as a public issue restored (Morgan 2006, Weinreb 2017). In Britain, school meals stop being food for the poor, provided 'soup kitchen' style during the Second World War to become 'part of Social Welfare, a social service for all children' (Fisher 1987: 190). While this change is probably evident to those involved in serving the lunches, less visible both pre- and post-war is the relation between school meals and agricultural production not just in the UK.

From the start, the US National School Lunch Program 'linked children's nutrition to the priorities of agricultural and commercial food interests, both of which carried more weight in the halls of Congress than did advocates for children's health' (Levine 2008: 4). In the US in the1930s, dealing with surplus/by-products of butter and cheese-making alters. Skim milk is diverted from on-farm use to feed livestock or discharged as waste to pollute waterways, with commercial uses being sought so that by the late 1940s it is being used in school lunches in dried form (Smith-Howard 2014). For several decades, the virtues of nutrition for children seems more like public relations for a school lunch programme 'designed primarily as an outlet for surplus food' (Levine 2008: 38). That it is run from the US Department of Agriculture is questioned in the 1960s; there is concern there is a conflict of interest between the aim of improving the agricultural industry and feeding children (and the poor). But by the 1990s, the programme is established as a significant market for the food-service industries with private companies stepping in after federal funding is reduced. The influence of food-service companies in schools spreads beyond just providing lunches to supporting nutrition education work using branded promotional materials. It is reinforced when federal regulation is relaxed to allow branded fast food to be sold in schools, with the cultivation of brand loyalty as an attractive commercial 'add-on'.

This is the background to what the American School Food Service Association calls the 'Junk Food Wars' of the early twenty-first century, with nutritionists, parents and educators mounting new campaigns to improve the quality of food in schools, echoing attempts already made during the 1960s to point out the conflict of interest within the USDA. A prominent initiative is mounted by celebrity chef Alice Waters, founder of the Berkley restaurant Chez Panisse. She inaugurates the *Edible School Yard*, in neighbouring schools, subsidized by her own foundation. As Levine notes, however, she mounts her own project (as do similar projects elsewhere) without 'address(ing) the public policy issues that produced school lunch difficulties in the first place' (Levine 2008:190; for the UK see Morgan 2006).

Jamie Oliver's television campaign – and its limitations

Several authors point to the efforts of the 'celebrity' chef Jamie Oliver to help tackle increasing rates of obesity by improving children's diets, in both his native UK and the US. *Jamie's School Dinners* is a four-part television programme broadcast in 2005 specifically geared to the improvement of school meals. Uttering an obscenity that is still not always broadcastable, he famously castigated 'turkey twizzlers' a highly processed specially manufactured school-dinner item.[6] Journalists and public health nutritionists were much struck by the way his ensuing campaign and petitioning prompted a rapid response by Tony Blair, the then UK prime minister (Zimmet and James 2006).

Oliver exports his mission to get people to eat more healthily to the US: ABC broadcasts his six-episode programme *Jamie Oliver's Food Revolution (JOFR)*. These campaigns to improve diets generally and to get children eating more healthily in particular, are not uniformly successful. His efforts in the US meet with considerable resistance, people reportedly not wanting to be told what to eat. Resistance is more muted in the UK; those involved in running school kitchens meet various obstacles to implementing Oliver's menus despite the difficulties of managing on very tight budgets.

Despite Zimmet and James' endorsement, the limitations of his endeavours can also be analysed social scientifically. The dominant ideology emphasizing individual freedom is criticized for downplaying structurally derived constraints on opportunities to effect change (Slocum et al 2011). The supporting arguments include the way that the programme is of a piece with a century-long line of well-intentioned efforts to improve the health of those on low incomes by teaching the working class healthy and thrifty eating habits (Gabaccia 1998). In addition, *JOFR* trades on shaming people about their diet and about their weight. Designed, it would seem, to shock the audience as well as the participants, the programme piles a week's worth of a household's food consumption on a table in a staged, ungainly heap of pizza, sausages and packaged foods. Slocum et al invoke public health and sociological literature to argue that shaming only makes matters worse: 'the bulk of the data shows that obesity stigma leads to a host of negative sequelae related to the health and well-being of the stigmatized individual' (2011: 182). Such limitations are further compounded. The programme is located in a region known for its white poverty in a city selected 'because of its designation by the Associated Press as the "unhealthiest in America," an estimation derived from the Centers for Disease Control and Prevention's (CDC) Behavioral Risk Factor Surveillance System (BRFSS) data' thereby obscuring social structural links with poor health (2011). Using shame is a tactic that assumes the overweight individual lacks sufficient self-control. It is based on the belief that everyone is free to choose to eat healthily or otherwise which, when coupled with too narrow a focus undermines 'its revolutionary aspirations' (2011: 187). In effect, Slocum et al's argument is that *JOFR* is not just a television programme, but an example of the same problematic features of wider US debates and food politics.

Conclusion – institution (school) eating and a thread towards the food system

Slocum et al's article is noted here as a convenient, swift illustration of alternative lines of thinking to those about inferior school food presented in most of this chapter. They use *JOFR* as a vehicle to convey their critique of individualistic approaches to dietary improvement that place undue emphasis on changing people's behaviour without paying any attention to social structural features limiting opportunities to make those changes.[7]

As to the connections between institutional eating and the food system, the work of Poppendieck and Levine (among others) would indicate that fruitful lines of enquiry would be to examine the social, political and economic forces at play in the practicalities and politics of procurement, currently typically outsourced to specialist catering companies. An example is provided by the geographer Kevin Morgan and the anthropologist Roberta Sonnino, both based in Wales, who compare two case studies of school food procurement, one in Italy, the other in the UK (2006). They point to the manner in which these two Member States of the European Union interpret its admittedly ambiguous regulatory framework in different ways, with contrasting implications for the healthfulness of school meals. Each does so, they argue, in terms of each nation's culinary culture.

In Italy, strong emphasis is laid on the local/regional along with appealing to established cultural traditions in food and eating in which schools are to play a part by educating the next generation in the self-same culinary heritage. By contrast, the focus on profit and efficiency in UK agriculture extends to forms of culinary cultural framing of school meals as primarily a commercial operation in which educating the next generation (and their parents) to eat well and become suitably informed consumers takes lower priority. Here the analysis moves well beyond the boundaries of a (total) institution to examine the regulatory framework, understand dominant commercial ideologies and attend to overarching culinary traditions in which food procurement takes place, to use it as a vantage point from which to assess the quality of school meals.

Box 17   Chapter 4 – Selected Key Points

1. Complaints about the quality of food in institutions – hospitals, schools, prisons etc – are widespread in many countries.
2. Erving Goffman's concept 'total institution' helps understand how meals become a focus for special attention for patients, students or prisoners, punctuating the day, limiting their choice of menu and/or companions etc.
3. Some degree of dissatisfaction is explicable as integral to the nature of the institution's internal social organization.
4. The history of school meals in the US and UK illustrates the way feeding children is turned from a private trouble into a public issue.
5. Herbert Blumer's conceptual scheme for studying social problems is relevant to identifying the social processes involved in the establishment of school meals.
6. The impulse for introducing school meals, milk etc. is not always solely out of public concern for children's nutrition or welfare, but also includes commercial considerations.

CHAPTER 5
FOOD PREPARATION COMPETENCE:
'COOKING SKILLS ARE BEING LOST BECAUSE PEOPLE RELY ON CONVENIENCE FOODS . . .'

'The slow death of the home-cooked meal'[1]

'. . . the dramatic decline in the country's cooking skills from one generation to the next . . . the rise and rise of the food manufacturer with an increasing range of convenience foods in his portfolio'[2]

'. . . kids are losing valuable cooking skills as their parents struggle with busy lifestyles and opt for takeaway or processed foods'[3]

'Women have lost cooking skills . . . mothers don't pass them on any more'[4]

This chapter's title is a recurrent, pessimistic refrain. It crops up in gossipy news reports when one politician's wife serves commercially prepared mayonnaise to another[5], or when an extremely well-known cookery writer publishes a book entitled *How to Cheat at Cooking* showing how to incorporate all manner of convenience foodstuffs into everyday meals.[6] The anxiety is repeated by other food writers and activists, some nutritionists and public health specialists and can be found as far apart as the US, New Zealand, Canada, and the UK. Cooking a complete meal at home from raw, unprocessed ingredients (colloquially known as 'from scratch') is said to be getting rarer as successive generations are supposedly not learning how to make such a meal and, with the proliferation of convenience foods, they do not have to. Indeed, the very availability of those convenience foods, whether just one ingredient, individual dishes or complete meals, can, in principle, result in doing away with any thought of needing to learn to cook.

While worries about the loss of home cooking may be found in several other countries, the reason given is not always the lure of convenience foods. In Singapore, for instance, people's cooking less and less is explained by the extensive employment of maids or simply as a result of going out for meals – according to at least one market research report which records that one-third of people eat out more often than they eat at home.[7] All in all, it is dramatically summed up by the journalist Michael Pollan who regards 'outsourcing our food preparation to corporations' as causing the 'decline and fall of everyday home cooking' (2009).

Such anxieties and what lie behind them are examined more closely in this chapter. Note that this is the first chapter that is as much about the food and the materiality of food itself as it is about studying food as a window on the social world. It involves asking what 'cooking skills' means; the independent researcher Frances Short finds it puzzling that neither 'cooking skills' nor a variety of associated terms is defined, arguing that they extend beyond cookery book specifications to include perceptual skills including 'the feel' of ingredients (2006). The chapter then turns to illustrate current research approaches to 'cooking skills' and 'convenience foods' by way of unearthing some of the associated complexities. For that, a historical perspective is essential, as is thinking about cooking and kitchens in far broader social and economic contexts. The chapter ends by considering the development of food and domestic technologies alongside kitchen design and the overall industrialization of the food supply. As to social structure, both gender and class are at issue throughout.

Are cooking skills really lost?

Before getting going, the question whether cooking skills are really being lost must be raised – and there is more than one answer. The first is that it is probably impossible to say, for there is insufficient evidence of the appropriate type. This lack is illustrated by a notable and now older contribution to the discussion by the English experts in food policy, Martin Caraher and Tim Lang (1999). They are confident that English cooking skills are declining, thereafter supporting their apparently pre-existing view by noting a wide range of factors coupled with assumptions in the absence of evidence (1999). They do add findings from various sources, often market research reports, e.g., noting that more young people can heat a pizza in a microwave oven than cook a jacket potato in the (conventional) oven. Missing from the findings they review, however, are time-trend data, for the very good reason that, as far as is known, such data do not exist. Yet Lang and Caraher neither comment on the lack of such data nor note the need for appropriately direct data to support their case. Note there are clear parallels with the need for, but absence of, time-trend data for the decline of the family meal (see Chapter 2).

A second answer to the question as to whether cooking skills are 'really' being lost requires asking what skills anyone has in mind or indeed what items are to count as the convenience foods claimed to be supplanting them. Caraher and Lang put together material from surveys of young people's capabilities, time spent in the kitchen or about how people learn to cook. Although they summarize 'theoretical perspectives and frameworks' for studying cooking, they do not address the question about either cooking or convenience food directly. By by-passing attention to the need for a historical angle on both, they do not take the opportunity carefully to test their prior assumptions.

Meah and Watson, however, firmly take account of additional more relevant aspects overlooked by Caraher and Lang to address the matter. They point out that:

(C)ooking has certainly been simplified and de-skilled in significant respects, through the availability of 'convenience' foods and innovations which speed up the process. Simultaneously it has also become more complex in terms of the volume of information available about how to cook safely, healthily, tastily, on a budget, for a family, for guests, for oneself, *and* in terms of the range of knowledge and skills necessary to negotiate contemporary technologies of food provisioning, from use-by dates to microwave de-frost programmes.

2011: para 1.8

In this fashion they extend the thinking about the definition of cooking, by pointing to the increase in amounts of information about cooking and attending to historical shifts—which are picked up later.

There are parallel difficulties with definitions of 'convenience' – as will be seen after considering the disquiet in question as both a public issue and private trouble.

The loss of cooking skills as a public issue and private trouble

There are several emphases in the public portrayal of the loss as a problem (Short 2006). One is about the appreciation of food, the celebration of the intrinsic virtues of cooking and good eating held to signal being civilized. This view is held by food writers, chefs and campaigners who invoke health and well-being into the bargain. It is a position central to the ethos of the Slow Food movement (Petrini 2001) and is similar to Pollan's view. A second emphasis holds that the lack of cooking skills – in particular those needed to use leftovers creatively – is one reason for the large volume of edible food that is wasted (WRAP 2014). Third, health practitioners, especially those concerned to support the general public or to inform dietitians, are worried that lack of home cooking and reliance on convenience food has an adverse effect on people's health (Barton, Wrieden and Anderson 2011). This is reflected by Canadian milk producers who fund a free newsletter for nutrition educators, and advise their readers that, in addition to educating their clients, or calling for policies and programmes to further food skills, they themselves 'can improve their own (personal) skill set through intentional practice and development' (Chute 2013).

Nutritionists and public health practitioners are particularly exercised, with research literature building up in these disciplines predicated on assumptions that being able to cook leads to more knowledgeable food provision, healthier eating and safer domestic kitchens (Chenhall 2010). That literature is developed against a background that includes not just an increase in eating fast food (typically higher in fat, salt and sugar and lower in fibre) but, according to the findings of one US survey of children's diets 'the increase in calories from 1994 to 2006 results entirely from an increase in fast food eaten at home' (Poti and Popkin 2011: 7).

The associated nutrition research literature includes examining the effect of cooking skills programmes. In Australia (Herbert et al 2014), studies seeking to determine the best age at which to introduce such interventions (e.g. in Northern/Republic of Ireland (Lavelle et al 2016)) along with advanced technical work to develop a tool to provide a standardized method of evaluating cooking skills to be used when devising and assessing multicentre cooking skills interventions (Barton 2011). This style of common sense thinking leads logically to instituting programmes for remedial education (notably running cookery classes for adults) as the solution. In other words, the public issue is commonly characterized as a loss of cooking skills coupled with assumptions, such as Caraher and Lang's, that children no longer have cookery classes at school, any more than they are learning to cook with their mothers in the kitchen. Such assumptions, however plausible, are nonetheless akin to common-sense thinking, for they neither rely on – nor even seek – systematic research about their suppositions.

Alongside such activities, the research effort linking poorer nutrition with higher use of processed foods serves as a basis for those seeking to publicize their concern (in newspapers and other media) that alternatives to cooking using basic ingredients at home are increasingly to be condemned. As Pollan observes, the 'fact is that *not* cooking may well be deleterious to our health' and that there is 'reason to believe' that resorting to commercially prepared alternatives has already taken a toll on our physical and psychological well-being (Pollan 2009). What Pollan does not mention, however, is who is to do the cooking that he argues is vital to health and well-being, prompting the tart observation:

(W)hile Pollan and others wax nostalgic about a time when people grew their own food and sat around the dinner table eating it, they fail to see all of the invisible labor that goes into planning, making, and coordinating family meals. Cooking is at times joyful, but it is also filled with time pressures, tradeoffs designed to save money, and the burden of pleasing others.

Bowen, Eliott and Brenton 2014: 21

The sociologist Michelle Szabo takes the point further in theoretical terms. She draws on the notion of 'social reproduction' (i.e. the value to the whole economy and to 'society' in general of unpaid domestic work, primarily undertaken by women). In other words, '(P)ut simply, without a (female) homemaker to cook, clean, take care of children, etc., (male) workers would have difficulty devoting the work day to paid work and economic production' (2011: 550). This allows her to point to the increase in households depending on two incomes and the corresponding need for increased planning and scheduling between employment time and time available for necessary unpaid domestic work.

This, she continues, is coupled with the perceptions of increasing pressures of time along with trade-offs with other values and valued activities. She concludes that 'significant and widespread changes in food provision at the household level cannot take place unless employment conditions, the shifting make-up of the household, and the gendered (as well as racialized and classed) division of labor are also considered, (2011: 549). This is the context in which both 'cooking from raw ingredients' and 'the use of convenience foods' must be understood by anyone such as Pollan (and Slow Food adherents) calling for more 'real' eating.

It is not surprising, then, to find that Pollan's dismay is not evident as a private trouble, and what can be found is not always a neat counterpart of its expression as a public issue. There is an exception reported by the anthropologist David Sutton in his subtle, extended studies of cooking on the Aegean island of Kalymnos (Sutton 2014). He finds that by 2005 supermarkets, a variety of frozen foods and ready-prepared meals, 'ethnic' dishes and TV cooking shows are established in that Greek island's life. He finds much head-shaking among older people deploring the younger generation's incompetence in the kitchen. These provide the background to his detecting a new echo of American concern over the loss of cooking skills. Sutton realizes, however, that so common a refrain is to be understood not as disapproval of kitchen activities but as 'one of the ambivalent fruits of "modernity" that has been threatening to overtake the island' for decades (2014: 6). Indeed, he observes that since the balance between 'tradition' and 'modernity' is one of the most significant moral questions facing islanders, expressions of concern at the loss of cooking skills must be understood not as mere description, but as a statement of a moral issue. In effect, this may not merely represent regret that is confined to matters of the kitchen, but is the vehicle for expressing a far more general alarm about alterations to a whole way of life on one small Greek island (but see Botonaki and Mattas 2010).

It is possible that the lack of a clear private trouble counterpart to public dismay at the loss of cooking skills may simply be that the topic is under-researched. Alternatively, it may result from there being only very specific circumstances when the lack is felt. One slender but suggestive study about a cooking class for men confirms that students (of a range of ages) found themselves newly in circumstances either of having to fend for themselves or of unexpectedly being responsible for cooking for children – typically those recently bereaved or just divorced (Coxon 1983).[8] Yet it is striking that Jackson et al's wide-ranging study of anxieties about food and celebrity chef's criticisms of people's inability to cook does not record a parallel concern among those 'ordinary' people whose actual cooking practices they study (2015).

Any 'private' difficulties that studies do record about cooking suggest that they have less to do with the supposed decline, more with the overall 'logistics' of food preparation at home. These range from making sure an eye is kept on the cost, serving food at a time to suit everyone involved, the general shortage of time for meal preparation and having to watch that everyone's tastes are accommodated (see Chapter 2). Even cooks who do prepare something special to accommodate individual dislikes, still find it frustrating and may be openly resentful about it (Beck 2007). One recurring private trouble is about time – or rather the lack of it (Short 2006: 57; Jabs and Devine 2006) although for Dutch adolescents, time is not an issue at all, getting round it by unconcernedly embracing convenience eating since it is quicker (Wahlen, van der Horst and Pothoff 2016).

The public view revolves around condemnation of those who supposedly cannot cook 'properly', making it unsurprising that those at whom the finger is pointed do not blame themselves. Remedy for such deficiency is to be education, whether mounted by those working in health promotion or obesity reduction programmes or via cookery books or chefs' campaigns by the likes of Jamie Oliver. In effect, there is a loose alliance of public health professionals, chefs, campaigners etc highlighting a problem which is not just about nutrition but also about people adopting what are socially considered to be unsuitable ways of feeding themselves and their children. However, those who make up such an alliance typically enjoy the economic and cultural capital that enables them to abide most closely by official healthy living advice. Distinctions involved are commonly not made explicit – although one of Johnson and Bauman's 'foodie' interviewees comes close, declaring that the use of packaged foods dumbs down the palate (2015: 190). More profoundly, inspection of the discourse of concern reveals systematic social structural patterning.

Cooking skills and convenience foods: the intersection of social structure, biography and history

C. Wright Mills' approach to sociology provides a framework for summarizing what Jackson calls 'moralizing' about the reliance on convenience foods (2015) – moralizing by the better off about those less so. Such attitudes have a long history, which play out in different ways in different places and can be seen by comparing just two examples: the US and Britain.

Cooking skills – history, class and gender

Public anxiety about the 'problem' is, then, not new. It surfaces in nineteenth-century commentary on the massive changes of migration in the US and urbanization and industrialization both there and in the UK. The key difference in mid-nineteenth-century food and eating between America and Britain is the sheer abundance of food in the former, which is considered to result in inferior, ignorant cooking (Levenstein 1988). While in Manchester (England) at around the same time, as Frederick Engels declares:

> it is self-evident that a girl who has worked in a mill from her ninth year is in no position to understand domestic work, when it follows that female operatives prove wholly inexperienced and unfit as housekeepers. They cannot knit or sew, cook or wash, are unacquainted with the most ordinary duties of a housekeeper.
>
> *1969 [1845]: 175*

Only a few decades later, it is not poverty but the ignorance of the foreign-born that is deemed primarily responsible for migrants' inadequate diets in the US (Gabacccia 1998) while in the UK, the urban poor are widely considered ignorant, with inadequate and wasteful culinary skills (Burnett 2014: 30). Rural areas in England suffer similarly: more than half a century later, George Bourne's 1912 account of life in a village in the south of England describes women working in the fields as having neither opportunity to learn domestic skills from their mothers nor to pass them on to their daughters (1984: 137).

In the US, the nutritional consequences of poor cooking are highlighted in the early twentieth century, held to jeopardize the whole nation's strength and health. Efforts to change the diet are couched in terms of attention to devising what American eating ought to be, with a national cuisine proposed as part of the newly developing domestic science. Notably, as Gabaccia points out, this resolves into distinct approaches to diet and two styles of recommended recipes – one for the better-off middle-classes, the other for new immigrants and poor Americans (1998).

The baleful consequences of a poor diet showed up in the UK in the guise of the poor health and fitness of army recruits at the end of the nineteenth century. So great was the concern that (as already noted above) a committee was set up to inquire into the problem. A landmark in the history of welfare policy (e.g. leading to school meal provision), among its views are accusations that 'British housewives' are 'tainted with incurable laziness and distaste for the obligations of domestic life' leading them 'to such expedients in providing food for their families as involve them in least trouble'. The effects of women's labour in factories may make 'bad wives and mothers' but it is coupled with the new 'production of tinned foods in enormous quantities' which has 'the effect of reducing the amount of home cooking' (1904 Committee: 40).

Notably, moral judgements are firmly reported; it is not simply that women are out of the house at work, it is also that they are idly evading cooking and resorting to the convenience foods of the day instead. In her study of English young women's leisure of the same period, Parratt reports parallel moral judgements '... girls and women who worked outside the home did not receive proper training in the necessary housewifely skills and consequently were unable to attend to their husbands' leisure wants' (Parratt 2001: 67). Walton detects similar disapproval of alternatives to home cooking, reporting that in the 1920s and 1930s take-away (take-out) 'fish and chips was attacked as an irrational way of spending limited resources and a cause of malnutrition in children whose parents – and especially their mothers – were too lazy or too ignorant to provide a "proper" diet' (1992: 150).

The nineteenth- and early twentieth-century married women being so roundly criticized are, however, not of the middle or upper classes in either the US or UK. Those of the latter in particular, did not cook, or indeed do any other routine domestic work, any more than they undertook paid employment outside the home – to do either would signal the shameful state of affairs that their husbands had not sufficient means to support their families and employ staff (it is only later in the century that fewer people become domestic servants as more attractive employment becomes available). As household manuals of the period indicate, while well-to-do women are expected, as part of their domestic duties to understand how to run a house, that means knowing how to instruct servants in what to do, not doing it themselves. The finger of blame is pointed at immigrant and working-class wives and daughters for falling down on their obligations and indolently failing to feed their menfolk and children properly.

Opinions on the matter today are possibly less explicitly condemnatory, and assumptions that women will do the cooking may be more muted, but powerful echoes of the same reproach of working-class women remain. Guthman arrives at a similar conclusion, albeit from the different starting point of examining the US trend for organic foods which, like calls for 'real' cooking, are contrasted with industrialized food provision. Fast food, she notes is about the taste of the masses, whereas 'craft production' is the preserve of better-off elites. Moreover, in respect to gender, the distinction, among other things, 'effaces the links between convenience food and women's massive participation in the paid workforce' (2003: 47–8). Similarly, the research of UK sociologist Julie Parsons shows how cooking 'healthy' meals from raw ingredients is a way of 'demonstrating a particular form of elite or established middle-class habitus' (way of life) in which an essential component of being a 'proper' mother in contemporary Britain is to provide the family with meals 'cooked from scratch' (2015b).

Cooking skills – biography, mothers and daughters

The gendering of blame carries through into the refrain that cooking skills are no longer being passed down the generations – also nothing new as Bourne's complaint above illustrates. But in addition to Short's pointing out that skills include perceptual and conceptual knowledge, UK geographers Angela Meah and Matt Watson (2011) show how only paying attention to mothers teaching daughters is far too simple. Certainly, they have data confirming the persistence of an *image* of some past 'golden age' when cooking was done properly with those skills passed on by grandmothers and mothers. Some, especially research participants in their thirties, highlight deficiencies in their own mothers' cooking including not using a chopping board or 'over-boil[ing] everything'. For them, new advances, such as microwave cooking, represent 'moving with the times' (para 3.3). It is when Meah and Watson move on to two case studies that the sheer diversity of sources from which people learn to cook comes to light. In both, the quality of mothers and grandmothers' kitchen work is judged as mixed, with only some things worth following. For the rest, participants learned from: temporary lodgers, picking up ideas when camping in other countries, learning from new student friends, cookery books and watching a television cookery competition that relies on professionals being given a surprise set of ingredients, who then demonstrate what can be done with them.

Watson and Meah's work illustrates the importance of using more than one data collection technique in a single study. They are clear that one on its own does not adequately reveal the complexities of cooking and associated skills. Adopting a qualitative approach, they begin with focus groups but then use food-based life-history interviews, which 'when combined with observations, invariably reveal a more complex and nuanced picture'.

Box 18 Focus groups

As a form of qualitative-group-interview focus groups consist of small numbers (6 to 10) of people brought together to answer and discuss questions posed to them by a researcher. Often a second researcher is present, observing and taking notes. Some groups are composed of demographically diverse people, others are selected to be similar (even recruited from friendship or work groups of those who already know one another) so that across the total number of groups held for any one study there is some rough correspondence to the characteristics of the population in which the researcher is interested. First introduced in the 1920s they were more intensively used by the sociologist Robert Merton in the 1950s investigating war-time radio propaganda. He always combined them with a quantitative method, regarding failure to do so as insufficiently rigorous and a misuse of the method (1987). Focus groups are extensively used in market research, opinion polling and political research and, for the last three decades, increasingly widely used across the social sciences and other academic work. Data are typically audio-recorded, transcribed as text and commonly analysed as if semi-structured interviews.

Certainly, they reaffirm that 'small scale intensive qualitative work can neither prove nor disprove long term population level trends in cooking skills' and observation introduces additional ethical issues. But as they state firmly: 'it is this sort of research that is needed to begin to disentangle the *diverse* influences and relationships which converge in cooking practices' which can then serve as an essential basis on which critically to examine 'claims about declining cooking skills' (2011: para 3.1, emphasis added).

Industrialization: kitchens and foodstuffs

In addition to illustrating how 'moralizing' about cooking is not new, attention to history is essential in identifying the changing contexts in which people learn to cook at home along with the development of alternatives. Indeed, extolling the very idea of successive generations of daughters being taught to cook by their mothers is contradicted by historical evidence. For the new home economics movement in the early twentieth century, first in the US then rapidly spreading elsewhere (e.g. Sweden, Ekström 2006) seeks to *replace* 'old-fashioned' traditional ways handed down by mothers, with the rationality of progressive domestic science applied to home cooking (Shapiro 1986).

In any case, despite the advertising slogans, women's use of modern kitchen technologies and foodstuffs does not necessarily bear out the promise of 'labour saving'. Reducing some burdens risks replacing any creativity in cooking with 'machine minding', reducing the time keeps women doing it at the same time freeing them to take on additional work (Driver 1983, Bose 1979, Murcott 1983c). It introduces new skills older generations could not possess while other skills become redundant. Few now could bake a cake in an oven without thermostatic controls instead using changes in the colour of white paper to determine the correct temperature. Two centuries' industrialization of available foodstuffs and of kitchen technologies is inextricably linked to kitchen practices – with class and gender as persistent themes. As oven technologies develop, the presentation of new cookers is strongly gendered, 'addressed to the housewife', or more precisely, to middle-class, increasingly servant-less, 1930s housewives (Silva 2000).

Kitchens

Tracing the development of kitchen technology must be set against the background of the evolution of the kitchen itself – an evolution which is neither uniform nor automatically worldwide (Sutton 2014). In addition, the use of the very word kitchen changes – the current use to describe a ready-made coordinated set of cupboards, units etc to be fitted into a room as semi-permanent fixtures is unknown in the 1950s. As the historian Sara Pennell demonstrates, somewhere with a source of heat and appropriate equipment to prepare meals as a necessary room inside a house only starts slowly to emerge in England from the seventeenth century (2016). Before then, such specialized domestic spaces are only for elite social groups, and then not always part of the living quarters, but built apart – then as now kitchens are the most likely places for fires to start.

Developments from the nineteenth century onwards starkly demonstrate the differences between middle- and working-class homes on both sides of the Atlantic. Turner records the contrasts in America of the late 1800s; middle class house design places a kitchen where the servants work apart, blocking off the dirt, noise and cooking smells from the semi-public areas such as parlour or drawing room. Working-class kitchens are not specialized spaces, but the main room of the home with table, chairs, fire, but also beds, the location of all activities, including paid work and sleeping. Significantly, people would not necessarily eat at a table, but wherever was easiest (2014: 38–9, see also Cowan 1983: 161–2). Indeed, no clear spatial demarcation of cooking etc from other daily domestic activities persists: kitchen-related items and activities extend beyond its four walls while simultaneously non-kitchen-related items and activities still happen within the kitchen space (Wills et al 2013).

As kitchens develop through the twentieth century, class remains significant. The introduction into domestic life, especially kitchens and cookery, of Taylor's ideas of efficiency in industry is taken up by pioneer home economists in the US (Silva 2002) epitomized in Margarete Schütte Lihotzky's 1926–1927 'fitted, ergonomically arrayed and rationalized "Frankfurt kitchen"' (Pennell 2016: 5). But although middle-class women in Belgium applauds the 'maximum productivity' to which such designs were geared, rural and working-class women are far less receptive. In any case, Belgian magazines aimed at the latter tend to ignore the question of kitchen design, and consistently 'workers' housing built between 1925–1940 does not incorporate the "rational" kitchen' unlike new housing for the middle classes (van Caudenberg and Heynen 2004). In Finland, by contrast, twentieth-century urbanization reduces class variation as homes are rebuilt. Nonetheless, images of the kitchen remain gendered (Saarikangas 2006).

Note the contribution to making these 'rationalized' kitchens possible made by the late nineteenth- and early twentieth-century innovations in the provision of clean water to individual dwellings, sewerage systems, along with the replacement of lamps and candles for lighting and wood and coal for heating and cooking, first by gas supplies and later electricity. In this way, domestic production is supplanted by industrial production – rendering obsolete the need for candle-dipping, home-brewing, homemade clothing etc. The similar switch from homemade production of sauces, stocks, ketchups and whole meals to industrially produced and commercially distributed replacements is self-evident – a switch that, notably, brings with it a high volume of 'moralizing' which is absent for handknitting or sewing. This can be accounted for by highlighting the material realm. Moralizing about home cooking, but not about making clothes at home underlines the fact that both foods and human beings are organic. Food is literally *incorporated*; sweaters and jackets only wrap round the body's exterior.

Foodstuffs – defining convenience

The switch from homemade cooking to industrially processed and manufactured food can be dated to the later decades of the nineteenth century, with the creation of a concentrated meat extract by the German chemist Justus von Liebig, adapted for industrial production and marketed using his name. The growth continues thereafter. Over a century later, US market research reports record that the highest sales growth categories in food and beverages have one 'overarching thing' in common: 'convenience'.[9] There is, however, no clear correspondence between reports as to which items come under this heading.

A broad definition is provided by the food scientist and nutritionist Arnold Bender: '(P)rocessed foods in which a considerable amount of the preparation has already been carried out by the manufacturer, e.g., cooked meats, canned foods, baked foods, breakfast cereals, frozen foods' (1975). Empirically however, convenience food is not nearly so clearly categorizable. As the historian Peter Scholliers shows, attention to 'convenience foods' first appears in the 1920 and increases steeply until the 1990s with a wide diversity of themes and items included under the heading of 'convenience' foods. He notes that 'most authors remain quite vague about what they mean by "convenience foods"' (2015: 3–4).

Scholliers' work is mirrored by that of Jackson and Viehoff (2016, Jackson and Brembeck 2018). Their review of recent research also illustrates a considerable diversity in the interpretations of convenience food as a category. They note that other researchers include 'fast foods, snack foods and packaged/canned/frozen/pre-prepared foods as well as to the idea of convenience in provisioning foods that do not require direct involvement from the consumer in the work of growing/raising/harvesting it' resulting in grouping together items as varied as fresh fruit cut in cubes, grilled sausages from the gas/petrol station, trans-fat fried chicken from the supermarket freezer and cartons of organic Indian carrot soup. Unsurprisingly, they highlight the considerable extent to which the use of convenience food is 'moralized'. Indeed, they are willing to go so far as to conclude by observing that the 'moralization of convenience food is, we suggest, a major obstacle in understanding the social dynamics of contemporary food consumption and a significant barrier in attempts to pursue a healthier, more sustainable, diet' (2106: 10).

Convenience – welcomed *and* rejected

Unlike the assumption in this chapter's title, historical evidence confirms that the introduction of manufactured foodstuffs in different places and at successive periods meets with a mixed reception. By the mid-1920s, American convenience foods are eventually enthusiastically adopted in Europe (Verriet 2015). The mid-1950s saw enthusiastic Finns along with 'early adopter' English people eagerly embracing American-inspired novelties and innovations in food production – even 'mousse' reputedly the result of a failed batch of commercially produced ice-cream saved by being marketed as an alternative delicious dessert, enjoying a brief period as 'the latest fashion'. As discussed in Chapter 4, contrasting political ideologies in East and West Germany during the Cold War imbue processed, pre-prepared foods with contrasting meanings – in the former signalling women's freedom from kitchen work to enter the workforce, in the latter to enjoy the experience of contemporary consumption while concentrating on home-making (Weinreb 2017).

Note, too, that factory-produced foods are greeted neither with enthusiasm nor outright rejection once and for all, but the reception can change over time. Amy Bentley's analysis of documentary materials (Box 21) shows how the idea of 'baby' (as distinct from 'adult') food is invented and subsequently normalized in the US during the twentieth century with Gerber's canned pureed fruits, vegetables etc moving from rarity to a 'normal' unexceptionable component of the introduction of mixed feeding during a child's first year (2002: 103). Bentley notes that the massive increase in sales thereafter coincides with the introduction of mixed feeding at ever-younger ages. She points to the indirect effect of the image on the packaging of a baby that looks no more than four months old, giving 'the implicit impression that babies this young should be eating solid foods' (2002: 109). She adds: 'it makes sense that Gerber and other baby food manufacturers would advocate the early introduction of their foods'. They are seeking to 'create and expand (their) market share' (2002: 109).

Since then, medical advice – endorsed in 1981 by the World Health Organization and continuing – deems six months as the earliest for infants to be fed anything other than breast milk. The notions of 'convenience' in preparation and use – babies can be fed 'on the go' – the 'selling' of baby foods as pure and wholesome, now conflict with nutritional guidelines. Lingering anxieties remain that somehow resorting to convenience rather than preparing food 'from scratch' means failing to live up to idealized ideas of 'proper family eating'. As a result, feeding an infant can be accompanied by dilemmas – a special case, perhaps of the tension between 'real' cooking at home and resorting to factory-produced food (Brembeck and Fuentes 2017).

Sociological thinking about 'convenience'

Alan Warde has made significant contributions to thinking sociologically about convenience foods (1997). He analyses the appeal of convenience foods as a novel conceptualization of time, which can be coupled with the properties of innovations such as freezers, e-mail, 'time-shifting' devices he refers to as 'hypermodern' (1999: 522). People respond to feeling short of time into which more activities are to be squeezed by trying to (re)arrange their sequence – the number of shopping trips can be reduced by 'peas in the freezer', also shortening preparation and cooking time.

Warde earlier undertakes a content analysis of every article about domestic food preparation in a sample of the most widely circulated British women's magazines (Box 21) in 1967–1968 and 1991–1992 to identify the way the tasks are represented (1997). This work forms the basis for identifying eight 'principles of recommendation', grounds for valuing one or other aspect. Magazine content can be categorized into these eight, which in turn, are paired as opposites – 'antinomies'. The word 'convenience' appears infrequently, referring most often to reducing the amount of time needed, together with, ease of preparation and capacity for a dish to be stored for future use. Opposing it is 'care', which covers recipes appealing to 'home cooking', cooking for 'the family'. Over 30 years, the emphases vary, but the antinomy, convenience *vs* care, persists, claims Warde. Note that in treating magazine content as a reflection of what 'really' happens Warde does not discuss how editorial policies may shape that content e.g. to avoid offending readers by criticizing their use of convenience foods or inducing guilt in any too short of time to cook from scratch – or that the publications' reliance on advertising revenue—may curb challenges to the quality of manufacturers' products (Box 6).

Warde's antinomies have been much cited by other authors who treat them as general interpretations of food preparation trends, in the process often detaching them from their origins as analyses of representations in magazines – although Warde tends to do so himself. At the same time, the convenience/care pair has been increasingly criticized. Meah and Jackson challenge the presentation of 'cooking from scratch' as an 'inherently more caring, healthy and sustainable alternative to the use of convenience food' (2017: 14). In the process they also challenge Warde's construction of convenience and care as an antinomy. Where his analysis includes 'convenience *or* care' and 'convenience *and* care' theirs examines 'convenience *as* care' drawing on 'ethnographically informed fieldwork' from a collection of UK households (2017: 3). They present empirical evidence for the use of convenience foods as: 'caring about' the world's food resources (e.g., the use of pre-prepared vegetables to reduce food waste); 'taking care of' e.g., using frozen vegetables so that children have the healthiest food possible within budget and time for shopping (also instance of Warde's time shifting); and 'caregiving' e.g. combining cooking with child-care in the short time between the end of school and the evening meal, using processed ingredients to oversee under-ten year olds making their own pizza. While Brembeck and Fuentes' analysis of web material from four European baby food companies with pages in their native languages as well as Swedish conclude that their marketing weaning foods adroitly '*unmakes* the conflict between care and convenience. In fact, it makes convenience equal to care' (2017: 171, emphasis added).

Conclusion – cooking skills, convenience food and a thread towards the food system

In this chapter, eating is centrally linked with the food system in the way previous chapters are not. One thread tying them together is market research, which is wrapped around convenience. It is a theme that has dominated the nexus between food production and consumption in the US since the Second World War. '(Q)uick 'n' easy', 'heat and serve' and 'ready in a jiffy' beat tattoos on the pages of the magazine and are echoed on the radio and TV' (Levenstein 1993: 116). This is the beginning of the period when, as Shapiro observes, the US industry is actively engaged in redefining the meaning of cooking as it seeks to persuade 'housewives' that packaged-food cuisine (as she calls it) will save them time, save them work and improve their lives immeasurably.

Looking more closely, however, suggests that if an opposition between cooking and the use of convenience food is set aside, different considerations emerge more clearly. By the penultimate decade of the twentieth century the US picture is confused. Levenstein summarizes the position citing *Fortune* magazine:

> The same working mother who repairs to McDonald's three times a week may settle down on the weekend for a bout of gourmet cooking. Diet sodas with pizza, health food for lunch and junk food for dinner – the trends in the market for food are precisely as consistent as the eating habits of Americans.
>
> *1988: 210*

His vantage point allows him also to conclude that a long list of social changes, from the rise of city dwelling, the steady decline in the availability of servants from 1900 onwards, public valuations of science are not enough in themselves to account for the transformation of American eating. This can only be achieved by the most powerful social institutions. In addition to the government itself via forms of education, are 'the giant food corporations ... with their influence over and advertising in the mass media' which together are 'the only forces with the necessary resources to spread the message on a mass basis' (1988: 211).

Behind food corporations' efforts lies market research crystallizing a direct link between the producers and their customers. This is well represented in an invaluable, late-1960s text, *The Convenience-oriented Consumer* which carries a foreword summarizing the state of studying markets for convenience foods by the Director of US Bureau of Business Research Studies in Marketing. Observing that 'the saving of time is "the high priority value" in the "changing life style of the American Family"' it notes that 'a new interpretation of convenience orientation is needed by marketers', for the absence of 'scientific studies' examining 'convenience-oriented consumer behaviour' constrains the marketer's efforts to meet the needs of the rapidly expanding convenience-goods market (Anderson 1971: xv). Such a view continues into this century among marketers. One study undertaken in Ireland examines the British convenience food market, a valuable destination for Irish products (Buckely et al 2007). The resulting data are divided to pick out those lifestyles with a 'positive perspective in relation to convenience foods to satisfy an increasing proportion of their food needs'. Their aim is to offer recommendations for manufacturers, for whom they claim the study is useful when seeking to use 'convenience' as a means of gaining a competitive advantage or for differentiation (2007: 614).

Here, then, is a short indication of market research clearly representing one of the links between this chapter's topic of cooking/the use of convenience food to the workings of the system supporting manufacturers' sales. It provides a thread leading inexorably to the commercial heart of the food system.

Box 19 Chapter 5 – Selected Key Points

1. Worries that people generally are no longer able to cook are found cross-nationally, with the conventional wisdom widely blaming over-reliance on pre-processed ingredients/dishes/meals but also (e.g. in Singapore) on reliance on being able to eat out cheaply and quickly and/or the ready availability of maids.

2. Adequate evidence supporting the loss of cooking skills/use of convenience foods is hard to find, partly because defining either is infrequent/unworkable/difficult and partly because appropriate data are unavailable.

3. Disquiet lest cooking skills are being lost is not new – evidence of disapproval is found in the US in the late nineteenth and early twentieth centuries and earlier still in the UK.

4. There is a mismatch between the public issue lest cooking skills are being lost and private troubles that include focus on adequately feeding the family, accommodating everyone's tastes, making ends meet and the general smooth running of the home.

5. Convenience foods are typically equated with industrially processed/manufactured foods, whose development has been integral to industrialization since the nineteenth century. Their reception by potential customers has varied from enthusiasm to suspicion and rejection.

6. Since World War II, industrially produced foodstuffs in the US, in particular, have been heavily marketed in the name of convenience.

CHAPTER 6
FOOD PACKAGING: 'THE PROBLEM IS THAT FOOD IS *OVERPACKAGED*'

'*My Food Bag* criticised by customers for unnecessary packaging'[1]

'Customers up in arms about excessive (food) packaging'[2]

'London chefs call for polystyrene packaging ban'[3]

Appearing just a few years ago, these headlines introduce articles which report complaints from the US, Australia and the UK respectively. The first reports customers' complaints of 'overpackaging' by a scheme that delivers, to order, suitable quantities of ingredients needed to make dishes according to the recipe also provided. The second blames both producers and customers, reporting shoppers' criticisms of two of Australia's biggest supermarkets. The third article is about four chefs and a food critic writing to London's Mayor wanting the city to follow New York, San Francisco and Washington DC and ban the use of polystyrene food packaging (widely used for fish, meat and other foods requiring refrigerated storage). Most recently, the pollution of the oceans by discarded plastic packaging is achieving new-found prominence, highlighted possibly as never before following the worldwide airing of the final episode of *Blue Planet II* a BBC television series presented by David Attenborough, the eminent English naturalist. In its wake have come initiatives from many quarters, senior politicians, food retailers, journalists, and discussions, which continue at the time of writing.[4]

In this chapter sociological thinking about food packaging starts by moving beyond a conventional wisdom shocked at apparently excessive wrapping of apples on a cardboard tray encased in transparent plastic film, to seek additional viewpoints. In the process, it notices the economic and social significance food packaging has for the character of the modern food supply. It continues to consider the difference the twentieth-century introduction of increasingly varied and complex food packaging makes to social relationships between manufacturer, retailer and customer.

Before reading any further, readers might pause and reflect for a moment to note the first thoughts that come to mind when 'food packaging' is mentioned. Is 'overpackaging' on the list, or 'waste'? Is 'advertising' included or finding there is insufficient information on the label to decide whether to buy the product? Does branding come to mind? Does the list contain any compliments or does it only consist of criticisms?

Certainly, criticism seems to feature more often in headlines. Letter writing campaigns, complaints and petitions are just some of the means via which people argue that much packaging is superfluous. Another way is to set up an anti-packaging enterprise to sell groceries loose, in other words, without any of the usual packaging by the manufacturers, processors or growers who nowadays wrap and supply their wares in units of a weight or size suitable for the customer to take home.[5]

Food packaging's ubiquity

The odd thing about food packaging is that although, at least once a day, the vast majority of people across the globe probably handle an example of it, for most people for most of the time it is completely ordinary, unremarkable and barely noticed. Packaging's presence can be assumed. As the journalist Thomas Hine memorably puts it, packaging is 'hidden in plain sight' (1995: 269). Mostly, food packaging is noticed only when it poses a problem. Apart from complaints about waste, the nuisance of litter, the needless cost, never mind the damage to the environment and wildlife, they also extend to accidents and injuries from trying to open packaged foods (Crocket 1985, Caner and Pascall 2010, Duzier, Robertson and Han 2009, Sudbury-Riley 2014). Such difficulties are, however, a tiny proportion of the number of times people handle food packaging every day. Ordinarily, it is hardly noticed.

Omnipresent, a taken-for granted, familiar, unremarked feature of daily shopping, cooking and eating this commonplace in everyday life, is also almost, but not quite completely, invisible in the history and sociology of food (Murcott 2018). Despite that absence, there are three good reasons for devoting a whole chapter to it. First it takes no more than a moment's reflection to realize that without food packaging, the modern food supply would look completely different, which is where sociological thinking might begin. For the comparative shortage of sociological research on the matter provides an occasion for 'thinking aloud' as to what such work could and should look like, illustrating a different angle on moving from conventional wisdom to types of sociological thinking.

Second, despite declaring that it is usually unnoticed, there are ways in which food packaging is *routinely* noticed and any messages it conveys duly recognized and, at times, any information printed on it inspected in some detail. Third it turns out that even though it is still small, the sociological contribution to food packaging expands an understanding of the food system, especially the junction between consumption and production where it is intricately entangled with marketing and food retailing. In any case, a sociological examination of food packaging adds to the way that sociologists are interested in food and eating both as a lens on other aspects of social life but also on the nature of food itself, its very materiality. So, the conventional wisdoms with which the chapter opens prompt sociological thinking that widens the angle of investigation quite considerably.

Food's materiality

Of the various approaches to thinking about the materiality of food, one is very familiar (see Chapter 1). Food is organic (as opposed to inorganic) and eventually goes bad. In other words, it is biological matter in which the passage of time is significant. There is a 'life cycle' of living organisms, including, of course, humans, whether a food source is of the kingdom of plants, animals or fungi. It is a biological progress from birth, via maturity to death. As soon as reliance on hunting animals and gathering wild plants is gradually supplanted by the establishment of permanent settlements some 12,000 years ago, humans have had to deal with food's materiality in a new way, associated with the domestication of plants and animals.

For, as soon as humans are no longer moving about looking for food to eat near enough there and then, when and where they found it, they have to take account of the passage of time on a different and lengthier scale. They do not simply have to tend the crops and herd the animals, they also have to plant the new crop and wait until it grows and be patient until the next generation of animals is born. It takes time to produce what will become food and once it has reached the point of being deemed edible, steps have to be taken to stop its continuing the biological cycle toward death (i.e. putrefaction and inedibility). Note that the stage identifying edibility is *both* biological and social, the meaning of 'ready to eat' is attributed to the foodstuffs when it reaches a certain biological point. Even in a small way, it is possible to recognize this by thinking of friends, some of whom will not touch a banana with the slightest sign of brown ripening on the skin (i.e. inedible) while others will only eat them once well darkened (finally edible). Not only does food have to be preserved in an edible form to prevent it from rotting, it must also be stored to provide enough to tide people over between harvests during the repeat stages of the cycle of new growth and next season's crop. Recognition of all this is highlighted by Freidberg's exposition of ideas of freshness along with commercial practices to secure it (2009).

With this basic view of food's materiality in the background, the chapter turns to consider how food packaging is identified.

What is food packaging?

Answers to this question come from two main sources: the food packaging industry itself, insiders' view and academic research in archaeology, history and anthropology.

The industry view

Unlike most who barely notice it, specialists are acutely aware of food packaging. The very fact that studies reporting problems even exist in the form they do, is part and parcel of their authors' professions that bring them into contact with people's packaging difficulties – and the need to report them. In addition to doctors' studies of accidents, authors record problems of waste, disposal, and debate the associated technical obstacles (e.g. Jambeck et al 2015) and discuss the branding opportunities packaging presents (Robertson 2005). They are qualified in disciplines from applied ergonomics, food engineering, food science, food technology to marketing, along with expertise in branding, design and advertising whose work informs food producers and the food packaging industry itself. For them, food packaging is particularly visible, right in the centre of their professional responsibilities, an integral part of the job, which is not simply about dealing with problems but also entails inventing, designing and manufacturing one or other type of food packaging.

This is obvious, especially for anyone either working in or representing the food packaging industry itself. Here is found the industry response to complaints of 'excess' packaging, an instance presented as 'packaging misconceptions': '(P)aper is not "better" than plastic or vice versa'. One of the polymers currently being attacked is expanded polystyrene – it has the lowest carbon footprint of any polymer 'because it is 98% air'. A more complicated 'truth' of a cost–benefit variety is added: '(P)ackaging that is difficult to recycle still delivers a net environmental benefit in protecting more resources than it uses and preventing more waste than it generates.'[6] More complex still is a discussion (entitled '(D)on't ditch the plastic just yet') about the value when transporting foodstuffs safely, securely and about innovations in materials that reduce the volume of plastics used.[7] Here, then, is the voice of manufacturers, retailers, in particular the food packaging industry itself, representing a counter to conventional wisdoms among the general public that condemns food packaging waste.

Industry's major defence of food packaging is that it reduces waste, even foodstuffs such as cucumbers, grapes or potatoes, as it slows the rate of decay, thus prolonging the period that they remain 'fresh'. The word has, however, different meanings: producers think of fresh in terms of time between packing and purchase, 'residency' life (on the shelf) and 'shelf' life including in customers' kitchens. Food system critics such as Pollan, or supporters of Slow Food and alternative food networks promote freshness via reducing the number of people, distance and thus time between primary production and purchase. Cookery books advise looking for a bright eye as an indicator of the freshness of fish and a perfume signalling a ripe melon (Jackson 2018).

The industry's argument about retaining freshness is integral to formal definitions, readily found in textbooks:

> the enclosure of products, items or packages in a wrapped pouch, bag, box, cup, tray, can, tube, bottle or other container form to perform one or more of the following functions: containment, protection, preservation, communication, utility and performance. If the device or container performed one or more of these functions, it was considered a package.
>
> *Robertson 2005: 2*

Academics' view

Very different is the approach of academic historians and anthropologists to identifying packaging. For them, if packaging is noted at all, the concern is not to identify food packaging's principles, practicalities and range of purposes but to document the types that are used for containing, storing and distributing food. Human beings have used some sort of containment for food for millennia, from temporary and flimsy to the ingenious and long lasting. For instance, anthropologists report the use of naturally occurring items – from paper bark (thin tree bark) among Australian Aborgines (Harvey 1941) leaves for wrapping in West Africa (Renne 2007) bamboo sticks containers with a plug of leaves or wood to seal the end in north-eastern India (Mao and Odyuo 2007) to baskets in Australia (Testart et al 1982) or clay pots, used for carrying food as well as for cooking on an island off Papua New Guinea (Young 1971). In Europe, and on a wholly different scale there is the historical evidence of Monte Testaccio. This is a small hill on the River Tiber, which consists of the broken pieces of 53 million amphorae that had contained olive oil imported from Spain to Rome between the mid-second to the mid-third century CE. The amphorae 'could not be re-used because the oil seeped in the fabric of the vessel and turned rancid' (Beard 2016: 508). On the other side of the world, in March 1827 on an island off the southern tip of New Zealand's South Island a traveller, John Boultbee witnesses the wholesale capture of muttonbirds by Maori. They then skin, bone and roast the birds, putting 'them into large bags, made by splitting the immense sheets of kelp which abounds here – these bags being fastened up and kept airtight, prevent the birds from being tainted, and I have eaten of them after they had been eight months in these bags, and found the meat as fresh as when put in' (Anderson 1995).[8]

The list continues with items that have remained much the same across Europe (and eventually its colonies) for many centuries: baskets and barrels, cloth bags and leather bottles. Foods are preserved in pots and jars of various kinds. The Romans made glass, with the techniques spreading across Europe as their Empire disintegrated, with evidence of glass making in America from the earliest colonial times. With the eventual establishment of small grocers' shops in early modern England, and later, general stores across the US (Strasser 1989) storage containers of various types are noted in surviving records: bottles, barrels, jars and tubs, with paper being especially important for eighteenth-century English grocers to weigh out spices or tea, and, by the early nineteenth-century paper bags, blue paper generally used for wrapping sugar (still being used in England in the 1950s) (Stobart 2013). The frugality of eighteenth-century grocers' economizing on expensive paper by re-using torn pages from unwanted books to wrap small items for sale is echoed in the frugality of those who sell snacks at bus stations throughout West Africa 'in slips of newspaper and recycled school exam papers' (Renne 2007: 620). Many in the UK still prefer their take-away fish and chips wrapped in newspaper in what to them is a time-honoured fashion. It was the technological innovation of the industrializing nineteenth-century that mark the beginning of a series of shifts that enlarged the variety of possibilities, adding tin cans, mass-produced bottles and jars, shifts that later continue into mid-twentieth-century developments in the use, above all, of plastics.[9]

Sociologists, too, have an answer to 'what is food packaging'. Elements of their thinking begin to enter the picture when considering the junction between food production and food consumption, where customer and retailer meet in the shops. In the process, historical changes to that meeting place must be considered, which requires reliance on the work of historians and business studies academics.

Food packaging between producer and consumer

Neither packaging nor even utensils figure in twelfth-century London street food of 'viands, dishes roast, fried and boiled meats, fish great and small, coarse flesh for the poor, the more delicate flesh for the rich such as venison and birds both big and little'. Instead, literally as the contemporary description puts it, these dishes are 'ready to hand' eaten in fingers there and then (Spencer 2004: 61). The paper of eighteenth-century grocers' shops survives into the 1950s, small white paper bags for sweets/candy, sheets of tissue paper around loaves in the bicycle basket of the baker's delivery boy, to this day still used in some small bakeries. It gives way to the food packaging innovations of the last half century. Little in the way of wrapping comes between retailer and customer in those older examples, in dramatic contrast to what prevails today. The earlier range of paper bags etc. has been massively augmented by artfully designed packaging that serves the functions described by the textbooks, decorated in full colour, printed with photographs, logos, alongside information both required by regulation to inform the customer and provided by the manufacturer to advertise the contents.

The difference goes further than the fact that preserved foods are mass produced and industrially wrapped. It is not just that Modified Atmosphere Packaging (MAP) is introduced to keep salads fresh for longer in the US, UK and elsewhere, or that oxygen scavengers are enclosed with packs of meat to increase residency/shelf-life, especially in Japan. It is also that the packaging, both the thing itself, the information it can carry and the meanings that may be attributed to it, is intricately entangled with a thoroughgoing transformation in social relationships of those involved, in particular between producers and consumers. How this comes about starts with considering the way that packaging is integrally associated with what, in marketing, is referred to as 'building a brand'.

Packaging and brands

Specific elements of creating a 'brand identity' on packaging itself are designed to convey special messages. Labels carry written messages, for instance nutritional information, the weight of the contents, lists of ingredients that may be required by law. Over and above that, they also carry other messages, 'packaging stories . . . narrative literary texts that go beyond labeling requirements—with the premise that food packages act not only as protective containers, but as important tools for marketing communications that convey values, ideas, associations, and messages to the consumer' (Kniazeva and Belk 2007: 52). They note one type of packaging story which positions

> the brand through a personal brand biography that seeks to convey to the consumer that it is a warm sympathetic character. Rather than providing impersonal information, the packaging narratives offer a dialog with the customer. "I personally guarantee this tea will meet your highest expectations . . . let us know how we can

serve you better," says the founder and chairman of Celestial Seasonings who leaves his signature on the package of Honey Vanilla Chamomile tea.

Kniazeva and Belk 2007: 57

The authors focus only on the words printed on packages. They not only leave out stories conveyed in pictures or diagrams that may either illustrate the words or provide a narrative in their own right, but they also by-pass any information or story that the actual shape, feel, even the weight of the package can be made to convey. A plastic milk carton in the shape of a ceramic jug, a PET[10] (which is very clear) bottle moulded into ripples that mimic those of a stream, a tin containing tea in the shape of a teapot, uses the very package itself as a bearer of information. Roberts shows how the quality of the packaging, the design and the brand names all come together to promote an image of Russia and 'Russianness' that appeals to a rosy image of the past via, for instance, a painting of Catherine the Great on a box of chocolates or Ivan, a fourteenth-century Tsar on a bottle of vodka (2014).

Adding to the work of business studies academics just discussed, the anthropologist Elisha Renne offers a detailed analysis of a more complicated set of messages on African foods on sale in the US aimed especially at expatriate customers who may miss the fufu or cassava couscous of 'back home'. The brand names and the designs decorating the packages evoke the way food is prepared in West Africa. Thus '(T)he trademark design for Ghana Fresh® products shows a seated woman, stirring a pot over a wood fire next to a grass-thatched hut' or the 'logo for Gold Tropics™ products depicts a woman using a mortar and pestle in front of grass-thatched hut' superimposed on an outline map of the African continent (Renne 2007: 619). The messages conveyed on the packages do not stop there, adding information about the contents, not pounded by a mortar and pestle but factory produced, sometimes part pre-cooked to reduce preparation time at home, sometimes announcing a recipe that is supposedly a healthy version. In this fashion, the packaging conveys a *transformation* of the original foods from Africa to versions that incorporate Americanized concerns of 'convenience' and healthfulness.

Packaging and relationships between producer/retailer and customer

The transition from grocers weighing out customers' requests into a paper bag to ready-packaged food on the shelves of today's stores is not straightforward. Initially, people find packaging suspect, worrying as to what it might be hiding. Describing his childhood in and out of his parents' corner shop in a northern England slum in the early twentieth century, Robert Roberts recollects that 'a drowned mouse decanted itself from a stone bottle of dandelion and burdock' resulting in a subsequent slump in sales (1971: 120). The significance of later, transparent packaging is self-evident.

This is where building a brand comes into the picture. The early years of Henry Heinz' eponymous food company make the point very simply. Horseradish sauce was widely used in Pittsburgh of the 1850s near where Heinz grew up.[11] By the early 1860s, a local trade in horseradish sauce had developed, put on sale in green or brown glass bottles. A contemporary writer remarked that the quality was poor and that 'dealers had adulterated it to so great an extent [by adding turnip and wood fibers as filler] that its use was rapidly diminishing' (Koehn 1999: 356). Knowing people's suspicions of food they could not see, Heinz used his mother's recipe to begin bottling unadulterated horseradish in clear glass. By realizing the value of clear rather than coloured glass, Heinz blazed a trail in both the decisions about what the packaging should be made from and the way it could be shrewdly coupled with the promotional information surrounding it. He also understood about branding, about the value of a logo that would become familiar and along with a memorable little slogan '57 varieties', even though by the time he invented that there were many more.

Buried in this discussion of branding is the development of a new, long-distance, relationship between food manufacturers and their customers. It supplants the earlier personal relationship between food retailers/grocers and shoppers. No longer are grocers standing behind their counter, busily weighing tea or spices to slip into paper bags or cutting pats of butter to wrap in paper sheets, recommending one or other to customers whose families they know or explaining what the foods contain or how best to store them. These tasks and that advice is taken over by the provision of foods *pre*-packed by the manufacturer. And though packaging cannot be said to *cause* self-service retailing, it helps make its development possible.

It was in 1916 that a Memphis grocer, Clarence Saunders, devises self-service shopping, based on a system he patents, reconfiguring his shop like a maze, familiar to all supermarket shoppers today, as the first Piggly Wiggly store (Hine 1995: 130). While it is another 50 years until self-service shops became commonplace, the significance of packaging is evident in a trade journal's definition of it in 1955: '(E)very item of stock must be *pre-packaged* and clearly price-marked and displayed within reach of the customer in an easily-seen, suitably-classified, quickly identified section of open shelving, bins, trays or gondolas' (cited in du Gay 2004: 153, emphasis added).

A trade journal of the 1940s argues that self-service benefits shopkeepers, for it reduces costs and saves labour (Sandgren, 2009). That is a point customers do not hear much about. Instead, as far earlier in Piggly Wiggly advertising, they are told they are now free from disapproving or impatient grocers making a virtue of the impersonal nature of self-service. The transfer of tasks of fetching and carrying from grocer to shopper is not mentioned.

So, over the last century one consequence made possible by manufacturers' packaging foodstuffs is the alteration of social relationships between suppliers and purchasers. Instead of a direct, personal relationship between the grocer and the customer, there is now an indirect relationship between distant, faceless manufacturers known by their brands, their logos and sometimes by the names and pictures of the supposed producers such as Aunt Jemima's or Quaker Oats (Strasser 1989). A twist to this indirect relationship is packaging's creating new possibilities for being selective in the information that is provided on the package, especially in remaining silent on environmentally unsustainable production practices or very low wage levels for agricultural workers (Wilk 2009).

Furthermore, packaging also makes possible transformations in the image or meaning of foods as they are transported along distribution chains. To workers in the fields and packing factories of Jamaica, a papaya is an object that requires careful handling, picked then weighed and graded in uncomfortable conditions. Packaging labelled with accompanying advice for the novice European consumer transforms it into something exotic (Cook and Crang 1996). The packaging remains silent on the difficult work of picking and the monotonous work of packing and instead promotes and persuades, part of the campaign advertising the deliciousness of the fruit.

Recent sociological thinking about food packaging

The French sociologist Franck Cochoy is one of the very few who has paid sustained attention to food packaging. He shows how something thought of as trivial or paltry, that will eventually be discarded, is a particularly powerful 'market device'. To talk of market devices points not just to things and words but also to the manner in which both co-occur in distinctive combinations in a market, here the grocery market. Market devices are 'a simple way of referring to the material and discursive assemblages that intervene in the construction of markets' (Muniesa, Millo, Callon 2007: 2).

Cochoy's work brings inanimate objects fully into the picture to be analysed, according them as much significance as the animate, the people and their social relationships (the 'new materialism' – see Chapter 1). This allows him to systematize thinking about the altered relationship between grocer and customer. He illustrates the way that the packaging goes further than changing the meaning of the product it contains, claiming, in effect that it alters the produce itself. 'It changes the product since, in hiding what it shows and showing what it hides, packaging transforms the qualification of the product' (Cochoy 2007: 120). Indeed, elsewhere he states that when shoppers look at the wares on sale, they 'are not really products, they are *packaged* products' (Cochoy 2004: 205). People would, he claims, be uneasy if confronted by unpackaged 'naked' foodstuffs. Gone would be any attractive images, guarantees of quality, codes allowing traceability, or the possibility of guaranteeing 'freshness'. Everyone has come to expect foodstuffs to be packaged. It is in this way, he argues, that packaging changes shoppers themselves 'since it makes them discover the invisible dimensions of products, for instance the presence of a guarantee or of an additive that they could not have identified without the mediation of the box. In other words, the consumer learns to exchange their preferences for new references' (Cochoy 2007: 120). In this respect, Cochoy comes very close to arguing that people no longer buy food, they buy the package and moreover, the package *is* now the food.

Cochoy's concerns are centred at the point where food production and consumption systems meet. Gay Hawkins, however, pursues the point further, to fasten onto what she calls 'the afterlife' of food packaging. To do so she augments Cochoy's work by 'following the thing' (Kopytoff 1986) past the market, beyond use as a consumer item on to the point of discard. Capitalizing on the analytic potential of packaging as a market device, she shows how it can highlight its 'performativity'. By this she means that such devices have a capacity, deriving from their material attributes, to make a difference in peoples' contact with them e.g. by resisting certain types of handling or creating possibilities of others. In this way things 'come to shape reality itself' (Hawkins 2013: 66). Here she points out that Cochoy does not take his analysis far enough: certainly everyone now expects foods to be packaged but, she points out, most are 'blind' to what happens to it afterwards.

To illustrate performativity, Hawkins uses the example of PET drinks bottles. In contrast to earlier drinks containers made of glass or aluminium, she argues that the PET bottle enables differences associated with their greater lightness combined with strength and translucence. Not only are they more practical, they also generate, she claims, an image of impermanence unlike older containers, suggesting 'the ways in which it can be drunk: on the move, convenience sipping with a light almost ethereal container made to throw away' (2013: 74). But when first introduced, the plastics recycling infrastructure was far less well developed than that for aluminium or glass, leaving users of PET water bottles inexperienced in their suitable disposal. Marketing efforts concentrate on convenience of the plastic bottle, using its surface for labels and logos to promote its virtues, providing information on, for instance, the water's source and purity. The trouble is, Hawkins points out, that the durability of the plastic itself outlives the marketing information which is only about sales and consumption. Thereby, the performativity of the plastic bottle, she argues, contributes to a problem of waste, and its very materiality carries it beyond consumption.

Food packaging and a thread towards the food system

Packaging is integral to the food system. Vast numbers of people connect with the system via shopping, but even more must come into contact with it via packaging. The topic well illustrates private troubles – from accidents through to mounting popular concern at waste and environmental plastic pollution – and indicates the way they are repeatedly intertwined with public issues, especially overflowing landfill and policy efforts to find sustainable solutions to world-wide waste. By implication, reflecting on food packaging and the food system provides a good basis for thinking of the latter in the plural, or at least of recognizing that there are other systems which are interlocked with the food system. A food production system overlaps and is entangled both with packaging production systems and packaging waste systems, as Gay Hawkins' discussion of the question of recycling and disposal of empty plastic water bottles well illustrates (2013).

Box 20 Chapter 6 – Selected Key Points

1. Standing back from one viewpoint complaining of excess food packaging and adverse environmental consequences of waste to include contrasting viewpoints from the food/packaging industries provides a fuller picture.
2. Food packaging has implications for the character of the modern food supply.

3. The twentieth-century introduction of increasingly differentiated and complex food packaging contributes to altering social relationships, specifically those between manufacturer, retailer and customer.
4. Franck Cochoy analyses food packaging as a 'market device'.
5. Gay Hawkins highlights its 'performativity' (i.e., that the materiality of food packaging makes a difference in resisting/concealing or enabling types of handling possibilities, thus making (in)visible positive/negative alternatives for disposal of used packaging).

CHAPTER 7
FOOD AND ETHNICITY, AUTHENTICITY AND IDENTITY: 'ETHNIC FOODS ARE EVERYWHERE'

'And why is Chinese food overwhelmingly the most popular ethnic cuisine in America?'[1]

'From fresh, bright, healthful fare to the exotic, with Pacific, African and Asian influences, ethnic and international foods seem to be everywhere'[2]

'Indian food is incredibly popular in Australia'[3]

This trio of headlines sounds as if they are not just reporting the ubiquity of 'ethnic foods' but also that they are very well-liked. That news media even carry such reports hints at something worth commenting on. The third, by a blogger in Australia who was sufficiently intrigued that he sought figures about the spread of ethnic restaurants, reporting that, like the US, the 'leading cuisine in every (state) capital city except Sydney is Chinese'.[4] That spread may not be so recent: the food writer, Michael Symons,[5] dates the beginnings of 'Continental' food (gelato bars, European breads) in a cosmopolitan area of Sydney from the 1950s (1984). In the same decade historians such as Panikos Panayi indicate similar origins in Britain (2008).

It is not that 'foreign' food was unavailable before then. Donna Gabaccia, another historian, notes the successive nineteenth-century waves of migrants which changed the 'eating patterns of American farmlands and cities' (1998: 7). A London coffee house advertisement records the provision of curries familiar to retired East India Company officials in 1811 (Collingham 2008) while in 1905, a royal commission in Australia hears a report of Italian shopkeepers' '"splendid"' window displays of fruit in New South Wales and Victoria (Symons 1984: 224). It is that from the 1950s the growth begins to *accelerate* such that, by 2016, a self-conscious search and fashion for the exotic is confidently remarked upon in the first headline, a view enthusiastically endorsed by participants in Johnston and Baumann's study of 'foodies' (2015).

This chapter pursues the reported ubiquity of ethnic food by examining three recurrent themes in sociological discussions of the topic. After briefly noting the mixed response to 'ethnic foods', it begins with 'authenticity' which leads to the second that examines the very question 'what is ethnic food?', proceeding to the third, 'identity', be it individual, cultural or national. Historical and cross-cultural perspectives are key to the discussion for they help limit the danger of essentializing (i.e. depicting phenomena as if their character is homogeneous and fixed) a risk that is particularly great when thinking about ethnic cuisines. This chapter also illustrates the distance between common-sense understandings and sociological thinking, which is perhaps especially wide in this instance (Banton 2015).

'Ethnic foods' – welcomed or shunned?

As the beginning of this chapter suggests, 'ethnic foods' currently appear to be welcomed. But eating foods from elsewhere or the inability to eat familiar foods when travelling is not always so positively received. Los Angeles residents in the early twentieth century fear Chinese food, suspicious of adulteration or being poisoned. Going much further back, a 1494 letter from Christopher Columbus to his royal sponsors, Isabella and Ferdinand of Spain survives. It reveals his unenviable task of having to explain 'why so many of the European settlers on the Caribbean island of Hispaniola had fallen sick and died'.

Luckily, the letter records a remedy, namely 'the foods we are accustomed to in Spain', an explanation which chimes with a widespread belief of sixteenth-century Europe. 'European explorers constantly complained that they fell ill when they could not eat familiar foods, and conversely asserted that only the restoration of their usual diet would heal them' (Earle 2010: 688). Worse, a European who eats a local diet risks turning into a 'local person', for the boundaries of the body are potentially dangerously porous. Surviving documents show explorers' suspicion of unfamiliar New World foods turns to scorn when realizing that indigenous residents 'eat hedgehogs, weasels, bats, locusts, spiders, worms, caterpillars, bees, and ticks, raw, cooked, and fried' supporting the European judgement that 'the inability to distinguish between the edible and the inedible was a sure sign of barbarism' (Earle 2010: 703). Sixteenth-century Europeans explicitly equate what they judge to be inferior food with their view of the inferiority of the peoples for whom it is their usual diet, which in the twenty-first century would be deemed blatant racism.

Different vocabulary euphemistically continues to allow the possibility of implicit racism. Later and further north, a similar impetus lies behind criticism of unfamiliar foodways in programmes deliberately designed to change them. As Gabaccia makes clear, late nineteenth- and early twentieth-century domestic scientists and dieticians sought to 'Americanize' immigrants' cooking, ostensibly in the interests of improved health. Italian migrants are advised against cooking combinations of certain ingredients (e.g. those of minestrone) in the belief that the mixture hindered digestion. Educators try to get Mexicans to limit the quantities of pepper and tomato, making dishes taste blander, considered less 'harmful to the kidneys' and tell Polish children that eating dill pickles is bad for the urinary tract. Such educational efforts have 'moralizing' (plus what once again would now be called racist) overtones in disapproval of Jewish mothers judged to be indulging their children rather than teaching them the virtues of (Protestant) self-denial (Gabaccia 1998: 128).

Quite the opposite opinion of ethnic foods, their popularity, is reflected not merely in the twenty-first-century headlines, but in cookery books and restaurant reviews. Yet, as anthropologist Emma-Jayne Abbotts shows, it depends whether the restaurant is 'at home' or 'abroad'. She reports the irony of US expatriates moving to Ecuador to escape the ills of metropolitan living and embrace a peasant way of life, only to be suspicious of the safety of local food, ending up resorting to US food imports (Abbots 2013).

Several reasons are commonly advanced for this trend of (mostly) wealthy nations. Some point to the increase in cheap travel; tourists return seeking to reproduce back home the tastes newly encountered while away. Others point to successive influxes of migrants. The food writer Colin Spencer notes the arrival in the 1960s of migrants from Hong Kong and the New Territories fleeing from the fear of Maoist China; by 1970 there are some 4,000 Chinese catering business in the UK (2004). Gabaccia takes the point far further, observing that the American 'penchant' to experiment with foods, to 'mix the foods of many cultural traditions' is a 'recurrent theme in our history as eaters' (1998: 3). It might be thought that something similar would apply to Australia, another country composed of some two centuries of migrants, until recollecting that although no longer a colony, even now it is not totally independent from Britain.

At this point, readers might pause for a moment to create their own list of familiar ethnic foods/cuisines, then compare it with the following four examples. The first belongs to the Australian blogger already mentioned when he enumerated the restaurants in each Australian state capital city. He has nine: Chinese, French, Greek, Indian, Italian, Japanese, Mexican, Thai and Vietnamese. The second list is found in the questionnaire in Warde and Martens' 1995 study of three English cities (see Chapter 3) which includes Italian, Chinese/Thai, American, Indian, almost completely overlapping with the blogger's list. Note that both rely on categorization based on national cuisines. Third, a student frequenting one of the food courts at the National University of Singapore will be familiar with a different set of categories. These identify foods to be had at the different sales counters above which are displayed the following names: Ban Mian/Fish Soup; Nasi Padang; Fishball Story; Mixed Vegetables; Western; Indonesian Express. The fourth list is a Japanese man's explanation that '(W)hatever is not Japanese, Korean, Chinese, Indian, American, French, Italian cooking, is ethnic', thus revealing his three categories of cuisine, the 'natural' (i.e. Japanese), the familiar but not his own, and the ethnic (i.e. unfamiliar food) (cited in Ray 2004: 77). Taken together the categories involved in these four lists are variously based on:

(a) ingredients (e.g. mixed vegetables, creating meat-free dishes);

(b) nameable dishes (e.g. Nasi Padang, steamed rice with various additions);

(c) national cuisines (e.g. French, Thai); and

(d) the far broader and less precise designation 'Western' (in practice, a menu whose inspiration is a US diner, burgers, grilled chicken, steak and chops).

In creating their own list, readers might reflect on Lisa Heldke's observation that the 'ethnic' or 'exotic' is identified from a specific (geographic) standpoint.[6] For Northern, European Americans, she suggests 'German food is ethnic, but Italian food is more ethnic, and Greek food more ethnic still. Foods from any part of Asia are yet more ethnic, and African foods are the most ethnic of all' (2003: 51). Readers comparing their own catalogue of ethnic cuisines against those presented in the previous paragraph might check whether they included that of any identifiable ethnic majority where they live as well as those of minorities, a point picked up again below.[7] But for now, bearing in mind this collection of categories, the chapter turns to the question of authenticity.

Ethnic foods and authenticity

Restaurant goers and tourists are widely reported to value the authenticity of ethnic foods when away from home. Those seeking a good ethnic restaurant are wont to declare they look for places patronized by diners who appear to be of the same ethnicity, a sign of 'insider knowledge' supposedly guaranteeing the authenticity of the menu – Japanese-looking people in a Japanese restaurant and so on. This tactic augments would-be diners' checking the 'branding' of the restaurant, its name, the language(s) of the menu, the utensils laid out on the tables (van den Berghe 1984). Authenticity is similarly sought and provided in dishes in ethnic ready meals, a sector of the UK market that marketing research reports say is becoming dominant[8] while authors of ethnic cookery books (or those marketing them) proclaim their recipes as authentic. Many of the academic articles in marketing or in hospitality and tourism journals confirm that diners find authenticity appealing. On that basis, authors point to the relevance of their work e.g. by offering restaurateurs recommendations about attracting customers: 'Mexican restaurants positioning themselves as "authentic" need to address their proximity to Mexico and alter their interior design and food offerings to match their consumers' criteria' (Wood 2009: 278) or arguing that since tourists regard local foods as authentic, then focusing on them 'has the potential to enhance the visitor experience by connecting consumers to the region and its perceived culture and heritage' (Sims 2009: 321).

Trading in authenticity

Such articles are explicitly geared to supporting practical and commercial interests, thereby differing from sociological contributions. The latter do not ignore commercial interests but are concerned to understand the social and economic circumstances in which they operate rather than endorsing/condemning them. So, the sociologist Krishnendu Ray stands back from promoting the virtues of portraying ethnic authenticity to point out that ethnic restaurateurs must 'trade in authenticity' in a fashion that goes beyond merely displaying the 'right' image. More is needed, for cooks in Manhattan's Indian restaurants have never prepared Indian food, whether on the subcontinent from which they migrated, nor at home, not even in a restaurant, until 'they get in the galley of a ship or a restaurant in Europe or North America' (Ray 2016: 179). As the historian Lizzie Collingham records, although described as Indian the first such restaurants in both America and Britain are set up and still run by migrants from Sylhet (now in Bangladesh). Migration is the occasion for learning to cook the foods supposedly of the country they have left behind. This echoes the origins of Chinese restaurants in the port of Cardiff in South Wales in the early part of the twentieth century, a time when the cooks on the ships that were in dock to un/load come ashore to continue cooking for the crew and enjoy a short period on dry land, with some simply staying on after their ship sails[9] (but see Liu and Lin 2009).

Generally, ethnic restaurants and cafés are established as part of the pattern of migration from one country to another. Once a migrant group grows, not only do some members need employment, but a demand is created for familiar daily necessities, be it clothing, foodstuffs or meals. More to the point, as Ray clearly points out, there are often distinct features to ethnic entrepreneurship. Setting up a small café requires modest capital requirements, and it can then be run using family members as staff who do not have to be paid employees' wages. Migrants tend to be familiar with the cuisine in question and understand the requirements of compatriots. Most importantly 'people who know each other have typically migrated from the same regions, work in and own similar enterprises built with money and expertise borrowed from co-ethnics' (Ray 2016: 15). This is of a piece with the way in which migrants from one country to another tend to move to cities (e.g. Indian or Pakistani households in Bradford in England, Greeks in Melbourne in Australia) or parts of cities (Turks in Kreuzberg in Berlin or in Stoke Newington in London, Chinese in San Francisco's Chinatown) where compatriots are already located.

Learning to like 'ethnic' cuisines

Such tendencies to residential geographic concentration might suggest that ethnic restaurants would display a similar concentration. But Zelinsky (1985) finds from his analysis of classified telephone directories up to the 1980s that the location of ethnic restaurants typically reflects affluence.[10] Yet the clientele of ethnic restaurants, apart from seeking authenticity, can be socially variable, some, such as elites priding themselves on their cosmopolitan outlook, as opposed to apparent caution of some lower down the social scale.

If the chefs have newly to be familiarized with ethnic foods to cook them (even of their own personal origins) so too do the restaurants' clienteles. They must learn to like them. Once established, the taste/fashion persists: American enthusiasm for French cuisine does not waver even though it is now just one of a proliferation of cuisines from beyond US borders (Johnston and Baumann 2015). Over several centuries, however, the English both hate and love the food of France (Mennell 1985). The English novelist John Galsworthy has one of his characters declare after dining at another house 'That's what I call a capital little dinner ... nothing heavy – and not too Frenchified'.[11] It may be fiction, but the author can be reasonably confident not only of the way that the wealthy upper classes in 1920s London prided themselves on being connoisseurs of French *haute cuisine* even at home, but also that his character's preference for 'plain English cooking' would be recognized by his readers.

As noted, people have to learn to like unfamiliar cuisines and for this to happen involves a process of mutual accommodation. Any initial suspicion of novelty (neophobia is the psychologists' term) must be converted into appreciation (neophilia). Waddington illustrates the way that for the latter half of the nineteenth century right through to the outbreak of the First World War the German sausage is used in Britain as a metaphor for profound suspicion of the German nation. 'Cultural and gastronomic stereotypes overlapped in a discourse that linked Germany and Germans to their national diet and aggressive nature, as well as associated German sausages with fears about diseased meat, adulteration, and the risks that eating them entailed' (2013: 1017). The fear of adulteration is also at issue in the instance that Liu and Lin record; in the 1910s, white American residents of Los Angeles discover that Chinese food is good 'and not at all poisonous' (2009: 136). There follows a long period, they report, in which Chinese restaurants supplied Americanized Chinese food such as chop suey, a widely known dish invented in the US, but, from 1965, pushed aside as new waves of Chinese immigrants arrive, when 'genuine' Chinese food begins to be served. This contrast is also recorded in Mexican restaurants in the same city, with some establishments providing Americanized dishes together with fake 'traditional' culinary arrangements. But others which provide 'genuine' Mexican food are in the more run-down areas where Mexican migrants lives displaying the incongruity of expensive cars in the parking lots of diners knowledgeable about real Mexican cuisine (Ferrero 2002). What may distinguish the first decades of the present century is *both* a proliferation in the provision of cuisines from elsewhere but also the social widening of that enthusiasm.

Sociological thinking and authenticity

A search for authenticity implies paying attention to the history of an ingredient, dish or cuisine, yet doing just that reveals the impossibility of pinning it down. Who is to decide on the criteria whereby to date the 'truly' authentic version? Sociologists have recourse to history to find a different lesson. Determining what counts as ethnic foods is part of a protracted process with components (people, ingredients, ideas for dishes, cooking techniques, whole cuisines) moving to 'new' places at different rates, and in varying volumes and combinations. The ingredients of what a 'food nationalist' would want to regard as an 'inescapable part of Indian cuisine today, came to India from South America' with recipes coming from elsewhere in Asia (Nandy 2004: 11).

The successive adjustments to recipes, new creations (never mind attendant 'branding') illustrated above is a powerful reminder of the *market* made between restaurateurs/chefs and their clienteles. As Johnston and Baumann point out, there are 'food fashion cycles'; a cuisine that is 'in' one year is passé the next (2015: 23). In any case, ethnic cuisine does not remain fixed either literally or symbolically but 'constantly gets recreated, transformed, and reinterpreted' (van den Berghe 1984: 393).

At times, the search for authenticity turns into a trap for sociologists (Murcott 2012b). Researchers must recognize that asking what is typical of one or other ethnic cuisine is a gourmet's preoccupation, belonging to the realm of common sense and everyday life. It adds little sociologically to leave it in such terms. Instead, the question must be re-made for the purpose of informed sociological enquiry. Authenticity is itself a social phenomenon to be understood, not a concept with which to analyse other phenomena. One re-made question might be: is there uniform interest in the idea across the social spectrum or is it found primarily among one stratum? Another question could be: are there commercial interests promoting the idea of authenticity and if so, how might they be uncovered and what might be the consequences for producers/consumers? More fundamental, if perhaps more difficult to tackle is: how does authenticity ever become a valued criterion? Here in particular is a sociologist's question. It turns on investigating the ways social groups display difference between, and distinctiveness from, one another (Bourdieu 1984). Versions of these questions run through this chapter and arise once more when turning to pose a broader, direct question thus far by-passed: what is to count as ethnic food?

What are ethnic foods?

Once market research starts reporting the increase in ethnic food consumption, some commentators begin searching for satisfactory definitions (Paulson-Box and Williamson 1990). But for sociological purposes, the term 'ethnic' must be considered first.

Sociological thinking and 'ethnicity'

In many public contexts, journalism, the civil service or political circles, the word 'ethnicity' now replaces the term 'race'. The purpose is to evade any hint of old, discredited theories of difference of skin colour etc. as signalling biologically fixed bases for, say, lower intelligence or inferior moral rectitude. Ray dates the origins of the replacement in the US from the 1950s such that ethnicity is now the 'dominant mode of framing difference without falling into the problem of race' (Ray 2016: 4). In parallel, the ethnic majority in the UK is said to have 'shifted in their understanding of the acceptable nature of terms such as "Negro", "coloured" and "black" over the past several generations' (Bradby 2003 :7).

Now the use of 'ethnic group' is well established in the compilation of official statistics in, for instance, the US, Australia, New Zealand, Singapore and the UK. Its definition is typically bland; e.g. a social group sharing a specific awareness of common identity and distinct sense of being different from other such groups, needing no reference to visible biological variations in skin colour, often including provision for people's own identification of themselves. A sociological definition follows suit. '(T)he usual characteristics distinguishing ethnic groups are language, history or ancestry (real or imagined) religion and styles of dress or adornment' (Giddens and Sutton 2014: 107) – and foodways and cuisine. A far more sophisticated recent sociological discussion of the whole field is provided by Michael Banton (2015) who insists that 'ethnic group' belongs to the practical world of policy and cannot serve as a term in the analytic world of the social sciences.

The key point is that ethnicity is social, not biological. And though it is widely used solely to refer to those who are different from the supposedly indigenous (i.e. non-ethnic) population this is mistaken – an expression of unwitting ethnocentrism – since 'ethnicity is an attribute of all members of a population not just some segments of it' (Giddens and Sutton 2014: 108). Ray is even more emphatic: '(E)thnicity is the perpetual schema by which Americans produce cultural difference' from themselves (2016: 10) just as do New Zealanders or the English.

In so saying he gets closer to a key element of ethnicity proposed here, namely that it is a product of a meeting, a consequence of social interaction, between members of two (or more) social groups who thereby become aware of group-related differences between them. A social group that never comes across another group need develop no special awareness of their own common cultural identity. They do not have to, for that shared cultural identity is the same for everyone and thereby goes unremarked. A version of this is illustrated in a study of consciousness of whether foods are halal. The question does not arise before leaving north Africa – all food there is halal. But it becomes evident when Magrebi migrants arrive in Bordeaux which, by definition, brings them into contact with other social groups whose foods are not halal (Bergeaud-Blackler 2004).

Sociological thinking and ethnic cuisines

Once food is added to Giddens and Sutton's list, then its materiality may be highlighted. It is one thing to notice another social group's clothes or language, pleasing or displeasing they may be evaded. It is quite another to become aware of religious activities which perhaps involve loud clapping or singing which could be experienced as intrusive or a nuisance by another ethnic group. Even more potentially disruptive is unfamiliar and disliked smell, objections to wafts of cooking or of garlic on the breath. 'The history of racism is full of complaints about the way that a particular group's cooking smells' (Wurgaft 2006: 57). Food's materiality is central to members of one social group learning to like the cuisine of another. It is, quite literally, a matter of taste. The taste of unfamiliar ingredients, the taste of unfamiliar combinations of them, the taste of their preparation in novel ovens or in different oils, the taste of the unfamiliar array of dishes served together is inextricable from learning that ethnic foods can be enjoyable, fundamental to learning to regard them as familiar.

It is self-evident that people do learn to like different foods, despite sixteenth-century explorers' repudiation of them. It can happen quite quickly even when migrating long distances geographically and culturally. Sri Lankans and Pakistanis taking up residence in Oslo adopt the Norwegian pattern of one hot meal a day, instead of three, switching to the local habit of bread in the mornings and at lunch. A quarter continue only to eat their 'own' dishes, with the majority adding Norwegian foods, and all reporting eating more meat (and with it more fats and oils) coupled with eating fewer legumes such as lentils – a matter of concern to the nutritionists undertaking the study (Wandel et al 2008).

As to the circumstances under which learning to like unfamiliar cuisines can succeed, van den Berghe is clear: '(C)onsciousness of eating ethnic cuisine, however, can only develop in a context of *interethnic contact* (1984: 392, emphasis added). He also suggests that becoming fully conscious of ethnic cuisine is most likely in multi-ethnic cities. More optimistically and less realistically, he comes close to suggesting that eating one another's food promotes inter-ethnic harmony: '(W)hat more accessible and friendlier arena of inter-ethnic contact could be devised than the ethnic restaurant?' (van den Berghe 1984: 393–394). A further example of optimism is evident in a study of South African migrants to Australia. For them, continuing to have food from home is important to their identity as they begin to settle. At the same time, it provides a means of introducing themselves to others, representing an 'important platform to enable migrants to integrate' leading, say the authors confidently, to greater social cohesion (Schermuly and Forbes-Mewett 2016: 2441, 2434).

This sort of discussion comes perilously close to another trap for sociologists. It is not just that the likelihood that inter-ethnic harmony may need more than meeting in a restaurant where the relationship between customer and staff is commercial and typically unequal (see Chapter 3) or that (remember the German sausage) the circumstances conducive to tolerably congenial exchange have to be established before migrants can introduce their food to others, a point none of the optimists cited above consider. The idea that someone is learning about another culture simply by eating the relevant food, is – and this is the trap – to imply that cultural identity *inheres* in the food. There is nothing inherent in any foodstuff that signifies anything, it is the meaning which people attribute to the foodstuff during its deployment in their lives that enables food to convey messages (see Chapter 1). To effect integration or promote inter-ethnic harmony meanings must be shared. The social circumstances, attendant social relationships together *and* the material circumstances of actually being confronted with the foods, have to be propitious for the emergence of that shared meaning over and above the actual act of eating. As Mintz repeatedly points out, the material precedes the symbolic (see Chapter 1).

In any case, to think that social cohesion or inter-ethnic harmony can be promoted by members of different ethnic groups eating one another's foods risks ignoring the historical evidence. As already seen, restaurateurs adjust their recipes to what they learn are the tastes of their clienteles, even inventing dishes that still get 'branded' as authentic. Ethnic cookery books start to emerge taking advantage of the pre-existing increased familiarity with and enjoyment of what are deemed ethnic cuisines. Eating one or other ethnic dish at home is thereafter augmented by manufacturers capitalizing still further in putting ethnic ingredients, sauces and then chilled/frozen ready-meals on the market. The consequence is, as Van den Berghe puts it: '(I)nevitably, ethnic food can fall victim to its success. Once its popularity earns it a place in the mass market, it loses all value as an ethnic marker, and thus becomes "de-ethnicised"' (1984: 394).

He could have said 're-ethnicized'. A 2000 report by the US National Restaurant Association considers that Italian, Mexican, and Chinese cuisines 'have become so ingrained in American culture that they are no longer foreign to the American palate' (Liu and Lin 2009: 158). In the 1990s, Willetts reports that residents in Lewisham in south London routinely think of pizza and pasta as British food, especially those families who come from the Caribbean who first encounter these foods in the UK (1997). To talk of this trend as 're-ethnicizing' emphasizes the manner in which all social groups are ethnic, not just minorities or newcomers.

Whose cuisines are 'ethnic'?

At this point, the discussion returns to think further about how far anyone's 'own' cuisine gets noted in a list of ethnic cuisines. When they do not, a question of the invisibility/ un-discussed assumption about whichever is the majority/dominant ethnic group is raised. To take that question further, it is useful to turn to the scholarly literature on 'whiteness'. Many credit Ruth Frankenberg's as one of the key contributions initiating an examination of the notion (Frankenberg 1993). Her concern is to show that white people in the US, of the dominant, majority, and more/most powerful ethnic group, lead racially organized lives as much as do those of ethnic minority groups whether their hair and skin is very blonde (e.g. Norwegian migrants to nineteenth-century America) or far darker (the descendants of West African slaves in the Deep South).

One way into thinking about whiteness in relation to ethnic cuisine is the historian Amy Bentley's dissection of what she describes as 'the Martha Stewart empire' (2001: 89). Focusing on Stewart's food as represented in publications, Bentley argues that the beautifully presented surface of her food hides its complex meanings.

Her examination of the recipes, the names of dishes etc. shows the food is *silently* marked as 'white', a 'class-specific whiteness' that has no need to signal its ethnicity. Unlike other women's magazines, Bentley reports that *Martha Stewart Living* (MSL) 'rarely features any food ritual or ethnic fare outside of mainstream America in general and New England in particular, prominently featuring Thanksgiving, Christmas, Fourth of July celebrations, church bake sales'. Some 'ethnic' dishes do appear e.g. matzo ball soup, Greek tsoureki but '(W)hen Martha Stewart publications do feature some ethnic fare, the

---

Box 21 Analysing documents

Sociologists (anthropologists and human geographers) increasingly analyse documents, hitherto primarily the materials of historians (Scott 1990). Such sources obviously include paper and anything on which people may make a mark creating text (e.g., Ray's use of newspapers to track the rise of restaurants in New York and Los Angeles (2016)). They also extend to images (e.g., of food packaging) (Cochoy and Grandclément-Chaffy 2005). The use of cookery books as documentary sources for sociological/anthropological understandings is now more common (e.g., cookbooks displaying ethnic identity in the US, Gvion 2009), identifying the availability of ingredients over time (Leach and Inglis 2003) images of kitchen technologies (Murcott 1983c) the making of a national cuisine (Appadurai 1988). It is essential not to assume that the contents of a document represent the reality portrayed.

entire process is glossed in a patina of whiteness'. Even a feature on an Indian dinner, 'unfolds not as an excursion into Indian culture and cuisine, but as a beginner's lesson in Indian flavors for her (white) husband and (white) friends. The result, not surprisingly and somewhat logically, is a lovely Indian dinner in the East Hamptons, Martha Stewart style' (Bentley 2001: 90).

Whiteness goes unremarked and thereby not noticed. Rachel Slocum's discussion of the work of a Central New York community food coalition shows how, unnoticed, white privilege runs through its activities, despite explicit efforts to promote an anti-racist stance (Slocum 2006). This is paralleled by Guthman's work on Californian farmers' markets and community-supported agriculture, illustrating the 'color-blind mentalities and universalizing impulses of alternative food discourse' (2006: 388).

Ethnic foods and identity

Panayi remarks that in Britain 'at the start of the twenty-first century, food nationality and ethnicity have a close association' but he could be talking about Seattle, Singapore or Auckland (2008: 36–7). Like Symons, he points to corporations as well as food writers as responsible for perpetuating that association.[12] Mid-twentieth-century anthropologists commonly talk of the way that food symbolizes group identity, another way of thinking about the rude names for different nationalities, French calling Italians Macaronis, Americans calling Germans Krauts (see Chapter 1).

'Food is central to our sense of identity' declares the sociologist Claude Fischler beginning what he calls a speculative survey of the matter. He continues: '(T)he way any given human group eats helps it assert its diversity, hierarchy and organisation, but also, at the same time, both its oneness and the otherness of whoever eats differently.' But, he adds, food is also central to individual identity in that 'any given human individual is constructed, biologically, psychologically and socially by the foods he/she chooses to incorporate' by eating them (1988: 275). His insistence at the beginning of his article that the human relationship to food is complex and multi-dimensional is particularly important and he valuably sets out several of the relevant dimensions.

What is striking, however, is that although he firmly distinguishes intellectual approaches adopted by psychologists from those of sociologists and anthropologists, and although he also discusses the cultural realm as well as the psychological, he nonetheless admiringly depends heavily on the inspiration of Paul Rozin, a psychologist. Ironically, Fischler ends up relying far more on psychology's than sociology's conceptions of identity. Moreover, as Ray has almost sarcastically pointed out: '(T)he psychological subject is also the most durable creature of common sense of both the American college and public commentary. It is a peculiarly universalized subject: an autonomous, free, adaptable individual who can eat anything he or she chooses' (2013: 363). In other words, psychology's conception of identity that describes a being who is rational, self-conscious, freely coming to their own decisions about how to run all aspects of their life, is the one that is most commonly assumed in all kinds of discussions both academic and non-academic. It is also the identity specific to the social stratum of well-off, white professional/middle classes. It is certainly the identity which is most widely implied in discussions of 'the food consumer'.

Sociological thinking and identity

Theorizing about identity is found in some of the earliest social sciences. The philosopher/sociologist George Herbert Mead (1863 –1931) argues that the self, and its associated sense of identity, is not inborn as a product of biology any more than it develops as the brain matures. Identity takes shape in the process of social interaction with other people which also means that identity cannot be studied without also studying interaction. How this works for all kinds of identities is well illustrated by considering the way Erving Goffman has studied those dealing with social difficulties, what he aptly calls 'spoiled' identities. In his study of 'stigma', someone's social and/or physical features which are de-valued, the object of social disapproval or discrimination, risking public shame or disgrace, are fundamental to the way someone develops a stigmatized identity, at risk of being 'branded'[13] as inferior and at the worst, outcast.

Crucially Goffman shrewdly observes that the development of a spoiled identity does not begin with the emotional or psychological effect of being stigmatized. It must start by learning what, in shorthand form, Goffman calls the 'normal' point of view, via what *other* people say/write about what counts as acceptable or unacceptable characteristics. Once the general point of view is learned, the person then turns to look at themselves whereupon they realize they possess the very characteristic deemed not normal. The instance of spoiled identities is a particular case of the development of identity generally but it shows the way that the development of identity arises in interaction between people and that learning first about general, shared understandings is integral to the process.

Appreciating that identity is formed in social interaction and thereby not fixed at birth opens up the realization that identity need not be stable or attained once and for all. By the same token, it is readily recognized that any one person may develop multiple identities: 'food and identity becomes a vast, rambling field containing national and religious claims, class and ethnic preferences, racial and gender distinctiveness' (Ray 2013: 163–4). This is not to say that any one of those identities is not experienced as real and 'true'. As Lu and Fine point out in their study of the presentation of food in four Chinese restaurants in the small city of Athens, Georgia, ethnicity is made real in interaction with others. At the same time the display of ethnicity, 'often becomes a marketing tool, part of an entrepreneurial market' adroitly displayed in simultaneous appeal to 'authenticity' and 'Americanization' (Lu and Fine 1995: 535). Tastes adjusted for the local clientele are presented as authentically Chinese.

Ethnic food as national food

A prominent idiom in which ethnic cuisines are publicly presented in documents of all kinds such as cookery books, restaurant menus, recipe websites and so on is nationality.

Here, in particular, the fluidity of notions of ethnic cuisine is apparent. Arjun Appadurai presents a detailed discussion of the way a national cuisine is artfully created, one which is both product and illustration of its time and place: 'the construction of a national cuisine is essentially a postindustrial, postcolonial process' in which 'the new Indian cookbooks are fueled by the spread of print media and the cultural rise of the new middle classes' (Appadurai 1988: 4 and Gvion 2012, deSoucey 2016). A different version is found in the promotion of American-ness in the nineteenth-century creation of Thanksgiving traditions (Wills 2003) more recently clearly demonstrated by Wilk in his discussion of the gradual invention of Belizean cuisine (1999). A specialist in marketing argues for the foundation of a Croatian 'gastronomic identity' since a 'unique and memorable gastronomic identity is an indispensable asset to any successful tourist destination' (Fox 2007: 546).

Note, however, that adopting nationality as the idiom in which to create an identity for a cuisine also illustrates the manner in which any identity is created when noticing difference. As Gabaccia observes '(o)nly in reaction to the arrival of immigrants in the late nineteenth century did the cultural elites of the Northeast attempt to define what American eating should be' (Gabaccia 1998: 125).

'Ethnic foods' and a thread to the food system

This chapter barely needs to pick up a special thread to the (globalized) food system. It runs throughout reflected in the myriad commercial interests in ethnic cuisines. They appear in the 'food service' sector via restaurants and cafés, never mind that 'ethnic' foods are popularized by adapting original recipes, 'domesticating' them, or inventing novel 'ethnic' dishes well away from the geographic and cultural origins with which they are to be associated. The purpose is to attract customers and stay in business. Manufacturers follow but also promote trends, via their market research aiming to identify customers' opinions and tastes and, like restaurants, find that 'ethnic' ingredients as well as 'ethnic' ready meals sell well. Cookery books, whether or not their owners cook from them, help spread positive images of 'ethnic' cuisines.

Box 22 Chapter 7 – Selected Key Points

1. 'Ethnic foods' have not always been as popular as they are reputed to be now.
2. Although ethnic foods and cuisines are marketed in terms of 'authenticity' and valued by restaurant goers, ingredients, cooking styles and recipes are moved globally and (re)invented to such an extent that securely establishing authenticity is impossible.

3. Defining 'ethnic food' is not straightforward, partly because 'ethnicity' is more a policy and practitioner term than a sociological concept, used, some argue, as a euphemism for skin colour.

4. Popular and academic discussions of ethnicity and ethnic food overlook whiteness as an ethnic attribute.

5. Associating cuisines with ethnic identity only becomes meaningful when different groups identifying themselves as distinct, come into contact.

CHAPTER 8

FOOD, NUTRITION AND KITCHEN HYGIENE: 'WHY DON'T PEOPLE JUST FOLLOW PROFESSIONAL ADVICE?'

62 percent of restaurant workers don't wash their hands after handling raw beef[1]

Only 12% of people wash their hands before eating[2]

Ask any Australian aged 14+ if they eat two serves of fruit and five serves of vegetables each day, and chances are the answer will be no. . . . only 2% of the population does – despite this being the minimum daily fruit-and-veg intake recommended by the National Health and Medical Research Council[3]

The problem is that most people don't know where to put what (in the fridge). They open the door and throw everything in[4]

Most people in Scotland are aware of healthy eating advice – but don't follow it[5]

This handful of headlines reflects a puzzle. Even though people are fairly well informed about how to eat healthily and more or less know what is needed to keep the kitchen clean, they still do not act accordingly, or so market research and opinion polls find. It is a puzzle that is also familiar to professionals, from nutritionists to food safety experts. For years, much of their literature has been devoted to assessing the effectiveness of efforts in many different countries to educate their general publics about the food they need to eat to remain healthy and/or about the steps to take to avoid foodborne disease (e.g. Bruhn and Schutz 1999).

Yet still, some of that literature confirms, that though the information is quite widely known and understood, people 'fail to comply' with advice – but why? Does it mean that people are stupid, lazy or wilfully disobedient? As adults, people are supposed to be responsible for taking care of themselves by listening to expert advice, limiting risks to their health and pursuing activities which prevent disease. This is the image of a good citizen of the overarching socio-political ideology of 'neo-liberalism' which suffuses the world of healthy eating and suitable kitchen hygiene just as it does other arenas under the public health professionals' heading of 'lifestyle and health'. The idea that people should know that following professionals' advice is the 'right way to behave' runs right through the question as to why people do not follow it. Note that this puzzle, or something like it, is not just reported by professionals in food safety, nutrition or public health, it also arises in other fields (Lockie et al 2002, Holm and Møhl 2000).

This chapter covers two ways sociologists tackle the puzzle. One is conceptual, dealt with in the first main section. It considers the way in which the puzzle is characterized and/or data are interpreted and reflects on the vantage point from which the puzzle is viewed, with implications for the way research is designed. It also includes attention to the social circumstances in which people are supposed to act upon advice, unlike the tendency in public health literature by nutritionists or food safety experts to focus on the advice itself. The way the whole research problem is conceptualized affects how studies are designed.

The second main section approaches the puzzle by concentrating on social structure, especially social class. It deals with correlations between class position and the likelihood of following professional advice, middle class more likely, working class less so. It goes on to consider how far economic circumstances and/or beliefs about health account for the difference or whether it has to do with the nature and source of the advice itself. But before turning to either, an alternative, sociological perspective on 'failure to comply' is introduced.

'Good' reasons for 'bad' behaviour

A central theme running through the rest of this chapter is an alternative perspective, namely, that whatever lies behind failing to comply might be reasonable and explicable. There may be 'good' reasons for 'bad' behaviour. This expression is adapted from the sociologist Harold Garfinkel's discussion of the reasons for patchy success in securing data for a study with nothing to do with food and society, but about the way patients are selected for treatment. Planning to rely on the records routinely kept in an out-patients' clinic of the UCLA Medical Center, he finds that they are too often so incomplete his plan would not work. Changing tack, he moved to characterize what lies behind those difficulties as 'good' organizational reasons for 'bad' records (1967: 187). The 'good' reasons for incomplete record keeping in which he is most interested are, in his words, 'normal, natural troubles'. These include commonplace features of the setting itself, such as the economics of running the clinic or the (inferior) status and lower importance staff attach to paperwork compared with other clinical work. In other words, he found that the reasons are elements integral to the social context in which the records are compiled, a task which is in any case part of ordinary clinic routine (1997: 191).

Note that to refer to the reasons as 'good' does not imply a moral judgement about the quality of the record keeping, any more than adopting Garfinkel's approach in this chapter implies blaming anyone whose actions do not follow nutrition advice or recommendations about kitchen safety. Calling them 'good' reasons refers to being able to recognize typical or ordinary features of the social setting in which the activities at issue take place. In this way they are made 'reasonable' and understandable whether or not they can be condoned.

Adapting Garfinkel's expression here indicates that to explain people's actions, it is insufficient to describe them as failing to comply or even wondering whether their not acting as advised results from poorly designed information campaigns. For many, this merely blames the victim. Instead, attention is to be devoted to the social context—not

Food, Nutrition and Kitchen Hygiene

Garfinkel's clinic, but the supermarket aisle, and especially the domestic kitchen. From the outset it means taking the view that what people do is readily understandable in that their activities are integral to the way daily lives are ordinarily lived. Invoking Garfinkel's sociological thinking also highlights methodological matters in moving away from an overall orientation to 'failure to comply'. The need to improve health and reduce disease is the public health task. Recognizing the force of that need does not mean it is sociologists' task to formulate their investigations in public health terms. On the contrary, that would be to inhibit making a fully sociological contribution to understanding the puzzle. Distinctively sociological research questions need to be devised requiring temporarily setting aside the public health viewpoint. Better still, in devising a distinctively sociological approach, that public health viewpoint itself should be incorporated into the picture to be studied.

Conceptual considerations – the puzzle

Equipped with this different perspective on 'failure to comply' with professional advice, this section concentrates on conceptual matters. Remember, these have profound implications not only for technical issues about data collection, but, far more broadly, for the way in which research is designed.

Considered first is the way the puzzle is characterized as a conundrum, something self-contradictory. This assumes that what people do will result from the advice they are given, leading to bemusement when this does not happen, a vantage point that leads directly to the judging of people as feckless, ignorant etc. They are viewed as deficient, leading specialists in science and technology studies (STS) to talk of a 'deficit model' to describe any public ignorance of scientific and medical expertise (Wynne 1995). This shines a light on the very vantage point from which such thinking is adopted.

'Deficit' thinking introduced – and evaded

Characterizing the puzzle as deficiencies in the public's knowledge or actions is a vantage point often found among experts in public health and food safety dedicated to improving dietary habits and reducing rates of foodborne disease. For example, a careful Australian study compares 40 Melbourne residents' answers to questions that test their understandings of food safety with what they were actually seen to do in the kitchen (Jay, Comar and Govenlock 1999). Video recording allows readily organized capture of what people actually do, as distinct from asking them to report what they do, and found 'a significant variance' between the two. The report uses a vocabulary of deficiencies: '(I)nfrequent hand washing; poor hand-washing technique; lack of hand washing prior to food preparation; inadequate cleaning of kitchen surfaces' (1999: 1243).

Their concern is clear: such activities are known to risk the spread and ingestion of microbes responsible for food poisoning and are thereby, logically, to be judged as deficient. The vantage point, however, remains at the stage of assessing the safety or

125

otherwise of what has been observed. Significantly, authors do not begin to ask how these activities come about, except to point out that they are often found to be at odds with what the perpetrators know should or should not be done. The deficit model can, it seems, go no further than such evaluations or beyond Griffith and Redmond's judgement that 'consumers' must take 'responsibility' for kitchen hygiene and that improvements are needed in devising public education and information campaigns (2001).

What has taken things further is a study which also uses video recording, along with interviews among additional methods. Here the starting point is a far wider perspective, deliberately including 'factors that many other studies of foodborne illness in the domestic setting have overlooked' (Wills et al 2015:119). Instead of thinking only of individuals and their actions *extracted* from the ordinary run of day-to-day life electing to focus only on any which are hygiene related, Wills et al characterize people's actions as just one part of ordinary everyday living. They view everything as a 'jigsaw puzzle of factors' among which are those that could be involved in the spread of foodborne disease. Furthermore, the study adds to what happens in the immediate context of food preparation by including people's biographies, their beliefs and values as well as their relationships with others inside and outside the home. In this way it shows how actions which are undeniably unhygienic as well as those which follow advice are *all* mixed up with many other, very familiar, actions which are interspersed with preparing food – from picking up a crying toddler or feeding the dog, to answering the phone or handing a partner a bunch of keys.

All this adds up to Wills et al's observing that food handling etc takes place entangled with encounters with other people and with non-food actions in a fashion that is very difficult to pull apart. In this way, the vantage point here is to set judging incontestably unhygienic actions to one side, instead attempting to grasp the reality in which they take place. This neither endorses nor condemns the observed actions, but shifts the emphasis away from evaluating to understanding them, not in artificial settings of test kitchens or of reporting actions on questionnaires, but in the actual circumstances in which they happen. It is in this way that Wills et al's portrayal of ordinary lives in the kitchen reveals that there are 'good', very familiar, mundane reasons for what food safety experts judge as 'bad' behaviour. This is not to suggest that public information campaigns should be abandoned. Rates of food poisoning might be even worse without them. It is, however, to suggest that blaming people or condemning their actions risks being pointless for anyone interested in helping changes to be successfully made.

From 'gap' to 'practices'

No matter how illuminating, adopting a vantage point that side-steps a deficit model does not dispose of what, on the face of it, is plausibly thought of as a puzzle. Various social scientists have characterized it as a gap between knowing and doing. Describing the puzzle in this way neatly fits with a commonsense view, as well as with attitudes among public health practitioners. Furthermore, it also fits with the assumptions policy makers and politicians commonly make (Shove 2010). Imagining the problem as a gap leads logically to supposing that the solution is to close it. In turn, this prompts research geared to understanding its nature to specify either what helps/obstructs the closing of it, very widely characterized as 'facilitators'/ 'enablers' and 'barriers' respectively. Theories of practice, a strand of sociological thinking, provides an alternative conceptualization.

Theories of practice

Picturing the matter as a gap between knowing and doing draws on the insights of the psychologists Martin Fishbein and Icek Ajzen's theory of planned behaviour (TPB) initially developed in the 1970s with subsequent further refinement (Connor and Armitage 2002). Identification of TPB's limitations (e.g. Gronow and Holm 2015) prompts an alternative approach, wherein lies the promise of sociological theories of practice. Pierre Bourdieu's 'classic' major foundational contribution to such theorizing continues to be debated and developed especially in respect of eating (see Chapter 1). Warde provides an invaluable discussion of several of these theories (2014). Various facets are noted, including the manner in which everyone undertakes commonly repeated, mundane activities, like grilling a burger, as if on 'auto-pilot' and attending to the way practices exist where individual cognition (thought processes) and collective conventions/social norms are interconnected.

Theories of practice highlight the importance of tacit and informal knowledge, the kind that everyone accumulates in their ordinary contacts with others. Intimately associated with tacit knowledge is embodied knowledge, developed via the senses, especially touch, including what some (especially professional chefs) call 'muscle memory'. Taken together, practice theorizing shifts the centre of investigative attention to the *combination* of knowing and doing, thus rendering irrelevant conceptualization in terms of a gap. Thus, any puzzle of contradictions between what people say and what they (report or are observed to) do simply disappears. 'Practices' replace 'behaviour' as the unit of enquiry.

Placed in the centre of an investigation, paying attention to the various facets of practices means Jackson can contrast deficit thinking with what people do/say in the kitchen (Jackson 2015). His research participants are frustrated by official food safety guidelines' selective attention to unhygienically risky activities, since they run counter to their own pre-existing knowledge (e.g. ruling out their own experiential and sensory judgements about the look or smell of, say yoghurt a day past its 'use by' date). Others are sceptical, if not suspicious, of 'use by' labelling; one talks of labels as 'a manufacturer's gimmick', another that date labels are 'a cynical ploy, "preying on your insecurities" and designed to "have you back in the shops" as soon as possible' (2015: 157–8).

Of course, food safety experts (and many others) may despair at these reactions, using them to argue that they only demonstrate how badly public education is needed. But sociological thinking offers a counter to that argument in that ignoring the contrasts thus highlighted does nothing to resolve them. On the contrary, it starts to specify the limitations of public education. If its limitations are by-passed, education campaigns are unlikely to be successful, and risk wasting money and time by not revising them.

Conceptual considerations – focus on actions in a social context

Recollect that Wills et al concentrate on the social circumstances in which people are expected to act on kitchen hygiene advice, differing from the frequent tendency in the public health literature by food safety experts who focus on the advice itself, the extent to which people are aware of it, etc. The same approach is adopted in relation to the provision of nutrition advice by Murphy et al, who take careful account of the context in which information about infant feeding is to be acted upon. Once again, thinking in terms of 'good reasons' for 'bad behaviour' is evident in the study's results.

'Good' reasons for not breastfeeding as advised – 'good' mothers, 'good' women

This instance of 'bad' behaviour is particularly widespread. A 2017 World Health Organization (WHO) press release reports that no country anywhere 'fully meets recommended standards for breastfeeding' which recommend for infants' first six months they be fed nothing but breast milk.[6] Not meeting these recommendations is unequivocally both a public and public health, issue, once again accompanied by a large literature in public health nutrition and allied disciplines investigating why, despite their awareness of the recommendation, women do not breastfeed as advised. But as becomes clear, it does not find a simple parallel as a private trouble: quite the contrary.

Murphy devised a different, and at the time, novel combination of research design and data collection method (1999). Her study included the same 36 women, followed from late pregnancy until the child's second birthday i.e. a longitudinal design. Instead of using a structured method of data collection her approach is qualitative. Over the two years, six open-ended interviews are conducted with each woman. The value of the longitudinal design meant that if a pregnant woman announced she would breastfeed but ended up formula feeding instead, subsequent research interviews represent occasions when she can be invited to discuss her change of plan.

Box 23 Research Approach, Research Design

A distinction is made between qualitative and quantitative research **approaches**. The former makes a virtue of study in-depth – typically involving smaller numbers of people, and fewer locales. The latter trades depth for breadth, involves much larger numbers and can have a wide geographical range. Which is adopted must depend on the type of research question being tackled. Questions about frequency or proportions are quantitative so the design must be quantitative e.g. Rozin and Fischler are interested in whether preferences for more choice are more/less frequent in different countries (2006). Those asking about how something comes

---

about or what a phenomenon looks like are qualitative e.g. Cochoy is interested in how self-service is promoted in the grocery trade (2015) and Bishop looks for conceptions of convenience (2007).

Studies must then be **designed** accordingly: a social survey for Rozin and Fischler; primarily qualitative content analysis/ discourse/ textual analysis for Cochoy and Bishop. Note that determining what is being measured in quantitative research is an essential precursor to counting how often it happens – the point at which the quantitative unavoidably depends on a version of the qualitative. Studies may combine qualitative and quantitative approaches: a common design is to undertake a small preliminary qualitive element to provide an informed basis for a larger quantitative component (e.g. Warde and Martens' study of eating out (2000)).

Murphy reminds her readers that 'breast is best' dominates the background against which women make decisions about feeding their babies, an official policy, promoted by health professionals and widely known among the general public. This means that a pregnant woman who says she does not intend to breast feed (planning to use commercially manufactured infant formula instead) is *publicizing* the fact that she plans to act *against* well-known advice. She thereby risks the accusation that she is a 'poor mother' who places her own needs, preferences or convenience above her baby's welfare. By contrast, the 'good mother' is deemed to be one who prioritizes her child's needs, even (or perhaps especially) where this entails personal inconvenience or distress' (1999: 187–8), images which fit with the predominant direction of official advice.

Interviewed before the birth, 29 women said they intended to breast feed, with six planning to use formula (and one a combination). Later interviews record that 31 actually initiated breast feeding with all but six stopping short of the official target of exclusive breastfeeding for six months. Although antenatally 29 planned to breastfeed as recommended, 24 did not sustain it beyond the first month. Note that in line with her research design and sampling procedures which cannot support doing so, Murphy does not generalize to any population other than the study participants. The number who do/do not do so is analytically beside the point. The way women talk about it is significant. Murphy notes that, during pregnancy, women are familiar with being asked about their feeding intentions in antenatal clinics as well as more generally. So being asked again in the research interview is nothing new. They all readily declared their intention and present well-rehearsed comments to support their decisions and all are aware of the official recommendation. One adds: 'I think it would be quite easy for somebody to feel guilty if they didn't' and another imagines friends would 'never speak to me again I'm not a real Mum' (2000: 302) Women endorse the official and general view of formula feeding as 'bad' behaviour, and by extension women who adopt formula feeding despite the advices are 'bad' mothers, thereby presenting themselves as 'good' mothers-to-be.

In order to make analytic sense of post-natal interviews with women, contrary to their original stated intentions no longer breastfeeding, Murphy analyses their statements as 'accounts' i.e. responses prompted when some action is the subject of evaluative questioning. She notes that such responses are a *normal* way in which people account for themselves as a suitably good person (Murphy 1999, 2000). They are statements made as a way of explaining untoward or inconsistent actions to render them understandable and thus reasonable. An adverse moral judgement is thus deflected. Inevitably hovering over Murphy's interviews is the unspoken reproachful question '"How could you as a good mother, knowing the risks associated with formula milk, have introduced this into your baby's diet?"' (2000: 304).

Analysing the interview material not as a window on actions but as actions themselves, shows what women who go against their antenatal declaration say to ensure they did not look bad in the eyes of the interviewer. Indeed, the material illuminates the way women stress that they are 'good' mothers, helping the child be more settled, sleeping better and be a happier baby. Other women who find they cannot breast feed describe their disappointment, 'good' mothers would obviously be unhappy about it. In this fashion, Murphy's analyses illustrate that, including the context framing infant feeding reveals not only that women's talk is aimed at parrying accusations of 'bad' motherhood but also that these represent 'good reasons' for 'bad behaviour'.

Social structure, (un)healthy eating and (un)safe kitchen hygiene

This section changes tack to consider the second approach to understanding how people might come not to follow professional advice. Here, the focus is on social structural variations in 'good' reasons for 'bad' healthy eating or kitchen hygiene and the terms in which it is often couched. Such enquiries are necessarily quantitative – social surveys, social epidemiology or in an earlier designation 'political arithmetic' (Murcott 2002). Time and again public health and nutrition-epidemiological studies confirm there is a consistent correlation: the higher the income/education level/social class, the greater the likelihood of healthy eating/kitchen hygiene being in line with recommendations. The picture, however, is not that simple. As soon as additional variables are introduced (e.g. region, parenthood, marital status, or different ways of assessing diet (macro- or micro-nutrient intake)) subtler variations complicating the picture show up (e.g. Roos et al 1998, Roos et al 2001, Friel et al 2003, Delva et al 2006) and black/white variations cut across other divisions, confounding matters still further (e.g. Bahr 2007).

Such patterns echo those about health in society more generally, mortality (death) and morbidity (disease) rates as well as use of health services. While the very broad contours of the changing patterns of disease in wealthy nations show a shift from infectious diseases of the nineteenth/twentieth centuries to the chronic conditions of the later twentieth/twenty-first centuries, there are variations throughout within the population. These variations run along socio-economic and demographic lines, commonly summarized as social inequalities in health (Smith et al 1990, Braveman

2010). Broadly, the lower the social class, the worse the mortality rates, from virtually all causes.

Although the pattern of disease and the thinking about its causes changes, so does advice on the types of policy for effecting improvements and more particularly, the thinking behind it which has an older pedigree. More than that, the long history of 'public health policy is characterised by a chasm between two central views of how population health may be improved through action to prevent ill health and promote health' (Baum and Fisher 2014: 214). One view concentrates on people's behaviour, aiming to change it in a healthier direction, a view which very broadly happens to be well aligned with psychology's focus on individual behaviour. The other concentrates on underlying or associated social and economic circumstances as the main determinants of poor health, one which happens very broadly to be aligned with some sociological work on social contexts, social relationships and above all social structure. Since the nineteenth century, the first view regards 'the poor health of the working class was the product of their own behaviour and 'immorality' while the second entails pointing to the effect of 'industrialisation and urbanisation on health among the working class and promoted structural and political reforms accordingly' (Baum and Fisher 2014: 214).

The former view chimes more closely with neo-liberal attitudes to individual's being personally responsible for their wellbeing and leads back to the expectations underlying solutions to the puzzle with which this chapter opened. Recollect the observation that if the problem is conceived of as a gap, it leads, logically, to the search for some way to close it. Correspondingly, much of the social epidemiological and public health work on nutrition inequalities is framed in terms of a search for whatever inhibits people doing as recommended or, better still, successfully identifying what makes it easy for them to do so (in order that may be supported and extended). A commonplace shorthand for these two is 'barriers' and 'facilitators'/ 'enablers' as noted above. The next section works through a study couched in these terms.

An example

The study is a survey of a nationally representative sample of 1,009 Spanish subjects older than 15, part of a Europe-wide study coordinated from Dublin (López-Azpiazu et al 1999). The authors introduce their study by observing that '(C)hanging food consumption is not an easy task' because of difficulties people have 'relating health with their own lifestyles or personal behaviours'. The aim of the study is to assess 'the perceived barriers' in trying to eat more healthily and get more information about people's views on benefits from doing so – not the same as investigating what enables eating more healthily. The authors convened an expert panel (nutritionists, 'food behavioural scientists' and industry market researchers) to discuss and then choose the barriers to be included in the survey. Inviting interviewees to select two from the resulting list of 22 (to which 'no difficulty' and 'other' are added) produces the distribution of responses presented in Table 8.1.

Table 8.1 Percentage (rounded) of interviewees mentioning 22 barriers, selecting a maximum of two

Barrier	%
Irregular work hours	30
Willpower	25
Unappealing food	21
Busy lifestyle	18
Price of healthy foods	16
Giving up foods that I like	14
I don't want to change my eating habits	13
Taste preferences of family or friends	12
Not knowing enough about healthy eating	9
Strange or unusual foods	8
Cooking skills	7
Too great a change from my current diet	7
Lengthy preparation	7
Limited choice when I eat out	7
Not enough food to satisfy hunger	6
'Experts' keep changing their minds	5
Healthy food is more perishable	5
Storage facilities	5
Limited cooking facilities	5
Healthy food more awkward to carry home	2
Feeling conspicuous amongst others	2
No difficulty	21

Source: López-Azpiazu et al. (1999: 210).

Cross-tabulated with social structural variables shows up class variations (e.g. '(U)nappealing food' and '(P)rice of healthy foods') as their main difficulties in eating a healthier diet increases in the lowest socioeconomic levels. Age-related variations are also evident (e.g. younger men more frequently record '(I)rregular work hours' and '(W)illpower' as difficulties, whereas older people more frequently select '(N)o difficulties').

The authors use their findings to advise nutrition educators that they should always be aware that the main perceived barriers to eating healthily are: an 'irregular and busy lifestyle, willpower and food-related factors (high prices, unappealing meals)' (1999: 214). They also draw attention to the 25 per cent of respondents from lower socioeconomic groups who refer to 'price' as the main difficulty, adding that this 'may be due to the fact that this group may regard the cost of food as prohibitive to eating a more healthy diet. Thus, it is necessary to ensure that foods which should be included in a healthy diet are not too expensive' (1999: 213).

Bearing only a minimal notion of socially structured opportunities and constraints in mind can introduce a more nuanced discussion. Consider the list of barriers itself. It may look plausible, but it is also arbitrary. Limiting arbitrariness can strengthen the utility of the analysis by, for instance, reorganizing the categories to reflect the degree of control someone must surmount or change the 'barrier' itemized, reallocating items to three new categories:

(i) *'Barriers' about which someone can do comparatively little*
Irregular work hours; price of healthy foods; lengthy preparation; limited choice when I eat out; limited cooking facilities; storage facilities; healthy food is more perishable;

(ii) *'Barriers' which involve others*
taste preferences of family or friends; too great a change from my current diet; feeling conspicuous amongst others

(iii) *'Barriers' over which an individual has personal control*
willpower; busy lifestyle; giving up foods that I like; unappealing food; I don't want to change my eating habits; not knowing enough about healthy eating; cooking skills; strange or unusual foods; not enough food to satisfy hunger; healthy food more awkward to carry home from shops.

Of course, the final category may well entail considerable effort, providing support for which self-help groups such as *Weight Watchers* are dedicated. It perhaps also relies on brusque, unsympathetic judgements like 'educate yourself' 'get over dislikes' or 'organise your life more efficiently'.

Beyond barriers and enablers

There is, however, another way of evaluating the list. The first category may be said to reflect economic circumstances, having no alternative to employment with irregular hours, inability to afford high prices, better cooking or storage facilities, alteration of which is not just out of the hands of respondents but also beyond the scope of nutrition education – taking public health into the heart of politics and government policies. Those in the other two categories may be regarded as reflecting *normal* social features: social conventions allow for the expression of individual preferences; sustaining social relationships is implicated in sensitivities to others when eating. Imagining these as barriers to be demolished runs up against routines of daily life which run through the everyday social organization of eating/meals.

As significant is the way those two counter other, valued, aspects of life which also limit the accomplishment of eating more healthily. To isolate some of these (especially difficulties deriving from economic circumstances) the sociologist Kathryn Backett shrewdly elects to study members of healthy, middle-class families sufficiently affluent for financial difficulties to be irrelevant. She is equally shrewd in opting to include as research participants *all* family members, not just the person responsible for food provisioning (1992). A strongly expressed value participants identify is *not* to be unduly concerned with health, itself regarded as 'fanatical' and thereby unhealthy. Balance is stressed, 'nothing in excess', the occasional excess regarded as 'good for you' now and then illustrating the view that 'life-enhancing' behaviours are not automatically the same as 'health-enhancing' ones. Indeed, fulfilling familial obligations or achieving harmonious relationships may be accorded priority, and thereby be defined as healthier than the achievement of physical fitness or a good diet (1992: 272). All in all, her work underlines the importance of examining the practical context in which professional advice is to be implemented alongside other important beliefs and valued activities. Thus far, the context is considered, but a different approach is to examine not so much the advice as its source.

Sources of professional nutritional advice

The sociologist Charlotte Biltekoff provides a fresh angle on efforts to persuade people to follow professional advice. Instead of looking at what people do, whether through the eyes of those aiming to change people's shopping, food preparation and eating in directions deemed healthier and safer, or from the viewpoint of those on the receiving end of recommendations, she stands aside from both to look very closely at the source of the advice (2013). She traces the early antecedents of twenty-first century dietary advice in America to late nineteenth-century domestic science. She couples it with the establishment of nutritional science as a fully-fledged discipline from the 1920s onwards.

Morality (do's and don't's, should and shouldn'ts), Biltekoff demonstrates, runs through both of these practical sciences. It is not just that there are right and wrong ways of cooking or that a suitable diet assures good health. Rights/wrongs are also social. 'Eating right' she argues, is also 'a process of self-assessment, self-improvement, and self-making that takes place in relation to particular social values, norms and ideals' (2013: 27). Early domestic scientists openly advocate dietary lessons 'as a way to inculcate social values related to particular ideals of good citizenship' (2013: 14).

Certainly, such explicit 'moralizing' disappears from professional advice about healthy eating or safe food handling. This is not because it becomes socially unacceptable (although it might also be so) but simply because it no longer needs to be included. The morality is already so well engrained, naturalized, as Biltekoff phrases it, that it slides silently into twenty-first century advice unnoticed. If someone does not follow advice, almost by definition there is something wrong, possibly, as already noted, even wrong with them as a person. Being able to identify what should happen, especially when backed by some sort of official sanction, is to occupy a powerful position. And therein lies the cultural politics of which Biltekoff writes.

It is not, however, only the activities of those whose position is backed in this way that can be similarly analysed. Biltekoff demonstrates close parallels among others also engaged in advocating 'eating right'. Indeed, one group of like-minded people set themselves against the types of advice about 'eating right' that is officially sanctioned.[7] These include such well-known Americans as Alice Waters and Michael Pollan. Recollect that Pollan is a journalist who in a series of very well-publicized books (e.g. 2006, 2008, 2009) has also criticized the idea that good food can be adequately described in narrow nutritional terms. Biltekoff pursues the widespread criticism that these alternative food viewpoints are elitist. She points out, it is not just that the way of eating they advocate is beyond the reach of the poor, it is because it also naturalizes a morality of the socially advantaged middle classes which casts the less healthy, lower classes as 'other', out of line and out of step.

Other researchers draw similar conclusions about healthy eating as expressing healthy citizenship, apparently unaware of previous, or one another's, contributions. Murphy's analyses of women's decisions about infant feeding has already been discussed. Julie Guthman's trenchant analysis of the politics of obesity parallels several of Biltekoff's arguments, including focusing on the manner in which the capacity to define the situation in one way, limits attention to alternatives which are just as significant (2011). Julie Parsons insists that ordinary daily foodways allow people 'to present themselves as responsible neo-liberal citizens, so that eating healthily, for example, demonstrates an engagement with public and medical discourses' thereby positioning oneself as 'responsible for her or his own health and well-being' (2015: 1).

Following professional advice and a thread to the food system

Detailed discussions of the most suitable way of turning answers to the question in this chapter's title into effective changes towards healthier eating or more hygienic kitchens are still in their infancy. This chapter illustrates, however, some of the 'good' reasons why people do not always simply follow professional advice. It ends by setting the discussion in the wider context of the food system, limited to introducing just one aspect.

The material on which the chapter draws reflects the content and tenor of the literatures in public health nutrition and the manner in which sociological research addresses it. Both, to varying extents, are silent on the commercial context in which all are couched. The professional advice people are to follow is not provided in a vacuum. It vies for people's attention alongside others' claims about different versions of good eating of which 'healthy' is but one: 'tasty', 'tried-and-tested', 'nice', attractive', 'new', 'convenient', 'modern', 'cheap', 'exotic', a 'treat', 'just like home-made', 'quick', 'good for weight-reducing' and, yes, within the law, healthy. Almost all those others are in the business of selling something, weight loss classes, advice, magazines, never mind foods themselves. Even charities, such as those associated with 'heart health', still 'sell' themselves to continue attracting donations.

What deserves fuller attention, then, is the overall picture of competition for people's attention about what and how to eat in which official professional advice is just one type. Worth asking is the number and nature of different types. Worth asking too is the relative power of different types. The size of multi-national corporations' advertizing budgets is liable to dwarf the spending of any national government's agencies mounting public health eating campaigns. Ironically, perhaps, both tend to use the same marketing techniques. And the corporations are on such a scale with budgets to match that they are able to mount effective lobbying campaigns of law and policy makers, thus working to shape the regulatory climate in which their business are run. Harkins and Miller claim the industries that produce alcohol, tobacco and junk food adopt the same lobbying strategies as each other. They are similar too, should there be any adverse health effects as a result of getting drunk, smoking or eating burgers: they blame irresponsible consumption and ill-advised choices on individual sufferers (Miller and Harkins 2010).

Box 24 Chapter 8 – Selected Key Points

1. Avoid 'deficit' thinking by looking for 'good reasons' for 'bad behaviour'.
2. Study the social context in which advice is to be acted on.
3. Replace talk of a gap between knowledge and action with 'theories of practice'.
4. Correlations are found between social class and likelihood of following professional advice – associated with economic constraints.
5. Study of the advice itself reveals that it reflects middle-class values and superior opportunities.

CHAPTER 9
FOOD WASTE: 'HOW DOES SO MUCH PERFECTLY EDIBLE FOOD GET THROWN AWAY?'

Every year, an average Malaysian household throws away more than one month's salary on food they don't eat[1]

Why Do Israelis Throw Away Half the Food They Buy?[2]

We (in the US) chuck out 31% of our food supply[3]

All these headlines rapidly come up when the words 'people throw away edible food' are typed into a search engine. Giving C. Wright Mills' dictum a bit of a twist, they represent efforts at making a private trouble out of a public issue. Each headline is written as if to invite a public outcry by shocking the reader: '*more* than one month's salary on food *they don't eat*'; '*... perfectly edible* food'. Each headline leads to a story reporting a problem that affects everyone, to be heeded by public authorities and especially private individuals.

As those headline signal, the scale is very great indeed. Although difficulties and inconsistencies across studies remain, techniques for measuring the food households discard receive ever more attention since Rathje's notable 1970s 'garbology', hand-sorting through household waste (Rathje and Cullen 1992). Yet there is disagreement as to whether it is increasing. So, between 1900–1920, Manhattan residents annually discard 160 pounds of food wastes/debris (including rinds, peel or husks) whereas in the early 1990s their successors throw out only 106 pounds (Alexander 1993: 5). Today, however, as will be seen many declare the situation has worsened.

Such observations form the springboard for this chapter's question 'why do people throw away perfectly edible food?' Publicity widely focusses on domestic consumption rather than commercial production.[4] In introducing the growing sociological literature on the problems associated with household food waste, it consolidates themes already established in previous chapters. Attention to history is needed yet again along with the relevance of public issues and private troubles, with the second section showing how thinking in terms of 'good' reasons for 'bad' behaviour makes better sense of familiar kitchen patterns of throwing food away than the 'moralizing' which hovers about (see Chapter 8).

Note that items are not waste by themselves. In just the same way that food is not food unless such a meaning is attributed to it and the social context recognized (see Chapter 1), so waste is only waste in the social circumstances in which it is so designated. Indeed, understanding food waste means understanding the *flow* of the actual items from one social context to another, one receptacle to another and even sometimes back again (O'Brien 2008). Food is perhaps a special instance of waste given that it is organic not inorganic, which, unlike other discards, means it is always in the process of being transformed biologically as time passes. Grasping why people throw away edible food requires thinking in terms of food's becoming waste, a *social* process of renaming which is integral to the social context in which it is located. New materialist approaches propose that rather than actually saying the words 'this is food waste' it may be an action (e.g. moving something from a shelf, table or fridge to a bin, saucepan or nineteenth-century market stall) that either names it as waste, (re)names it as 'new food' for needy people, or deems it something usable for pig feed or garden compost. When Roe discusses the socio-cultural definition of items becoming food via the way they are *handled* rather than by the way they are talked of or named, she could as readily be referring to the way foodstuffs become waste (2006) (see Chapter 1).

Food waste as a private trouble and public issue

The extent to which what has come to be called food waste is either a private trouble or a public issue varies sharply over the last century or so. Thinking this through introduces various elements – hunger vs waste, when/where foods are named as 'leftovers' rather than 'waste' – and reintroduces Blumer's conceptual scheme about the making of social problems.

Food waste, hunger and donated leftovers

As a private trouble historically, food waste has probably been eclipsed by the far more severe troubles of hunger, shortage and the threat of starvation. Hungry people do not throw edible food away. If anything, they eat what is otherwise considered close to *in*edible food – putrefying road kill in New Jersey (Kempson et al 2002) or centuries of 'famine bread' made of tree bark in Finland. If lucky, the hungry might be given others' leavings. During the 1930s, prosperous farmers of the upland Carolinas enjoyed enormous holiday feasts prepared by black cooks and helpers. The meals were far too big for the white guests to finish. So, as a contemporary writes, large quantities were 'sent to the colored folk in the kitchen and on the back porch' (Gabaccia 1998: 40). Earlier still, the very hungry poor are given scraps of batter left in the fryer after cooking the fish (Walton 1992) or the dregs from the saucepan in which 'mushy peas' are boiled, thanks to the fish-and-chip shopkeepers of Britain's industrial cities (Spencer 2004: 266).

In the twenty-first century initiatives to divert surpluses from shops and cafés as donations to charities for those in need are springing up. Possibly one of the longest established anywhere is City Harvest begun in 1982 in New York City (Poppendieck 1998: 127). A London scheme is run by the fast take-away chain Pret à Manger themselves, whereas Food Share in Dunedin is an independent organization especially dedicated to redistribution.[5] While such schemes seem an attractive way of diverting surplus to help those in need, there are drawbacks and restrictions. Closer investigation highlights the way schemes do not necessarily run smoothly, with imbalances in the relationships involved and tensions between maximizing profit, limiting waste and brand control (Alexander and Smaje 2008). In 1990s UK, a more expensive food retailer only donates surplus to selected charities of their choice.

Rather different but instructive, is an example of a conjunction between hunger and waste as *both* private trouble *and* some sort of public issue in heavily socially stratified nineteenth-century Paris. This time food leavings are not donated but traded.

Food waste, hunger and leftovers on sale

Paris is a city whose population in 1830 grew from 800,000 to 1 million in only 20 years with a stark divide between the very rich, ruling elites and the desperately impoverished classes (Aron 1975). Food leftovers are bought and sold across that divide. '(L)eftovers formed an important part of the Parisian diet in the nineteenth century' (1979: 99).

In part it is that leftovers are in any case a distinguishing feature of classic French cuisine – the croquettes, fricassées, ragouts, ingenious concoctions that can be made by using up surplus ingredients or the remains of the previous day's roasts. It is also that there is a nineteenth-century trade in the leftovers from the tables at embassies and famous restaurants, government ministries and smart hotels, often the 'object of secret transactions'. Aron refers to this as the public trade (i.e. selling to the public) contrasting it with the thriving private trade (i.e. between specialist food producers, the macaroon makers who buy the surplus egg whites from the bakery chefs specializing in making parfaits and ice-creams which only need the yolks).

The public trade is well organised; zinc-lined carts following a known route through the city, resulting in collections arranged by the traders – nicknamed 'jewellers' – on platters, more expensive examples of which have

> attractively displayed poultry legs, a lobster claw, a filet of sole, a bit of pastry and some pistachio custard. Or else a half a pig's foot, with truffles alongside a slice of galantine, a breaded cutlet, and a fish head, crowned by a chocolate éclair. Or even – for there was an admirable variety of jewels available – sauerkraut keeping company with crayfish in Bordeaux wine, sautéed rabbit, calf's head, roebuck filet, and apple charlotte.
>
> *Aron 1979:101*

As Aron observes, ingredients lose their form in the indiscriminate mixtures on those platters. The customers of those nineteenth-century Parisian 'jewellers' ranged all the way 'from people working for starvation wages to women trembling with fever to minor clerks and on to housewives from lower-class neighbourhoods' (1979:101). Wares were put on sale in the corners of markets dotted around the city on stalls specializing partially or entirely in 'this strange trade', feeding the hungry poor on the discards of the very rich.

Regulating trading in food

Neither traders nor their customers would be the kind of people to create a record of this market. For his evidence Aron is, however, able to draw on two sources. First, are the observations of Fréderic LePlay, the nineteenth-century social scientist. Second, there are contemporary records preserved in the Police Archives documenting seizures of rotting foodstuffs illegally on sale – food and eating are simultaneously private and public. Indeed, it is publicly manifest via the law. Currently, for instance, the law has something to say about food waste in the European Union, part of the regulatory concern with food in general, its purity and safety, something to be honestly traded.[6] Some of the oldest laws in England deal with the relationship between those who put food on sale and those who buy it. The Assize of Bread, 1266, provided, among other things, for assuring the weight of a farthing loaf (calibrated to reflect the prevailing price of wheat). This simultaneously protects the public from unscrupulous bakers selling short weight while recognizing that the latter's livelihood is affected by movements in grain prices (Burnett 1963). While not centred on food going to waste, this mediaeval attitude to controlling food on public sale none the less testifies to an interest on the part of governments and the state both in having a care as to what the population has to eat and in fair shares to suppliers.

Current urban foraging

Eating discarded food is not, of course, simply a feature of the past. In wealthy as well as poorer countries, across the US, Europe and elsewhere homeless street dwellers forage in urban trash cans for anything half eaten. Not so different, older people facing the diminishing value of their pensions are prompted to scavenge at the close of the day's trading in Turin's Porta Palazzo market (Black 2007: 145) But urban foraging varies. The pensioners in the market do not frequent the nearby soup kitchens patronized by middle-aged unemployed men. They, correspondingly, do not forage at the market.

Both are different again from those Black records foraging in the Croix-Rousse market in Lyon. These resourceful French, are young, self-consciously displaying an 'alternative lifestyle', fierce critics of wastefulness (2007). Their North American, Australasian and UK counterparts are found 'dumpster diving', recovering food thrown away by supermarkets from dumpsters/bins/skips. It is sometimes associated with 'Freeganism', the protest movement dating from the 1970s in rich nations based on as limited as possible economic engagement with consumerism. It may be small, but it illustrates another way in which the private matter of acquiring food is converted into a public issue via actions representing condemnation of the huge scale of food waste. In engaging in such acts of resistance (mostly) by choice rather than need, freegans seek to bring several problems to public attention, ranging from demonstrating the reprehensibility of throwing away still edible items to criticizing aspects of the contemporary global food system (Edwards and Mercer 2013).

Creating a private trouble

Freeganism reflects the political stance of two campaigners' very recent efforts to make food waste a private trouble for every household. In *American Wasteland*, US journalist and blogger Jonathan Bloom summarizes his view of the antecedents whereby most Americans waste more than their own body weight in food every year:

> America's gradual shift from a rural, farming life to an urban, non-agricultural one removed us from sources of our food. Our once iron-clad guarantee of inheriting generations of food wisdom became less so, as busier lives forced many of us to leave the kitchen or spend less time there. Convenience began to trump homemade, and eating out drew level with dining in. We have higher standards for our meals, but diminished knowledge about how to maximize our use of food. Many of us don't even trust our noses to judge when an item has gone bad. Yet our awareness of pathogens has multiplied, and we apply safety rules to food with the same zealous caution that we apply to allergies, kids walking to school, and most everything in modern life.
>
> *Bloom 2010: xii*

His book appears only a year after *Waste: Uncovering the Global Food Scandal* by an English activist Tristram Stuart, an award-winning book turning a spotlight on the volume of edible food that is discarded in the UK (2009).

Both are impassioned campaigners. Stuart's book is illustrated with arresting colour photographs: acres of surplus oranges or tomatoes lying on the ground to rot; vegetables, pies or bread rolls tipped higgledy piggledy into dumpsters/bins outside shops and supermarkets, bread and fruit still in their original plastic packaging, cartons of milk and boxes of ready-meals unopened – a mess echoing the indiscriminate piles of leftovers on sale in Paris. Bloom summarizes widely repeated diagnoses of the problem of food waste which, like Stuart, he couches in broader terms of what both see as ills of modern food systems. Their view is that people have become disconnected from, and are ignorant of, the way foods are produced and distributed, echoing the position adopted by Pollan and Petrini (ch 1).

Current popular discussions are heavily judgemental. Bloom uses vocabulary such as 'squander', seeks to get his statistics to 'hit home' and declares that 'there is culpability in waste' by contrast recommending remedies including buying 'wisely' and storing food at home 'sensibly' (2010: xi–xiiii, 207). Stuart also 'moralizes': people 'have simply become lazy and negligent about food' listing annual totals of more than 400 million 'unopened pots of yoghurt, 1.6 billion untouched apples (27 apples per person)' and '2.6 billion slices of bread', among the 'most startling instances of consumer indifference to wasting food' (Stuart 2009: 78, 71). Both seek to shame people into changing their ways, trying to create the private trouble of a pricked conscience.

More food wasted than ever before?

Even if eating leftovers is both old and new, many commentators think that the volume of food currently wasted by households (as well as retailers and caterers) is without historical precedent. Currently, it is claimed that today waste is far more 'visible' with food 'being wasted on an unparalleled scale'.

How far the claim reflects what is actually happening or whether it results from louder debate is a question to which the discussion now turns (Campbell, Evans and Murcott 2017).[7] This requires a change of register, moving above the level of previous chapters of meals, domestic social relationships or keeping kitchens clean. Looking at an altogether different plane both geographically and temporally, it returns to the food system and the length and complexity of twenty-first-century globalized food chains (see Chapter 1). This considers nearly two centuries of major transitions affecting agriculture and food production.

Such transitions are captured by 'food regime theory', the highly influential sociological account of food history in these areas developed by Harriet Friedmann and Phil McMichael (1989). Despite its name, it is not so much a theory, more a schema organizing different trends with mutually contradictory consequences into a single conceptual framework. It is this which makes it useful and has kept it at the centre of the sociology of agriculture and food production for over two decades. Food regimes are considered on their own in the next sub-section to provide a basis for thereafter doubling back to ask about the visibility of food waste.

Food regimes

Undeniably anchored in a perspective from wealthy nations, food regime theorizing helpfully summarizes a significant food history periodization in a way that attempts to deal with considerable complexity and trends pulling in different directions. It comes from the sub-field of agro-food studies[8] as a means of characterizing a collection of changes that occurred in the agricultural systems of certain countries. In particular, these were the countries which initially still had colonial empires but which were subsequently becoming configured in relation to one another as nation states, all at the same time as agriculture/food-processing were becoming industrialized (Friedmann and McMichael 1989).

A key to food regimes is appreciating the shifts away from empires as the main mode of global government toward the subsequent rearrangement of international relations of trade in food between nation states during the nineteenth and twentieth centuries. In many ways, a food regime approach is not so much about agriculture and food as about a way of thinking about the world order in which food is produced and traded This is an important reminder that food is not produced in a political or economic vacuum and that the food system is not simply a set of practical arrangements but the objects of vested interests.

A significant element of a food regime approach is that it captures the way global arrangements for the production (and consumption) of food involve rules and regulation. It then shows up the history as successive periods of comparatively stable sets of trade and other relationships interspersed with relatively unstable periods when political arguments develop and disturb arrangements. Researchers working in this analytic tradition are agreed that there are at least two food regimes. Friedmann and McMichael's 'First Food Regime' (later also referring to it as the Imperial Food Regime) refers to the distinctive period following the food shortages of the 1840s that includes the 'heyday' of the British Empire, stretching from agriculture, food and eating in the Victorian era almost to the outbreak of the Second World War. This is a period when industrialization was securely established in Europe, most especially Britain, when urbanization in Europe and the US proceeded apace and when the populations were 'fed' by the agricultural production of erstwhile colonies. Dubbed the 'workshop of the world' Britain, the first nation to industrialize, was supplied with lamb from Australia, wheat from Canada and butter from New Zealand. Together with sugar from the Caribbean (Mintz 1986) these basic commodities, wheat in the form of bread, provided manageably priced food for the factory workers turning out the manufactured goods for trading back to the colonies as well as onto the world market. Affordable food helped to hold wages steady, if not low, keeping those nineteenth- and early twentieth-century factory hands and their families going on the calories and comfort of tea heavily sweetened with sugar accompanied by much bread and treacle, little meat, of which the man of the household as the breadwinner got the lion's share and, if lucky, weekly fish and chips (Walton 1992).

Then come crises of war and economic depression, overturning the stability of the first imperial food regime. Emerging from that instability and the immediate post-Second World War reconstruction Friedmann and McMichael recognize a new period of relative stability, the second food regime (AidSurplus regime) typically reckoned to run from around 1950 to the 1970s. This is characterized by the production of vast agricultural surpluses from the US (erstwhile British colony/'settler-state') and a change in the nature as well as rate of industrialization with a shift from 'final use to manufactured (even durable) products' (Friedmann and McMichael 1989: 103). A mainspring of this change of regime is, they argue, a collection of simultaneous mutually influential and above all far reaching mid-twentieth-century shifts that significantly alter the food system to convert it to something recognizably new. Note that they single out the invention of 'durable foods' as of particular significance.

Food regimes and the visibility of food waste

This summary of a food regime approach to history does not just introduce it as an important element of the literature in the sociology of food. It is presented here primarily to serve as a basis for evaluating whether current rates of food waste are unprecedented. Householders as well as supermarkets throw out food still in its original packaging. To say that food waste is far more 'visible' encapsulates both the reported increased volume of waste itself (literally made visible in photographs and on websites, as well as in representations of charts, graphs and statistics) and the combination of increasingly loud protests, campaigning groups' activities, with so widespread a formal response and policy attention. Echoing a food regime approach, this is describable as a transition from invisibility to visibility, while the attempt to grasp whether it is new is aligned with the periodization of food history characteristic of classical 'food regime theory' (Campbell, Evans and Murcott 2017). A difficulty in trying to develop such an analysis is, however, dogged by the patchiness, if not complete lack of evidence for earlier historical periods. Almost by definition, if food waste is invisible, concern is liable to be absent thereby prompting few if any to devote resources to collect relevant information. This means having to rely on oblique and incidental sources.

Two types of source can be found for the periods covered by the first food regime. One is the records created for administrative and similar purposes by authorities (e.g. local municipalities, armies providing for troops) to inform the activities with which they are charged. Some of the earliest arise from pressures on local governments responsible for rubbish disposal. So, for instance, Melosi can rely on contemporary sources to record the per capita generation of garbage in the small increasingly crowded island of Manhattan of 1900 to 1920 (Melosi 1981). Primary work in archives across, say, the US and the UK would possibly add to the list of such sources. But even were a larger collection of early statistics available, the chances of being able to use them to decide whether wasted food had increased over the last century, remain small, for the simple reason that waste disposal opportunities change over time and definitions of waste are neither agreed nor consistent.

The second set of oblique resources is not in the form of statistics but texts. 'Food waste is especially visible when its prevention is being counselled' (Evans et al 2013: 12). English language cookery books from the latter part of the nineteenth century in the US, New Zealand and the UK not only include recipes but commonly extend to advice on how to organize the kitchen/shopping along with general guidance on how to run a home economically. For instance, Miss Beecher's *Housekeeper and Healthkeeper* published in the US in 1873, repeatedly talks of being frugal by using up '(R)emnants of cooked meats' (1873:80) or 'remnants of bread . . . potatoes, hominy, rice' (1873:71). Thrift remains key in advice on 'making the most of leftovers' into the 1930s. But it seems to fade, and by the time Second World War rationing ends in the 1950s cookery books no longer routinely include advice on using up leftovers (see Box 21).

Biography linked with history

Relevant here, however, is the significance of C. Wright Mills' insistence on examining the conjunction between biography and history. Those who lived through wartime privation, especially in nations suffering enemy occupation or blockade tended to learn a distinct attitude to food. Survivors still recollect the way that what pre-war would have been animal feed is redefined as an essential part of the human diet (acorns or 'broom corn' (a type of sorghum) during the Athens famine of 1941–1942 Matala and Grivetti 2007) and carob, also recorded during the siege of Malta (Campbell, Evans and Murcott 2017). These elderly people can only shake their heads in disbelief at the profligacy of their grandchildren. But it is not the age of that older generation but their membership of a cohort living through a distinct historical period that has them do so.

Food waste seems to shift from being visible to invisible: visible in late nineteenth- and early twentieth-century cookery books' urging that every last scrap must be used up and in governments' rationing and associated campaigns to conserve food during times of war; invisible as it not only disappears from cookery books after the Second World War but also off the political agenda. This coincides with the surpluses and cheap food policies of the second food regime. One distinctive food waste transition can be identified in the middle of this particular period. And this may mark it out as quite different from its predecessors. By the millennium, it appears that throwing away obviously edible food sometimes still in its unopened package is increasingly acceptable, ordinary and, initially, not much noticed, the attitude to food which Stuart calls 'indifference'.

Unprecedented?

The discussion thus far does not help decide whether food is really being wasted as never before. Instead, it ends up complicating the picture still further, with a multiplicity of facets to be taken into account. Setting aside the technicalities for present purposes, one clear conclusion can be drawn. The emergence of modern ways of measuring household level food waste and contemporary modes of publicizing them bear little comparison with the rougher attempts of the early eras of the first food regime and Victorian cookery books' strictures about thrifty kitchen management. That effort is increasingly devoted to such measurement itself helps make food waste visible, perhaps even more so as campaigners and other major public opinion formers refer to the problem. At the same time, there is no getting away from the huge differences between the daily lives in the twenty-first century and that of their grandparents and great grandparents with first hand memories of wartime. And it is at those younger generations that Bloom's and Stuart's 'moralizing' is directed. The problem of how to make sense of such 'bad' behaviour presents itself once again.

Throwing away perfectly edible food: 'good' reasons for such 'bad' behaviour

This final section of the chapter returns to the more familiar, domestic level and the question of why people throw away so much perfectly edible food. There appears to be a recent upsurge in reports of empirical investigations confirming that people throw away food that is still fit to eat with the central interest focused on why. Yet people are widely reported to disapprove of such failings in themselves as well as in others (Schanes, Dobernig and Gözet 2018). Reasons people give for discarding food include: buying too much food, portions are too big, items stored in the fridge or freezer for too long, the food no longer tastes, smells or looks good or it is past its use-by date (e.g. Lancfranci et al 2016: 3059). Uncovering such reasons is important, but it fails to go far enough, only prompting new, more profound queries. Why does anyone come to shop in that way or to cook too much in the first place, what lies behind the infrequent checking on the freezer's contents?

Processes of becoming waste

The search for 'good reasons' for throwing usable food away builds on the observation that food waste is not a fixed category. Items become waste by people's actions which move them to a place designed to receive waste, whether or not they name the action as they do so. Focus on this type of sociological thinking now allows concentrating on the process of transformation from food to non-food (waste) locating it in the social circumstances under which it occurs.

Such an orientation to how people come to throw food away is adopted by several sociologists. In his ethnographic study of household food waste in the north west of England, David Evans pays detailed attention to how food becomes waste. He points to what he calls 'the dynamics of everyday life and the ways in which waste is embedded in these flows and practices' (Evans 2014:11). His work exposes to view several ordinary and very familiar practices of routine domestic provisioning. Evans' work illustrates one answer to how people come to over-cater. An interviewee reports that having made a dish with cauliflower calling only for part of the vegetable, some is left unused. She considers there is not a lot else she can do: it 'isn't the same without cheese, none of us really like it on its own without' so it is thrown away. Note that she adds 'I worry a lot, not being able to use the food that we have bought' (2011: 432). Another interviewee explains that her job can take her away from home unexpectedly. Returning late, tired and hungry, unable to recollect what is in the fridge she simply goes shopping on the way home picking up food that is quick to prepare. The surplus thus created gets thrown away a few days later. A further instance is an interviewee who points to a saucepan on the hob explaining to Evans:

> (T)hat's from stew that I made a few nights ago [. . .] I meant to put it in the fridge after it cooled, you know, and then have it another night [. . .] but it's probably not safe to eat as it's been out for a few days now [. . .] I really hate wasting food.
>
> *2011: 437*

Although these examples provide 'good' reasons for over-provisioning. they do not account for interviewees throwing the surplus food away: they could, after all, keep it for longer and use it up later. Evans finds, however, that the 'unifying feature' throughout his study for all foods is 'an acute awareness that food harbours the potential to make people ill and that this risk accelerated evaluations of food as past its best' (2011: 437).

This illustrates a dilemma. The public issues and discourse about food waste which so roundly castigates those who throw too much away comes right up against other public issues and discourse about food which urges care in kitchen hygiene, not allowing food to go bad and observing 'use-by' dates, which, unlike 'best-before' dates (which are about quality/freshness), warn that food kept longer risks not being safe to eat. It is hardly surprising that people tend to rather 'being safe than sorry', with the public advice implying it is preferable to discard food which may have 'gone off' rather than risk food poisoning.

Watson and Meah enlarge on these conflicting public discourses and present ethnographic data to argue that people's provisioning practices require navigating a path between them. They find two views of use-by dates. One regards them as a firm instruction to be obeyed to avoid getting sick. The other is cynical dismissal, regarding them as 'manufacturers' gimmick' and a ruse to enhance sales. Either way, they argue that 'use-by' dates are 'one piece of information assimilated alongside many others in assessing whether something is still food or has become waste' (2013: 112).

Note that both studies concentrate on the foodstuffs themselves and what people do with them. This is a major contrast with studies which solely depend on what people say about how they provision or reasons they offer for discarding food. In so doing, they exemplify Roe's materialist approach which concentrates on the manner in which actions, not words, define items. By 'following the thing' both studies well illustrate the way items become food waste happens via what people *do* with them. In turn, what people do is part and parcel of people's daily negotiating the small, mundane but complicated demands of ordinary living, especially when it all takes place in the shadow of contradictory public information. One of the important features of both studies is their evidence that runs counter to claims that people are indifferent to the value of food, or are lazy, thoughtlessly failing to use up the food they have bought. The circumstances under which stuff which starts as food when it is bought, to become stuff that is wasted, are everyday and familiar, providing a grasp of the 'good' reasons for 'bad' behaviour which, in campaigning to draw attention to the volume of discarded food, too many commentators by-pass.

Household food waste and a thread to the food system

Revealing the processes whereby food becomes waste is a valuable antidote to blaming people for the volume of food wasted. Yet understanding these 'good reasons' needs visualizing as a component in the food system as a whole. As Jellil et al observe, household food waste is 'more than a behaviour issue but rather a symptom of a bigger societal problem shaped by an unsustainable production and consumption system that relies on oversupply, consumerism and competition on cheap prices' (2018: 2). This work points out, first, that manufacturers and retailers have considerable power for they primarily control the transit of food products from producers to consumers. This gives them considerable influence over both production and consumption (2018). Although these producers are closely focused on improving efficiency etc, this is only in respect of their own industrial operations, stopping short at the point of purchase.

For Jellil et al, this represents 'a major flaw' in the food system that highlights a 'disparity' between production and consumption. This can only be rebalanced by effecting changes such as: the abolition of best-before-dates which are largely for traceability and for manufacturers'/retailers' stock control; adopting innovative technology such as temperature-sensitive smart labels or bio-reactive tactile labels that makes detecting spoilage more precise or developing packaging technology still further to extend shelf-life.

Whatever the details or indeed viability of Jellil's suggestions for improvement, her discussion highlights the need to shift analytic attention from household activities. Failing to do so risks myopically neglecting the manner in which those activities are embedded in the food system as a whole, intimately linked to and shaped by the operations and technologies of the manufacturing and retailing industries.

Box 25 Chapter 9 – Selected Key Points

1. Food waste is a public problem campaigners, policy makers etc are trying to turn into a private trouble.
2. Like food, food waste is socially defined, a product of cultural convention/social context.
3. Food leftovers/surplus are put on sale (e.g. nineteenth-century Paris) donated, (twenty-first century by supermarkets etc to charities).
4. Is the current rate of food waste unprecedented? Food regime theory helps consider whether it has simply been invisible.
5. Familiar 'good reasons' for wasteful 'bad behaviour' in everyday kitchens at home.

CHAPTER 10
FOOD POVERTY: 'POOR PEOPLE SHOULD EAT PORRIDGE NOT COCO POPS',[1] IT'S FAR CHEAPER

Feeding America's clients live in working households ... most face wrenching choices between paying for food or heating their home, buying medicine for a family member, or making the mortgage[2]

'Food bank use across UK at record high, reveals report'[3]

'I had a large bowl of porridge today. It cost 4p. A large bowl of sugary cereal will cost 25p'[4]

The first quotation is from a report on the numbers and circumstances of US users of food banks, the second reports parallel increases in food bank use in the UK. The third quotes remarks made by Anne Jenkin at the press launch of a report 'Feeding Britain: A strategy for zero hunger'.[5]

Baroness Jenkin is a member of the UK upper house and serves on the All Parliamentary Group which produced the report. She hits the headlines with this observation which she prefaced by saying '(W)e have lost our cooking skills. Poor people don't know how to cook' (see Chapter 5). But later the same day she publicly apologizes for any offence caused, observing that her words were ill-chosen and explaining that she was trying to say that home-cooked food can be cheaper than pre-packaged.[6] She is not alone in criticizing the shopping and eating habits of those on very low incomes, and, as will be seen, this type of remark is nothing new, any more than it is confined to the UK (Poppendieck 1998).

The kernel of such remarks, however, strikes a chord; it can seem only common sense to seek less-expensive alternatives when money is short. But, striking the same chord, there are other commonsense views on the matter which can be found on social media in response to Jenkin's comments. Often bluntly expressed they are posted by people well versed in being short of money/living on state welfare/going hungry because other fixed costs must take priority.[7] Many explain that to follow her advice, they need to (a) have enough money to make the initial outlay on a pack of porridge; (b) have a receptacle in which to cook; (c) have access to a hob or microwave oven;[8] (d) be able to afford the cost of the fuel required to run it; (e) be able to afford anything to make the porridge more palatable (sugar, milk, salt etc); and (f) be confident everyone likes porridge so none is wasted. If money is so short that one or more of these cannot be achieved, then it is common sense to take the less-expensive option of buying a small packet of cereal that does not need cooking, is palatable with no need for additions and is liked by everyone waiting for breakfast.

Instead of regarding buying sugary cereal as profligate or born of incompetence, those alternatives can be viewed in the same light as recognizing other practical responses to an immediate shortage of money. In the US, nutrition researchers in New Jersey record other responses for coping with insufficient food, including activities which nutritionists consider unsafe or risky to health: 'removing spoiled sections, slime, mold, and insects from food; eating other people's leftovers; and, eating meat found as road kill' (Kempson et al 2002: 1795). From a century earlier in the city slums of Salford in north west England, Robert Roberts records an age-old tactic, this time played out at the factory gate at the end of a shift: 'every evening stood some of England's young starvelings, each asking hopefully, "'ave yer anything left from yer dinner, mister?" as children begged for leftover scraps from workers' packed lunches (1971: 117).

Looking back, the second headline quoted above shows yet another alternative for those without enough, namely recourse to emergency food provision. 'Food bank' is a comparatively new expression in the UK describing a new solution to an old problem. Both expression and solution are borrowed from the US where Janet Poppendieck (1998) reports a sudden increase in the number of food banks, food pantries and soup kitchens in the early 1980s (also evident in other wealthy countries at the time). What makes the increase[9] so widely remarked is its occurrence amidst such plenty, then and now. As just one UK headline puts it: 'Why can't people afford to eat in the world's sixth richest country?'[10]

Sympathetic journalists point to the so-called demonization of food bank users, reminiscent of Jenkin's remark. They report users' experience, criticizing failures in the organization of public welfare provision. Such difficulties are summarized by two social policy researchers and a GP who ask whether current UK policies are 'economically and politically efficient given the impact on people's health and well-being' (Purdam et al 2016: 1084). Though published in a journal of sociology, their article ends there, neither suggesting any kind of remedy nor beginning to discuss a sociological approach to analysing the problem.

This chapter picks up where that discussion stops short. It is devoted to asking what the styles of sociological thinking presented in this book might look like when applied to food poverty.[11] Note that, most certainly, many nations have a system of welfare support for those in the direst need. But the systems vary. The Supplemental Nutrition Assistance Program (SNAP), federal provision, replaces paper vouchers to buy food with electronic cards (like a debit card). UK support is provided via a range of benefits, which are being reformed with entitlements reorganized or reduced (Lambie-Mumford 2015). By comparison other nations (e.g. India and Singapore) have less extensive welfare provision. This chapter is concerned less with such important variation but with overarching considerations about food poverty, notably, the recurrent 'moralizing' about poor people evident irrespective of what/whether local welfare systems exist. As Turner tartly observes: '(U)ltimately many of their writings are tinged with a moral disapproval of the working class for being insufficiently middle class in their behaviours and priorities' (Turner 2014: 26).

The chapter begins with illustrations of the personal troubles of insufficient food, then brings those illustrations together with food poverty as a public issue, highlighting the place of research in the juxtaposition. Not only does it point to the intersections of biography, history and social structure, but it also highlights both the material and social consequences of insufficient food. The discussion stresses the way that food poverty is thought about, noting the various terminologies devised and the understandings involved. For, as Blumer points out (see Chapter 4) unless and until food poverty is named, then deemed a social problem, no response will be forthcoming. Recollect that how the problem is characterized frames the type of solution that is proposed. As the historian James Vernon puts it, the 'changing ways in which we have understood hunger matter, because they have shaped the systems used to address it'. Reflecting Vernon's contention that Imperial Britain 'played a formative role in changing the meaning of hunger and the systems for redressing it in the modern era' (2007: 3) this chapter emphasizes the British case. Bear Engel's 'law' (see Chapter 1) in mind, that those with lower household incomes spend a higher proportion of it on food than does anyone better off.

Personal troubles of food poverty

This section first presents material about the experiences of poor people themselves, providing biographical viewpoints, before going on to illustrate one or other authority's responses to the personal troubles of food poverty.

Poor people's viewpoint

There is now more than a century of detailed, dependable descriptions of the living conditions of people in extreme poverty. Seebohm Rowntree's pioneering, systematic study of the English city of York provides graphic examples. Using a range of data collection techniques that is much the same as today's, he includes case studies of families at three (low) income levels. The case studies are based on records specially kept for his investigation by 18 housewives of selected working-class families who note the household income, the amount spent on rent, a detailed account of all expenditure and what the family has to eat and drink at each meal.[12] At the lowest income level, Mrs D records a weekly wage of 20s (approximately £100 today[13]) for a family of four. Here is part of the picture of food poverty based on her notebook, augmented by the visiting investigator's notes:

> The father drives a lorry: he is now in regular work but was out of work for six months last year. During that period the family incurred a heavy debt, which Mrs D. is now striving to clear off. Questioned as to how they lived during these six months when Mr D. was earning no regular money, Mrs D. replied that she didn't know; her brother was very kind to her and bought shoes for herself and children, her mother gave her odd things, and for the rest they got into debt . . . The mother lacks method, and always apologises for the house and children (aged 5 and 2) being dirty . . . The

only place for keeping food in is an unventilated cupboard under the stairs. There is a water-tap in the living room, in a corner behind the entrance door, but as there is no sink or drain the droppings from the tap fall on to the floor, which consists of red bricks, badly broken and uneven ... The fireplace is usually untidy. A square table (generally covered with dirty cups, saucers, plates, etc.) occupies the centre of the room, around the sides of which there are two wooden easy-chairs, a sofa covered with American cloth[14] and a large chest of drawers ... The house is situated down a narrow, cobbled thoroughfare, and being faced by a high brick wall it gets very little sun ... The meals are fairly regular, Mr. D. coming home for them ... Although Mrs D. lacks method she has great ideas of keeping her house, etc. nice, and always imagines that when they 'get round a bit' it will be easier to do so.

Rowntree 1901: 231–2

Rowntree's dietary measurements record that this family's diet is 9 per cent deficient in energy and 18 per cent deficient in protein. More than twice the amount of the household income goes on food than is paid in rent. For the week ending 22 February 1901, the family's breakfast consists of tea or coffee on alternate days, bread daily, bacon three times a week with butter on other days. Dinner in the middle of the day consists of bread or potatoes, bacon or a bit of pork, eggs once a week with the addition of onions and Yorkshire pudding on Sunday. Tea (the early evening meal) always includes bread and butter, with shortcake at weekends accompanied by tea to drink, with an occasional piece of bread or cup of tea later in the evening. Breakfast and tea also have additions on Saturday and Sunday.

What is not recorded is how the food is distributed round the family. It is highly likely that Mr D. receives the lion's share (the family depend on his being able to work), any income-earning children fed next, then other children while the wife/mother stints herself (see Chapter 2). This arrangement is recorded for another of Rowntree's cases – one slightly better off than Mr and Mrs D:

'If there's anythink extra to buy, such as a pair of boots for one of the children', a woman ... told one of my investigators, 'me and the children goes without dinner – or mebbe only 'as a cup o' tea and a bit o' bread, but Jim (her husband) ollers (always) takes 'is dinner to work, and I give it 'im as usual; 'e never knows we go without and I never tells 'im'.

Rowntree 1901: 55

What is striking about Rowntree's case of the D family's circumstances is how similar it is, not only to records kept for poor working families of south London two years later (Pember Reeves 1913) but to detailed records of the subsequent century of research reporting the condition of the impoverished trying to get food.

The same sort of scrimping is reported among the unemployed in Marienthal in 1930s Austria. An unemployed man reports that '(C)ats keep disappearing ... Cat meat is very good. Dogs are also eaten'; '(S)ome families reported that they had not had sugar in the house for two years'; 'Frau M. L. always plans her housekeeping very carefully ...

When shoe repairs become necessary, the cost is worked out beforehand and the money saved on food' (Jahoda et al 1974: 26, 27, 31). In late 1960s UK, a major study of poverty includes a detailed set of case studies which, like Rowntree's, uses several different data collection techniques (Townsend 1979) reporting remarkably similar examples. Having to cope with debt remains for many already having difficulty, illustrating points made in the 1900s coverage of poverty that outgoings on housing are fixed, whereas what and whether to eat is not. Exactly this feature, along with others Rowntree records, are well illustrated in the cases reported for a twenty-first-century study in three cities in the English Midlands, glimpsed in the following quotations from interviews:

> '... mortgage comes before anything else, then the bills, and then food comes last, because you can adjust food, you can adjust how much you eat.'

> 'My food shopping has changed a lot ... (husband) used to have steak every week, lamb cutlets, all that kind of thing. I still try and make sure he has it, but I manage with something different ...'

> 'We've got a canteen at work, so I pay, it's subsidised ... to have a proper meal at lunchtime ... I'll eat very little [in the evening]. Because I'm not having to go to the shops to buy food, I can't be tempted to buy something that I don't need ... I'm saving on gas, I'm saving on electric, I'm not heating the water up to wash up, so it actually works out so much cheaper ....'.

> *Goode 2012: 16, 20*

A mortgage instead of rent, hot water instead of a dripping cold tap mark the century that separates the cases of Goode's and Rowntree's. But the deprivations and tactics for coping are much the same.

Deprivation is obviously of food itself, with adverse consequences for health. But deprivation is also social. For working-class women with minimal education and little employment experience, whose main position in life is as a mother, 'being unable to provide for your children and having to ask for a referral to a food bank is the ultimate disgrace; admitting defeat is most mothers' worst fear. I have known women who have told me that they would rather "go on the game" (become a prostitute) than go to a food bank' (McKenzie 2015: 109).

Recording the shame of receiving charity is a long-standing refrain in novels, journalism as well as academic studies about poverty. This is found in different places (e.g. van der Horst, Pascucci, Bol 2014 for The Netherlands) and is nothing new. Reminiscing to Irene Glasser about his gratitude for a soup kitchen during the Great Depression of the early 1930s a New Jersey man explains that '(F)or 5 cents or less one could have a quite satisfactory meal, without any hint of charity, because money was demanded and paid' (Glasser 1988: 16). Her study of a soup kitchen run as part of Christian ministry reports additional positive experiences of its guests, in the way that its non-judgemental organization counteracts loneliness, creating companionship, valued for the sake of it, over and above the central focus of providing something to eat.

Being a guest at soup kitchens is not necessarily anything like so congenial – illustrated in the ethnography of soup kitchens in Jerusalem (Cohen, Krumer-Nevo, Avieli 2017). Being an inmate in an institution, even on a temporary basis such as eating at a soup kitchen, can be socially demeaning and depressingly uncomfortable. Recollect that the authors refer to Goffman's discussion of total institutions noting that staff required diners to accept whatever was on the menu. Here the value of Cohen's electing to participate to observe not as a volunteer or member of staff, but to eat as a diner is well illustrated. For she is able *bodily* to experience and describe the revulsion she felt at being presented with cold, unappetizing-looking food, a component she argues that is part of diners being treated as inferior people.

Authorities' and professionals' responses to the private troubles of poor people

Researchers are one type of professional who consider poor people's personal troubles. Some assessments come close to the 'moralizing' of Rowntree's investigators and Pember Reeves who evaluate women's housekeeping competence. Other researchers' reports include the responses of formal authorities. Sympathy is reflected among those who are still employed/not going hungry in the Austrian village of Marienthal in the 1930s: 'Violations of the fishing laws and even minor thefts of coal from the railway are ignored by the authorities' and '(W)hen the farmers find that cabbages and potatoes are disappearing from their fields, they hardly ever take action. A young farmer said to us, "What can we do? The poor devils are really desperate"' (Jahoda et al 1974: 2). A more striking instance arises when hunger-related criminality in post-Second World War Berlin becomes 'a mass phenomenon': Cardinal Frings 'suspended the seventh commandment "thou shalt not steal"' in his 1946 New Year's Eve Sermon (Schmidt 2007: 69).

As striking is the way a medical investigation of hunger in 1980s America is written up to include the reactions of the doctors conducting the work. Despite a local doctor's declaring otherwise, members of a Harvard University Physician Task Force on Hunger in America conducting a mid-1980s field trip to the Mississippi Delta to see for themselves, report that 'there is substantial hunger in this rich agricultural region' (Physician Task Force 1985: 6). They, too, assess poverty-stricken families' housekeeping/budgetary competence

The four doctors were visibly shaken by what they saw. Inside the remnants of a house alongside a dirt road in Greenwood, lived a family of thirteen people. Graciously welcome by the mother and father, the doctors entered another world – a dwelling with no heat, no electricity, no windows, home for two parents, their children, and several nieces and nephews . . . No food was in the house. The babies had no milk; two were crying as several of the older children tried to console them. 'These people are starving' the local guide told the doctors. Twice a week she collected food from churches to bring to the family. It had been this way for two months while the family waited for the local food stamp office to determine whether they were eligible for food stamps . . . The parents . . . had not eaten for two days. The children had eaten some dried beans the previous evening.

1985: 27

Sympathy or shock are not the only responses recorded among authorities. Although often unpaid, those who run soup kitchens, food banks and the like, report deriving personal satisfaction and pleasure in what they do. Jan Poppendieck records the enthusiasm of volunteer gleaners among whom is a high proportion of retired people 'What we're doing is fun. I'm in it for the fun, the companionship . . . And I think it's great that we can take food in so that anybody who really needs some can get it. It's a good feeling' (1985: 176).

So authorities' and professionals' responses to private troubles of food poverty also tend to be individual/personal, expressible with reference to emotional reactions. This contrasts with those of the public sphere, discussed next.

Food poverty as a public issue

That such personal troubles of food poverty are recorded and made publicly available in the academic literature is a result of their collection's being defined as a legitimate part of research. Rowntree's study features as a landmark not only in histories of British sociology (Halsey 2004) but also as establishing a scientific basis for measuring hunger by drawing on contemporary nutritional understandings to calculate what constituted a diet adequate for what he called 'physical efficiency' (Vernon 2007). From Rowntree's study onwards, both nutrition and social research on poverty implicitly and explicitly address wider societal definitions and meanings of not having enough to eat, both responding to pre-existing discourses and contributing to them.

It is not that hunger and/or poverty (however defined or whether it is measured) have never been a matter of social concern. Chapter 1 notes that hunger is a shadow perennially overhanging human existence. In any case, proper attitudes to poverty, wealth and material goods are represented in the teachings of the great world religions, never mind that before Rowntree's study, nineteenth-century English novelists such as Charles Dickens and Elizabeth Gaskell drew attention to the dreadful plight of the urban poor in England. But the concern in this discussion is with the idea of hunger/poverty as a certain type of problem with implications for a society-wide solution.

Defining/measuring poverty

Rowntree's study provides an austere image of food poverty. He identifies a 'poverty line' against which to determine the proportion of the city's population that is poor. Adopting an extremely parsimonious approach, his estimates are based on the necessary minimum expenditure that is 'even less generous than that allowed to able-bodied paupers in the York Workhouse, and that *no allowance is made for any expenditure other than that absolutely required for the maintenance of merely physical efficiency'* (Rowntree 1901: 133, original emphasis). He is emphatic, exclusions explicit (e.g. no bus or rail fares, no buying postage stamps, no donations to the Church collecting plate, no saving, no children's sweets, or father's tobacco). 'Finally', he adds 'the wage-earner must never be absent from his work for a single day. If any of these conditions are broken, the extra expenditure involved is met, *and can only be met*, by limiting the diet' (1901: 134). By that measure, he concludes that '15.46 per cent of the wage-earning classes in York, and (equal to) 9.91 per cent of the whole population of the city' are below the line (1901: 111).

Rowntree knows perfectly well what he is doing when creating so strict a definition, despite subsequent commentators misunderstanding his purpose. He is shrewdly aiming to evade criticism that the impoverished condition and inadequate diets his study reports are caused by unwise budgeting or profligate spending. He wants to make it very hard for anyone to dismiss the gravity of his findings of such high levels of poverty. He stresses his measure assumes that all earnings are 'judiciously expended upon necessaries' (1901: 111). Then as now, the idea of the 'deserving' and 'undeserving' poor is pre-eminent, not just in England, but in the US and elsewhere, and he is determined to evade any suggestions that those he classifies as poor are to be judged as having brought their difficulties on themselves – which make possible justifying withholding sympathetic help. In effect, he aims at a definition of poverty that, in by-passing moral evaluations, makes his findings hard to dismiss. Thus, he turns the discussion of poverty into a political exercise. Much later, the historian Selina Todd draws parallels between the 1930s and today in her sharp remark that there is 'a persistent assumption made by the powerful and privileged that the willful idleness of the poor caused poverty' (2014: 62).

Definitions have been further developed since Rowntree's distinction between primary and secondary poverty: the former where 'total earnings are insufficient to obtain the minimum necessaries for the maintenance of merely physical efficiency' and the latter where total earnings would be sufficient were some not spent on other things 'either useful or wasteful' (1901: 86). The moral overtone is clear. Twentieth-century work pursues the question of defining poverty. Notably, Peter Townsend's comprehensive 1979 study distinguishes 'absolute' (insufficient resources for basic necessaries for survival) from 'relative' poverty (identifying a standard or style of life considered usual for a particular country at a specific era). He devises a 'relative' poverty/deprivation index, based e.g. on whether interviewees' households have 'gone through one or more days in the past fortnight without a cooked meal' (67.3% of the population) or 'does not have a refrigerator' (45.1%). In principle, neither is necessary for survival, but in 1970s UK both are regarded as part of an appropriate 'style of living' (Townsend 1979: 249–50). Relatively, what counts as poverty reflects the historical period in which it is defined.

A different type of research is provided by an often undeservedly neglected study of an impoverished area of Nottingham, a city of the English east Midlands in the 1960s. Recognizably aligned with 'the rediscovery of poverty' (so-called first in the US to attract public attention to the problem) it was run with virtually no funding, with data collected by volunteer students (Coates and Silburn 1970). The study has minimal discussion of hunger and food poverty directly, but makes it plain that poverty is all encompassing, affecting every aspect of life.

Two important features of the work warrant more attention. First, while reviewing other researchers' definitions of poverty, the authors are clear. It is impossible to understand poverty without also, simultaneously, thinking about wealth; in other words, poverty has to attend to society-wide economic inequalities. Second, throughout, the authors show how their data about poverty underline the powerlessness of the poor; poverty is the absence of power. Taking to task those who record low levels of aspiration for improvement as evidence of poor people's individual failings, the authors point out that lacking knowledge about, or experience of something, makes aspiring to it a difficult feat of imagination. Why aspire to possibilities 'given that they had so little power at their disposal to change them' (1970: 167). Echoes of those authors' argument continue: '(P)art of what defines poverty in any era is the inability to make free choices about necessities such as food' (Turner 2014: 7).

New/old thinking

A new mode of thought is evident in public discussions of food poverty, although it is an old idea in a new guise, echoing the distinction between 'deserving' and 'underserving'. Responsible citizenship (see Chapter 9) is invoked: people are expected to be knowledgeable, to exercise informed choice to assure healthy eating and to manage domestic food preparation safely. As Whiteford observes, 'responsible citizens make reasonable choices – and therefore "bad choices" result from the wilfulness of irresponsible people, rather than the structural distribution of resources, capacities and opportunities' (2010: 194). He goes on to point out that it is not simply a political and policy assumption about how people ought to behave, it is also implicit in measures 'to reconfigure citizenship' (2010: 195).

Whiteford traces the way this plays out in policies designed to support the homeless, notably by introducing charges for homeless people to buy a hot meal at a day-centre in southern England. The intention behind this is to encourage service users to take 'responsibility' for their own welfare. Whiteford records that not only do some of the service providers have mixed feelings about the plan, but so do service users. While several of the latter recognized the fairness of the idea (recollect the way that the New Jersey man's reminiscence about paying for a meal during the 1930s counteracts the shame of receiving charity) they also were very well aware that sometimes it was simply impossible to find the means. Whiteford concludes that charging for meals does not clearly engender responsible citizenship any more than it deals with the persisting problem of poverty, hunger and homelessness.

Researchers and campaigners alike issue a warning. To regard soup kitchens as 'the great panacea for hunger' risks, as Poppendieck clearly declares for the US in the 1980s, 'relieving the pressure for more fundamental solutions'. A similar warning is offered about the reported increase in food bank use in the UK in the 2010s, lest they lead the public, politicians and policy makers into thinking that their existence disposes of the problem of hunger. Their very existence can lull the powerful into the false sense that food poverty is being dealt with.

Food poverty and a thread to the food system

Individual volunteers are not the only ones reporting a benefit in contributing to helping run food banks or soup kitchens. There are financial and reputational benefits to be had too for producers and manufacturers. As Poppendieck sharply observes, corporate welfare is always a business decision; 'soup kitchens and food pantries, and especially food banks and food rescue programs, have proven extraordinarily useful to business . . . (falling) under the general rubric of "cause-related marketing," the use of association with a good cause as a marketing strategy' (1985: 159). She is talking of what would now be called 'corporate social responsibility' and which is, no doubt, a factor in food retailers' decisions about diverting their 'food waste' to charities. Indeed, an important feature of Poppendieck's study is her relating public responses to the ups and downs of the food supply; publicly owned stores of cheese in danger of spoiling are suddenly made available to feed the less well off, diverting farm surpluses via a convenient route for dealing with a problem that simultaneously enhances reputation (1985: 88, 143).

Box 26 Chapter 10 – Selected Key Points

1. Despite variation between national systems of support for those without enough food, 'moralizing' about poor people's way of life recurs.
2. There is a mismatch between personal experience of troubles of food poverty and characterization of the problem as a public issue.
3. 'Moralizing' is not new; the nineteenth-century distinction between the 'deserving' and the 'undeserving' poor persists.
4. A definition of (food) poverty as powerlessness is neglected.
5. Critics argue that the success of food banks risks creating misplaced reassurance that they solve the problem of food poverty.

CHAPTER 11
FOOD AND POWER: POLITICS, THE FOOD SYSTEM AND 'CONSUMER CHOICE'

New Traffic Light Food Labels: Much-Needed Intervention or Nanny State Interference?[1]

Public opposed to nanny-state approach in battle of obesity[2]

Should governments make their citizens exercise more and eat less?[3]

Many people assume they are free to choose from a very varied, safe and affordable supply of food without 'interference' from governments. If a problem arises, such as the March/April 2018 E. coli outbreak linked to romaine lettuce from Arizona, affecting 149 people across 29 states and resulting in one death, with six more ill in Canada,[4] then many people also assume there are authorities responsible for ensuring systems exist to contain it, measures to deal with culprits and services to help victims. Restoring safety also restores the freedom to choose. But behind anyone's ability to make such assumptions lie centuries'-long histories of all kinds of governing activities and negotiations involving politicians and food industry interests, lobbyists and campaigning groups of modern food systems.

'Consumer choice' is a conventional wisdom that runs throughout these current assumptions, serving as a touchstone and rationale for many of the relevant food system decisions and activities. Freedom to choose lies at the core of a much-repeated argument represented in the trio of headlines above. Ought governments curtail 'consumer choice' to improve people's health/reduce obesity, or does that treat people like children needing a 'nanny' to care for them when, rightly, they are free to choose for themselves? Public health practitioners, nutritionists and some in professional classes along with some (Democrat/left leaning) politicians typically take the former view, some sectors of the general public along with (Republican/neo-liberal/right leaning) politicians, the opposite.

Sociological thinking in this chapter divides into three, dealing first with governments' position making it possible for people to assume a safe and reliable supply. A second section illustrates industrial interests in governments' activities, turning, third, to discuss 'freedom to choose', highlighting ways in which it is limited, exposing 'consumer choice' as an example of political ideology.

That food and eating are simultaneously private and public assumes a new prominence in this chapter. As noted, one expression of this is individuals' expectations that government is to provide a regulatory framework at least for food safety, although the industry may also be judged to bear a responsibility (Henderson, Coveney and Ward 2010). There is, however, a tension between private/individual and public/government responsibilities, with repeated arguments about where the dividing line is to be drawn. In wartime, for instance, publics accept, more-or-less grudgingly, that governments take control to an extent they would not in peacetime. That control may not only involve (more/less stringent) food rationing as was instituted during the Second World War in the US, across Europe including Germany and neutral countries like Ireland as well as occupied Singapore and Japan itself. Government intervention may also include nutritional and culinary advice on what to eat, on being thrifty, urging saving food scraps to feed chickens, foraging for berries, growing vegetables and advising how to preserve the results (Collingham 2011). Governments' interests controlling the food supply in times of crisis is not only a way of feeding the population, but of preventing unrest (Oddy 2003: 72) providing compelling reasons for shifting the dividing line towards authorities' limiting individuals' room for manoeuvre, moving the line back once the crisis is over. Where that dividing line is to be drawn is an integral component of political ideologies: neoliberalism, for instance, seeks, among other things to minimize the state and limit what is seen as its encroachment on matters that are, from that political perspective, properly personal and private.

Governments' responsibilities for food and eating

'Feeding the population (is) one of the primary duties of government …' observes a bishop who sits in the upper chamber of the UK Parliament.[5] The Director General of the UK's Food & Drink Federation (a trade association) declares that food is

> not a trivial issue. Food is a matter of national security. If you can't feed the country you don't have a country. Our shoppers and consumers over the last thirty years have grown used to a real, massive amount of choice, a huge number of different products at all price points, so maintaining that level of choice, that level of enjoyment in food in the UK rests on a stable and contented workforce.[6]

His reference to 'national security' is, of course, significant. Unrest, civil disorder and criminality (e.g. in the shape of black markets) threatened by worsening food shortages or steep price rises, face governments which neglect that primary duty to which the bishop refers. Food riots, in extreme cases, turn into revolution – think only of France 1789–1799.[7] But, as the historian E. P. Thompson argues, food riots are to be understood as evident manifestation of the expression of wider grievances (1971, Patel and McMichael 2014), as illustrated when following the news from Venezuela during 2017–2018.

Feeding the population can be subdivided into three major topics: having enough, food that is safe to eat and the right kind of food (to which may be added others, e.g. food that is honestly traded, ensuring information is made available). The way twenty-first-century national governments interpret such responsibilities varies somewhat, as illustrated by the websites of food standards authorities in different countries. For instance:

Protecting the public health by assuring that foods (except for meat from livestock, poultry and some egg products which are regulated by the US Department of Agriculture) are safe, wholesome, sanitary and properly labelled.

Safe food, healthy animals and plants for Singapore.

Our primary concern is consumer protection – making sure that food is safe to eat, ensuring consumers know what they are eating and improving nutrition. With that in mind, our vision is to deliver a food and drink environment in Scotland that benefits, protects and is trusted by consumers.[8]

Assuring the food supply is not only a wartime concern. A peacetime and distinctive historical example is Soviet Russia between the Russian Revolution of 1917 up until the German invasion in 1941. In this period the Soviet government claimed control of every aspect of the supply of food but was unable to do so reliably. What the historian Mauricio Borrero calls a 'politics of scarcity' developed. Bolshevik ideals of egalitarianism plus the practicalities of governing ended up in 'rationing policies alternated between notions of food as a right to be given to all and as a privilege to be awarded by the state to selected groups of people' (2002: 259). And, detailing the complexities of the government's management of chronic food shortage, he goes on to point out that the difficult decisions about food distribution lead to the emergence of priorities based on work performed, in effect, as payment, accompanied by slogans such as 'he who works, eats' (2002: 265). In this instance, controlling the food supply is also an explicit means of controlling the population.

The immediate precursors of twenty-first-century organization of government responsibilities for the purity and safety of the food supply in the US and across Europe intensify from the nineteenth century onward. Upton Sinclair's 1906 novel *The Jungle* prompts the passage of the US 1906 Food and Drugs Act to assure the safety of the food supply (see Chapter 1). As the last two centuries' geographic distance between rural food production and the growing urban populations to be fed lengthens, so does the sheer scale of the task of safeguarding supplies. Legislation that applied to the earlier pre-industrialized food market is no longer appropriate for changed times. Dealing with widespread fraud and the growing conviction that foodstuffs are ever-more adulterated becomes more urgent (Scholliers 2007).

The incorporation of those responsibilities in political institutions is, however, slow and uneven. In nineteenth-century England, milk is regularly watered down, 'bobbed' or 'washed'. But the speed with which effective regulation to control it can be introduced is, partly, associated with the slower development of the science which makes dependable assessment of any adulteration possible (Atkins 1991). In late nineteenth-century Germany the gaps left by patchy local authority preventive monitoring are filled by the so-called 'associations against adulteration of food' set up by citizens (one in Leipzig is started by a writer of comedies, songs and adventure stories) acting as interim arrangements, eventually made redundant by the establishment of municipal authorities (Hierholzer 2007). Scholliers illustrates the way that the creation in 1856 of a municipal analysis laboratory for Brussels to curb fraudulent activities in 'food and beverages' has to deal with anxious interested parties (notably millers, bakers and grocers) to provide assurances that the purpose is to regulate the quality of the foods, not the activities of their distributors (Scholliers 2014).

Organizing government responsibilities for a pure food supply develops, dealing in the process with the historical shift in focus from adulteration to safety. At any period, the emergence of a novel 'food scare' can act as a spur to major action. A recent example is what is widely regarded as the UK government's serious mishandling of bovine spongiform encephalopathy (BSE) popularly known as 'mad cow disease' (Morgan, Marsden and Murdoch 2006). The Ministry of Agriculture, Fisheries and Food (MAFF) was fiercely criticized for prioritizing the farming industry's interests over the health of the public. Stopping the potential epidemic (eating BSE-infected beef is invariably fatal) required the slaughter of more than 4 million cattle and the imposition of a suite of controls on beef entering the human food chain, the last of which was lifted only in 2013. It culminates in the establishment of a public enquiry whose report runs to 16 volumes (made available *in toto* online), leading to the reorganization of government obligations. Responsibility for safeguarding the public was removed from MAFF and transferred to a new 'arms' length' organization (i.e. independent from government). The Food Standards Agency (FSA) became operational in April 2000 enjoined to 'put the consumer first'.

The list of government responsibilities for the population and its health is simpler to put on paper than to put into practice, not least because none of the other responsibilities of government have yet been mentioned.[9] As already seen in the case of BSE in the UK, responsibilities both for feeding the people properly and attending to the economy can often conflict. Another government responsibility revolves around the importance of the business sector, guarding jobs and recognizing the value of the food industrial sector to an economy overall. 'Food & drink' contributes £28.8bn to the UK economy, the sector described as 'a national asset'.[10] In other words, a further government responsibility is to ensure there is employment (staff for the industry supplying the food) and wages for people to be able to buy it. Over and above managing such tensions, government responsibilities do not exist in a vacuum. Governments are (more/less) accountable and others have a view. An especially interested party is the industrial food sector.

Governments, industry and NGOs

Here the meaning of 'private' (personal or individual) swivels to the different usage, the corporate/industrial sector as distinct from the public sector. Ostensibly, of course, the food industry is not political but commercial: a business producing food. But any company no matter what they make/sell operates within circumstances not of their making, including the regulatory framework and fiscal regimes in whichever region they buy/sell. To the extent that governments seeks to alter either regulation or fiscal regimes so the food industry is interested in the state's responsibilities for feeding the public. It would be perverse if the companies involved did not want the situations in which they conduct their business to be as favourable to the success of their operations as possible, even if, or perhaps especially if, they produce items high in ingredients government dietary advice counsels against (i.e. foods low in dietary fibre and high in fat, salt and sugar such as potato chips/crisps or chocolate bars, fried chicken or pizza).

Some aspects of the fast food industry's activities (no different, it should be noted from other industries) that seek to affect the circumstances in which they conduct their business are described by Miller and Harkins as attempts 'to resist meaningful progress on public health measures to tackle consumption related harms' (2010: 564). They argue that lobbying as part of corporate strategy is an important element of these attempts, one of the means they have at their disposal to influence government policy. Employing public relations (PR) companies that specialize in promoting favourable images of the businesses involves more than simply presenting government with a case (by for instance responding to public consultations on a food related matter). It also includes making sure to 'secure and capitalize on favourable assumptions by offering incentives in the form of travel and hospitality, paid and unpaid advisory positions, and – the big prize – board memberships once politicians and senior civil servants leave public service' (2010: 568).[11] In this fashion, companies seek to have influence in indirect ways, trying to 'dominate the information environment' to affect thinking and governmental decision making.

That study of lobbying relies on publicly available information. Marion Nestle, the eminent nutritionist at New York University, also uses publicly available information in *Food Politics.* Her book documents the same activities in the US geared to influencing a favourable regulatory and fiscal environment for the sale of foods high in sugar, salt etc. As a senior academic member of her profession, however, she can augment published material by drawing on her first-hand experience of actions of the food industry while serving as a nutrition advisor for the Department of Health and Human Services and on various federal committees on food/nutrition policy. This grants her access to discussions and documents about food companies' efforts at creating commercially advantageous environments which are ordinarily hidden from public view. Nestle is, however, unable to quote from these, since most are subject to confidentiality agreements. Although her public service gives her good contacts, she notes that 'I could not find *anyone* who would speak to me "on the record" for this book' (Nestle 2002: ix, original emphasis). Although colleagues in the industry and government offer their help, they always add the proviso that the information they provide be unattributed. The control of information is itself an aspect of power.

The food industrial sector is not the only party with a special interest in governments' responsibilities for feeding the public. Another is the more diffuse, far smaller sector consisting of organizations campaigning against the adverse public health consequences of industrialized food products which are high in salt, sugar and fat and low in dietary fibre and/or whose production has detrimental environmental consequences, organizations such as *GE Free NZ* or *FIZZ* in New Zealand and *Action on Sugar* or *LEAF* in the UK.

Clearly such organizations set themselves in direct opposition to much the food industry does and stands for. These non-governmental organizations (NGOs), neither public nor private, may succeed in being 'noisy' achieving media coverage out of proportion to their small scale. But they cannot begin to match the food industry in terms of funding their own PR activities. Where food companies engage in PR as part of their corporate strategies allocating funds from the business to carry them out, NGOs are typically non-profit and reliant on charitable donations.

Governments must, then, honour their responsibilities for feeding the population in what can be highly charged circumstances. How governments proceed in steering between these two groups of interests (among others) is shaped by the political ideology prevailing at the time. An expression, simplistically put, of neoliberal commitment to a small state, is avoiding regulating industry and instead relying on businesses' voluntary co-operation in discharging responsibilities for feeding the population properly. In this fashion, regulatory responsibility can be said to be devolved. England provides a good recent example in the announcement on 18 August 2017 of a programme 'to remove excess calories from the foods children consume the most'.[12] The media coverage picks out the way that government is relying on food companies to effect this voluntarily, albeit with the threat of legislation should they not comply.

Industry does not always welcome voluntary regulation. For instance, an industry representative is reported to argue that government should go beyond voluntary agreements. Major, socially responsible companies would comply, they argue, but others would not, making competition unfair. So regulatory measures are welcomed to ensure everyone complies. But what of the private responsibility of individuals for feeding themselves properly?

'The food consumer' and 'food choice'

A strand running through Chapter 8's discussion of people's following (or not) official nutritional advice is the expectation that people are responsible for themselves and their own healthy diet. This finds an equivalence in expectations that are integral to the twenty-first-century version of the idea of 'the consumer'. More-or-less firmly established in food and nutrition policy documentation and in the discourse of food and nutrition policy communities, the current image of 'the consumer' widely reflects the conceptions of classical economics. In this view, consumers are distinct from producers, both actors making a market in which they act rationally in their own interests, consumers making choices that maximize their welfare.

Readers may, however, have noticed that many writings on food and society (newspaper reports, government documents, or even some social scientific publications) commonly refer to 'consumers' rather than the 'public' or even 'citizens' (Wilkins 2005). This book does not. Referring to 'people', 'members of the public' etc. it thereby seeks to stand back from any alignment with those whose activities and commitments lead them to use the name 'consumers' to allow readier investigation of the economic/political circumstances and consequences of such naming.

Readers may also have noticed that as often, such writings refer to 'food choice', as does work in public health nutrition, also in the study of human–food-related behaviour in psychology.[13] This book does not. 'Choice' is a technical term in economics, closely associated with 'consumer', when studying supply and demand for goods and services: it is assumed that consumers are rational and are free to satisfy their preferences for whatever meets their needs. Other social scientists do at times adopt a similar usage that treats 'food choice' as if it were a neutral description of the foods people put in their supermarket trolley/shopping cart, or that they select from the menu of a works canteen. So doing, however, risks narrowing their field of analytic vision losing the opportunity to investigate empirically the extent to which people are able actively to choose (i.e. to make an unconstrained choice) to be discussed after considering the notion of 'the consumer' a little further.

'The consumer', varying images

The idea of 'the consumer' that is current nowadays emerges unevenly historically and only over the last two centuries (Trentmann 2006: 19). The image alters from eighteenth-century economists' conception of consumers as unorganized individuals needing protection against organized monopolies, to the current emphasis on governments' responsibilities for consumer protection as an element of 'feeding the population,' particularly in respect of the sale of food (e.g. Foreman 1989). Yet the idea of the 'consumer' remains elusive and variable (Autio and Heinonen 2007). Wahlen reports that at least in the 2000s the notion is rarely apparent in German documents and where it is, safeguarding consumers appears to be the most common concern (2009). By contrast, a differently designed cross national European project analyses constructions of 'the food consumer' (derived from open-ended interviews with food policy communities' members, including producers, manufacturers, retailers, public authorities, scientists, media and consumer organizations). It identifies additional ideas of the 'food consumer', summarized as: 'the trusting consumer' (Norway) 'the complex consumer' (Denmark) 'the quality conscious consumer' (Italy) 'the unprotected consumer' (Portugal) (Halkier et al 2007).

Notwithstanding such variation, Julie Guthman declares that, in the neo-liberal era of the last few decades '(P)robably the most central organizing theme in contemporary food politics is consumer *choice*' (2008: 1176, emphasis added). She points out that the 'devolution' of responsibility to individual consumers (matching that of devolution to industry) is integral to that theme. Responsibility is the other side of the coin to the presumption that consumers have freedom to choose, thereby defining any ill-advised choices as consumers' fault. Certainly, authorities acknowledge the possibility of unwitting ignorance, hence the sustained efforts at public and school education (see Chapter 8), thus concentrating neo-liberal government responsibility on the provision of dietary education and continued information in the form of labelling, notably nutritional labelling (Frolich 2016). The regulatory balance has tipped with responsibility moving to lie more with individuals (and industry) than with government. As a result, a responsible consumer, once educated, is one who keeps themselves suitably informed, duly and dutifully exercising choice in line with professional advice on healthy eating and on safely preparing food in their kitchen. As Unni Kjaernes observes, this reveals that

'(C)onsumer choice' is part of a regulatory regime based on voluntarism, market solutions, and the State acting at a distance. But this is not only a matter of commercialization. The focus on lifestyle choices as a private matter and consumer choice as a dominant value represents an ideology of moral management of the self.

Kjaernes 2012: 147

This line of sociological thinking suggests that using the expressions 'consumer' and 'food choice' is neither neutral nor innocent of political ideological overtones. Avoiding alignment with either helps study the manner in which people act as 'consumers' as well as considering the extent of any constraints surrounding how and what they eat. The next section considers shopping by way of example.

'Consumer freedom to choose'?

Shopping is not just extremely familiar, it is also ubiquitous. Very many rely on the market, in some guise, to acquire what they eat. Shopping can be regarded as a lens through which to view 'the intersection of individual choice, cultural production and the larger political economy' (Koch 2012: 13). Considering shopping also leads back to focus on the food system (see Chapter 1) illustrating the way it not only comprises food production from field to shop but also food consumption, and, indeed, waste and recycling bins beyond the table. One of the bridges among myriad interconnections in the global food system linking production and consumption is represented in the image producers have of 'consumers', members of the public as shoppers. This, as will be seen, is an integral component of their thinking and actions in their operations as producers.

Shopping: customers and retailers meet

Shopping is a key vantage point from which most populations needing to eat view the food system. Food retail in the twenty-first century means paying full attention to supermarkets not least because of their ubiquity in wealthy nations occupying a rapidly increasing share of the grocery market (Koch 2017). Their development is accompanied by and responsible for major shifts in the contemporary global food system, contributing, it has been argued, to its fundamental re-shaping (Pritchard 2013). Along with its component food chains linking the farm to the plate, the system lies behind the encounter between shopper and check-out staff. This is the system which continues to remain opaque, with elements veiled by commercial secrecy whereby companies legitimately seek to conceal what is considered to confer their competitive advantage, the semi-visible system of which the vast majority of customers are unaware (see Chapter 1).

Note that studies introduced on earlier chapters' topics either do not mention shopping at all or treat it as unremarkable, leaving it unexamined on the sidelines. Perhaps the most attention shopping gets is its inclusion in lists of domestic tasks typically undertaken by women. Switching to put shopping in the centre of the picture means this chapter now approaches 'the meal at home' from a vantage point by-passed in much sociological research on domestic meals. It does, however, have to rely on the far smaller sociological literature in a field that is, in any case, limited (Hallsworth 2013).

A notable point of that literature challenges a simple version of the idea that supply meets demand and demand is satisfied by supply. Instead, the suggestion that customer's needs are met by retailers' provisioning is deemed deceptive. As Mintz stresses, it is not simply a matter of studying 'supply and demand' but also of attending to 'supplier *induced* demand' (1985). If someone has a product (or service) to sell they want to be sure of persuading people to buy theirs not anyone else's. Moreover, that impulse is dynamic, not once and for all, competition does not stand still. Two themes beginning to emerge in this literature are picked out here. The first is that despite talk of streamlining, efficiency, cleanliness and modernizing image of supermarket food retailing to improve 'the customer experience', shopping requires work, it is a labour, and has been from its inception (Deutsch 2010). The second considers the argument that far from simply responding to customers' needs or wants, supermarkets work to *shape* shoppers' behaviour.

Supermarkets

Undeniably, supermarkets appear to dominate, in the US, Australasia and Europe. They have come to occupy a particularly powerful place in those parts of food systems involved with the distribution of food. They merge wholesale and retail, have moved 'upstream' to incorporate food processing and develop direct relationships with primary producers (Dixon 2007).

Care is needed, however, not to assume the patterns of supermarket food retail and practices of shopping are similar everywhere; the range varies cross-nationally. Even within the US the density of alternatives is notable. Although '90 per cent of American consumers shop primarily at either a supercentre . . . or at a supermarket', many also have access to upmarket organic stores, chain stores, grocery stores, at national and local retailers, locally grown produce from farmers' markets, speciality foods at small health-food shops as well as independent delicatessens or convenience stores (Koch 2017: 111). This is before listing organic vegetable box schemes ordered online direct from growers, or deliveries of menu, recipe and ingredients for a pre-specified menu ready to cook at home, 'Blue Apron' in the US, 'Hello Fresh' in London.

Similarly, not everyone everywhere shops at a supermarket. Based on over 20 years' fieldwork in South India, the anthropologist James Staples notes that supermarkets are primarily patronized by the wealthy, or students from overseas (Staples 2018). Ten years' fieldwork in Marrakech provides Katherina Graf with very similar anthropological evidence; supermarkets are not centrally located in the city, carry both non-food and food items, of which only a small proportion is fresh. The fresh food is displayed unpackaged, on stalls just like street markets, but inside the huge warehouse-style superstores. There too supermarket shoppers are wealthier people, including those keen to signal their 'European-ness' and to avoid mingling with 'lower' Moroccan residents, sometimes considered dirty, in dirty street markets (Graf 2018). Moreover, detailed anthropological research in rural South Africa allows Lizzie Hull to demonstrate the supermarket expansion is neither inevitable nor linear (2016).

Shopping, hidden labour

Shelley Koch's study of shopping is firmly placed where eating at home is linked to the food system (2012). Her institutional ethnography (see Box 27) is located in the American Midwest.

Added to interviews with 20 shoppers and others with store managers, she analyses the discourses about how to run a house aimed at women responsible for domestic provisioning that originate in institutions' documents lying beyond shopping.[14] She includes magazines, texts representing official government sources advising on healthy diets, more deriving from home economics about being an 'efficient housewife' as the one who writes shopping lists and knows about prices.

Throughout her study, she highlights the work, the effort involved and its organization, required even for modern supermarket shopping. It represents a shift, historically, of labour from supplier to customer. Before the advent of the supermarkets' self-service, shops divide into smaller, separate specialized outlets, butcher, fishmonger, dairy, grocer, greengrocer etc. In such stores, in the US, across Europe and in colonies such as Australia and New Zealand, for more than two centuries up to the first decades of the twentieth century and though starting to decline, still evident until after the Second World War, shop assistants do just that, they assist. They fetch goods from cupboards, shelves and storerooms to show customers; they carry and wrap purchases, often delivering to their homes without the shopper ever needing to touch a single item along the way.

This is replaced by self-service, with the assistant doing all that labour long gone. Now the shopper does it. Readers may like to stop and count the number of times they pick up/move a purchase between the moment of walking into a supermarket until the moment of arriving back home (around six or seven?). The change also entails a shift

---

Box 27 Institutional Ethnography

Institutional ethnography is an extension of ethnography initiated by the Canadian sociologist Dorothy Smith (2005). Originally focused on features of daily life combined with analyses of the connections to practitioners' and policy makers' advice (e.g. on child-rearing or kitchen safety) it can be adopted to study other institutions' links with everyday activities. Institutional ethnography emphasizes attention to work, not just employment, but any and all types of labour, thereby directing analytic attention to the way that 'institutional ideologies typically acknowledge some kinds of work but not others' (DeVault 2006: 294).

away from the sales staff being the customer's source of information about purchases. The main source of information becomes the manufacturer directly to the shopper, without the sales staff between the commercial producer and the purchaser. The means of conveying the information is the labelling on each package, the 'market device' of brands, pictures or logos together with any statutorily required details of the contents' ingredients and/or nutritional value (see Chapter 6). A dominant motif of this shift from retailer to customer is its liberating people to enjoy 'freedom of choice'. Such freedom is double-edged, for it places responsibility for making a 'good' choice by following professional advice onto purchasers' shoulders (see Chapter 9). But that advice pays no attention to the added effort involved in keeping up with the latest information or of squaring it with the amount of money available to spend on food when budgets are tight.

The initial work of shopping does not stop at thinking about what to buy but includes having to decide where to buy it. The sociologist Christopher Carrington shows how detailed this is in his sophisticated ethnography of San Francisco lesbigay households. In the process he illustrates a virtue of ethnographic work that allows the generation of multi-faceted data relying not on asking one, undeniably obvious, question (where do you shop?), but instead conversing with research participants *during* the task of planning and *accompanying* them on a shopping expedition to provide a far more nuanced understanding of the labour of shopping. He refers to shoppers as planners to highlight the management work required.

Planners shop at several stores, displaying detailed strategies weighing up 'menu, parking, time availability and quality' (Carrington 1999: 40). Add to these concerns with foods' healthfulness, a concern that he clearly shows reflects social structural variables of class, income level, gender and sexual orientation, etc. Emphasizing ethnic identity is evident too in decisions to patronize Latino markets even though they may be more expensive than other retailers who undercut them. And this is all before even going into a store. Once inside, there are others' likes/dislikes to remember. Things change: new items come on the market. So planners need to keep up with the marketplace. Planners read flyers grocery stores put in newspapers or send in the mail with 'much of the provisioning work tak(ing) place in one's mind, the place where much of the hidden work of monitoring' happens (1999: 44). Things change at home too (e.g. household members' timetables change at short notice).

Customers' labour is only one form of hidden work in shopping. In any retail enterprise, there is work behind the scenes, out of sight of shoppers, often out of hours too. In supermarkets this is heightened, prompted by the idea that in the name of consumer freedom to choose, the complete array of items must always be on display. So, to remain fully stocked, shelves must continuously be monitored and replenished both amongst daytime throngs of shoppers but also overnight when the store is closed. The manner in which supermarkets are arranged, 'the way aisles and shelves are organized and products are labelled and presented, are based on experience with, and meticulous studies of, consumer behaviour' (Jakobsen 2015: 252). But the labour employed to ensure a continuing well stocked display is typically poorly paid as well as mostly being hidden. Also partly hidden is what Koch calls 'consumer control'.

Do supermarkets 'shape' shoppers?

One of the themes emerging from this literature is the suggestion that far from being 'free', shoppers are guided and their activities 'shaped' to such an extent that supermarkets can even be said to be controlling them. As indicated, Koch's and Carrington's evidence reveals shoppers' mental and physical effort, representing unpaid labour not just undertaken on behalf of the household but also representing a service for the market. This inverts the conventional assumption that suppliers work to provide a service to customers. Instead, Koch regards shoppers' activities as shaped by others including retailers. She reports that grocery store managers refer to their tasks of selecting products, advertising their wares via the local press or flyers, as passively 'merely responding to customer needs and wants' (2012: 207). On the contrary, she argues they are actively shaping those needs and wants, an example of supplier-induced demand (see Chapter 1).

Think back to the discussion in Chapter 6 of the invention of self-service, arguably a key element in the origin of the supermarket. Remember the maze Clarence Saunders created in his 1916 store in Memphis, Tennessee, inventing routes through the shop, guiding customers past all the shelves from which they help themselves. Saunders paid exceedingly close attention to securing as much control over bringing shoppers face to face with the goods on sale as he possibly could, so much so that he took out a patent in the US for 'A Self -Serving Store' in 1917.

It is against this sort of history that Koch devotes the institutional element of her study. She shows that what managers call 'customer demand' is the basis for their decisions about what to stock, how to display goods etc. Yet her examination of what happens in the store runs counter to their explanation. '(M)anagers report that if they put out a sign that says "new item", especially one sticking out from the grocery shelf, people are more likely to look at it' (2012: 89). Or again, capitalizing on knowing people are more likely to buy what is at eye level, managers decide on which shelf to place products with reference to the height of the average American woman (2012: 90).

Supporting what happens in supermarkets, Koch points out the importance to management of gathering as much information about customers as possible. In addition, she notes efforts at keeping customers by the provision of coupons; sorting through them is another source of labour for shoppers. The use of loyalty cards/points cards/ rewards cards/store cards, may be an advance on the provision of vouchers, stamps or other forms of discount to entice shoppers (e.g. US Green Stamps were the model for Green Shield Stamps in the 1950s UK). But modern IT systems allow the collection of prodigious volumes of electronic point of sale (EPOS) data about shoppers' demographic characteristics and purchasing patterns, data, many consider, that benefits retailers far more than shoppers. Koch records how marketers stress the value of such technology as a 'key to serving customers' (2012: 945).

Koch records the trade press as a further source, behind which sits the academic marketing literature. She quotes from a *Supermarket News* article of 2010 which discusses the additional management task of engaging efficient shoppers who make lists, study advertisements, collect coupons and check websites to arrive at the shop with clear decisions about what to buy:

> ... if the market is doing its job, then point-of-purchase programs – tie-in displays, in-store sampling, multiple-buy offers, promotions or other inducements – are likely to prompt even list-makers to beef up their market basket and *buy more than what was on their list.*
>
> *2012:107 original emphasis*

Shoppers are thereby revealed less as individuals actively and freely exercising choice as they buy their food, but more as 'targets' of major efforts at directing their choices toward choices which serve the retailers' (and behind them, manufacturers') commercial interests. Though taking over more and more of the grocer's labour, shoppers paradoxically have become passive, the object, it is suggested, of supermarkets' attempts to shape and control what they put in the shopping cart/trolley (Deutsch 2010).

Box 28 Chapter 11 – Selected Key Points

1. Resistance to official dietary recommendations as needless 'nannying' co-exists with the expectation that state-organized authorities/regulation will assure the safety of the food supply.
2. Governments have major responsibilities, developed most rapidly since the nineteenth century, for the nutritional quality, safety and reliability of the food supply.
3. Food producers have an interest in the regulatory circumstances in which they conduct their business, and lobby governments to shape those circumstances in their favour.
4. Campaigning NGOs also seek to lobby governments, but typically have fewer resources than food businesses/trade associations.
5. Requiring individuals to take responsibility for themselves/the healthfulness of their diet finds equivalence in the twenty-first-century idea of the 'consumer' which, coupled with 'freedom of choice', represents central elements of the contemporary politics of food.
6. Studies of shopping – the labour involved, the invention of self-service – illustrate the limits of 'consumer freedom of choice'.

CHAPTER 12
CONCLUSION: SOCIOLOGY, FOOD AND EATING

This chapter brings *Introducing the Sociology of Food and Eating* to a close by recapitulating the book's prime intention of illuminating contrasts between 'conventional wisdoms' and 'sociological thinking'. The former, 'what everybody knows', received wisdom, common sense explanations, take the form of statements to do with food and society. A predominant feature of moving to the latter is increasingly close attention to evidence, gathered systematically and interpreted as rigorously as possible. To help make this move, the inspiration of C. Wright Mills' 'sociological imagination' is invoked – he brings private troubles and public issues together, pointing to the significance of the intersections between social structure, biography and history.

Reminding readers of that move is illustrated in the next two sections. It consists of a succession of questions that highlight, step by step, how to proceed to sociological thinking from an example of conventional wisdom.

From 'conventional wisdom' . . .

Having located a statement of conventional wisdom, the first set of questions begins with: what sort of statement is it, who is making it, does it 'moralize', to whom is it addressed? This helps distinguish between more routine news reports of, say, trends in eating out or the ubiquity of ethnic cuisines, from campaigners' complaints of overpackaging and from practitioners' anxieties at people's not following professional advice. Move to asking about anything else that can be discovered – where is the statement located, is the same sentiment to be found in other places, are they all of the same sort, or is there some variation? Is there anything special about the location, some affiliation to a political party, an NGO, how well known is it, what kind of reputation does it have? The source of the first headline opening Chapter 5 is *The Washington Post*, judged by some to be left leaning/Democrat, whereas the fourth of the same chapter is carried by *The Daily Mail*, a UK newspaper usually deemed on the right/Conservative – but both carry similar views on cooking skills.

A second series of questions considers the basis for the statement. Is it the result of reporters' asking a chef's opinion of a recent research report about fewer family meals, or inviting nutritionists to comment on a study reporting children's not knowing where bananas come from? If so, what sort of qualifications does the commentator have? Are food writers or campaigners trained to evaluate research of any kind? Are nutritionists authorities on cooking skills? Is it possible to distinguish between conventional wisdoms that primarily seem to be opinions and those which (apparently) report facts? Of wasted food, Stuart lists facts about annual totals of '484 million unopened pots of yoghurt, 1.6 billion untouched apples (27 apples per person)' and expresses his opinion that people 'have simply become lazy and negligent about food' (2010:78), which when checked against sociological evidence is not borne out. Knowing how much food is wasted cannot support a statement about why it is wasted. Pointing out that porridge is cheaper than Coco Pops is factual, but as the bloggers point out, this is not the only relevant fact about the cost of getting breakfast.

The third group of questions builds on the second. If the example of 'conventional wisdom' not only contains facts but records they derive from research, it is essential to consider the type of research and its purposes. For instance, many reports of families not eating together are based on market research. It may be illuminating to discover who commissioned the research – after all a key purpose of this form of work is to reveal aspects of sales and the retail food market. Is it a manufacturer or perhaps a magazine? Is there note of how the study is conducted? *Good Housekeeping* ran a survey of its readers reporting that family meals are 'the daily norm' for almost half – how typical are its readers of the whole population, and are those who respond to such a survey self-selected, perhaps most interested in family meals? (Murcott 1997).

. . . toward sociological thinking

Turning to focus on academic alternatives to market research, public commentary and journalism represents the point where questions move into the realm of sociological thinking. And these questions go in different directions. Some reflect C. Wright Mills' reminders. Does his intersection of biography, social structure and history help to develop productive questions? Is a criticism that poor people live beyond their means by buying expensive food anything new? Asking whether complaints that cooking skills are declining have been made in previous eras reveals that they go back well over a century. Does asking whether those repeating the conventional wisdom include themselves in its strictures, or only 'others'? Recollect Wilk's stinging criticisms of those who disapprove of families not eating together as 'moralizing' about those different from white, nuclear families, and his indictment as reflections of unequal social structural distributions of opportunity. Similarly, public issues and private troubles turn out to be useful touchstones for organizing an examination of the literature – if they are not aligned with one another, what does that say about the realm in which 'moralizing' conventional wisdoms persist?

A further set of questions proceeds in another, more technical direction. Is the research design and approach suitable for the kind of research problem/question being posed? Asking why people throw edible food away is less well served by a quantitative design (e.g. a social survey). That design is the best for tackling research problems about the number of people who say they throw out edible food or enquiring which socio-demographic groups are most likely to admit they do while simultaneously disapproving of their own (and others') actions. Ever more detailed technical matters arise when recollecting the National Center on Addiction and Substance Abuse studies about links between (ir)regular family meals and the incidence of tobacco, alcohol or illicit drug use. How dependable are telephone interviews? Does each teenage respondent mean the same thing by family meal? Have intervening variables such as education or income been controlled for? Are conclusions drawn which make the cardinal error of mistaking correlation as cause?

The last group of questions arises from thinking which is already sociologically informed. An instance is the introduction in Chapter 8 of 'good reasons' for 'bad behaviour', an orientation to enquiry inspired by Garfinkel's discussion of problems he encountered when setting up a research project. The key point is that Garfinkel did not look for good psychological reasons such as people's motivations, attitudes or temperaments, or for failures of training, but at the social organization of daily life. In this it is profoundly sociological. Adopting such a way of looking at an existing body of research – some sociological, most not – which has hitherto sought psychological or educational reasons for 'bad behaviour' shifts the research effort in a new and more sociological direction. So, it makes sense of the social organization of circumstances which militate against people following dietary advice and/or information about kitchen hygiene. So, it can also make sense of the process whereby food becomes waste. It shows that there is less a deliberate decision to throw away edible food, more a set of pathways, or conduits of disposal in Evans' vocabulary, along which items 'travel' from being defined as edible food to being put in the bin, an action thereby defining them as waste (2014). And the pathways consist of readily recognizable small dilemmas of daily kitchen life – only half a cauliflower used one day, the remainder not fitting with other ingredients for the next, the unexpected change in an evening's timetable leaving food unused in the fridge. Storing them signals intentions to use them, but other plans leave them longer than expected until the weekend's routine shopping and regular purchasing patterns bring newer, brighter, fresher-looking ingredients in to replace them.

Also sociologically informed is the quest for different meanings, for 'unpicking' pre-existing notions, for looking critically at different usages in different contexts and at their history. So, Trentmann's history of the idea of 'the consumer' helps initiate a line of thinking that exposes its current politicized connotations (2006). So, Ray's commentary points out that 'ethnicity' is the current way of referring to groups whose skin colour is other than white without recourse to the discredited terminology of race (2016). So, 'eating out' can be unravelled the more fully to be able to view those high-level sociological questions about where people eat as part of the general sociological enquiry about the social organization of eating introduced in Chapter 1. So, the anxieties about the apparent loss of cooking skills can be recast to recognize not only the way in which skills change over time, but also to relate them to the history of kitchens and associated technologies. More to the point, as the example of divided Germany shows, links between modes of cooking (using more and less factory- vs home-produced food) and overarching political ideologies and associated economic arrangements can thereby be revealed – providing an instance of the study of food serving as a lens on broader societal features (Weinreb 2017).

This conclusion seeks to compress the overall intent of *Introducing the Sociology of Food and Eating* by providing a kind of checklist. It is selected as an exemplar, but similar quick ones could readily be produced by choosing other chapters and different statements of conventional wisdom. Readers are thus now equipped with a grounding based on what has been accomplished in the field over the last 30 years, ready to follow developments for the next 30.

****

There can be no conclusion to this book. I wrote it to invite readers to think differently about so much they are already familiar with and to *continue* thinking differently. In any case, research does not and should not, stand still. Disciplines go on developing and new interdisciplinary fields emerge, especially as new topics, questions and problems arise. If any readers are inclined to contribute to that continuing research effort, I should like to speed them on their way by urging: 'don't do as I did, do better'.

NOTES

Preface

1. Hilly Janes (2014) *The Three Lives of Dylan Thomas* London: Biteback Publishing.

Chapter 1

1. These are the opening lines of Dylan Thomas' *Under Milk Wood: A Play for Voices* London: Dent, 1954. Janes was living and working in Swansea in South Wales where he and his friend Dylan Thomas were born and where Janes was when he made this painting.

2. See http://necsi.edu/research/social/food_crises.pdf (last accessed 3 October 2017).

3. See https://uk.reuters.com/article/uk-venezuela-looting/wave-of-looting-shutters-stores-spreads-fear-in-venezuela-idUKKBN1F61MD (last accessed 21 January 2018).

4. It is not only a matter of family memories. A link has been established between early pregnancy during the famine and increased weight in adulthood of the offspring (Lumey 1998). Note that the 20 million deaths during World War II from starvation, malnutrition and associated diseases equal the 19.5 million military deaths (Collingham 2011: 1).

5. See www.weforum.org/agenda/2016/12/this-map-shows-how-much-each-country-spends-on-food/. See also *The Economist.* Available at: www.economist.com/blogs/graphicdetail/2015/09/daily-chart-9 (last accessed 12 December 2017); see also www.ons.gov.uk/peoplepopulationandcommunity/personalandhouseholdfinances/expenditure/bulletins/familyspendingintheuk/financialyearendingmarch2016 (last accessed 23 December 2017).

6. So prominent are 'consumer anxieties' about food that just a few serve as the basis for research developed by the geographer Peter Jackson. He advances the argument that 'food-related anxieties should not be understood at a purely individual level' but instead attention must be paid to their social dimensions (2015).

7. Note that in contrasting sociological thinking with conventional wisdoms, this book does not claim that the latter are wrong. They are different and do different things. Equally, the book does not suggest that to pay heed to or believe in conventional wisdoms is somehow mistaken or ill-advised.

8. See http://metro.co.uk/2016/09/20/41-of-children-dont-know-where-eggs-come-from-6140549/#ixzz4NGFS6XAf. See also www.abc.net.au/news/2016-03-10/stephanie-alexander-survey-children-do-not-know-food-origins/7235536 https://primaryito.ac.nz/news-and-features/children-who-dont-know-where-food-comes-from-are-the-future-of-primary/ (last accessed 13 October 2016).

9. See www.huffingtonpost.com/margarette-purvis/beyond-the-grocery-store-_b_1070259.html (last accessed 13 October 2016).

10. See www.express.co.uk/life-style/food/599401/Children-of-Britain-food-apples-problems-education-issues (last accessed 4 November 2016).

11. See https://primaryito.ac.nz/news-and-features/children-who-dont-know-where-food-comes-from-are-the-future-of-primary/ (last accessed 4 November 2016).

12. See www.return2health.net/articles/kids-food/(last accessed 22 October 2016).

13. See www.channel4.com/programmes/food-unwrapped (last accessed 3 February 2017).

14. See www.prnewswire.com/news-releases/nationwide-surveys-reveal-disconnect-between-americans-and-their-food-130336143.html (last accessed 13 October 2016).

15. Such as considering whether alarm is displayed at children's/adults' ignorance of other topics, asking about levels of children's levels of media literacy generally, or if they display any scepticism about food advertising or packaging (Elliott 2009).

16. Upton Sinclair (1985 [1906]) *The Jungle* New York: Penguin p. 43.

17. See www.dailymail.co.uk/news/article-2566242/The-market-butcher-forced-stop-displaying-meat-game-townies-object.html (last accessed 24 February 2014).

18. See http://data.worldbank.org/indicator/SL.AGR.EMPL.ZS (last accessed 3 November 2016).

19. See www.un.org/en/development/desa/news/population/world-urbanization-prospects-2014.html (last accessed 4 November 2016).

20. See www.ers.usda.gov/data-products/ag-and-food-statistics-charting-the-essentials/ag-and-food-sectors-and-the-economy/ (last accessed 3 January 2017).

21. See www.gov.uk/government/publications/food-statistics-pocketbook-2017/food-statistics-in-your-pocket-2017-summary#agri-food-sector-employees-gb-q1-2017 (last accessed 14 May 2018).

22. See www.reuters.com/article/us-europe-eggs-idUSKBN1AR0EZ (last accessed 10 August 2017)

23. See http://web.princeton.edu/sites/pei/pdf/CarloPetriniBio.pdf (last accessed 22 January 2018).

24. Online sources accessed 19 January 2017: www.cdc.gov/foodborneburden/2011-foodborne-estimates.html; www.food.gov.uk/sites/default/files/multimedia/pdfs/fds2015.pdf; www.who.int/foodsafety/publications/foodborne_disease/fergreport/en/; www.healthycanadians.gc.ca/eating-nutrition/risks-recalls-rappels-risques/surveillance/illness-estimates-estimations-maladies/yearly-annuel-eng.php; www.fda.gov/food/resourcesforyou/consumers/ucm103263.htm www.karger.com/Article/Abstract/415556.

25. A plant related to the banana.

26. See http://ec.europa.eu/taxation_customs/sites/taxation/files/resources/documents/taxation/vat/how_vat_works/rates/vat_rates_en.pdf (last accessed 23 January 2017).

27. The manufacturers of a 'snowball' successfully securing a legal ruling in Scotland that their spherical products whose desiccated coconut covering explains the name, are cakes (subject to zero-rate tax) not confectionery (subject to tax at the standard rate). See www.dailyrecord.co.uk/news/scottish-news/scots-bakers-lees-tunnocks-win-3778835 (last accessed 4 October 2017).

28. See www.craftbakersassociation.co.uk/uploads/vat_information.pdf (last accessed 4 October 2017).

29. See www.scotlandnow.dailyrecord.co.uk/news/editors-picks/haggis-banned-usa-6736230 *Scotland Now* (last accessed 6 November 2015).

30. See www.fda.gov/AdvisoryCommittees/CommitteesMeetingMaterials/FoodAdvisoryCommittee/default.htm In the US, novel foods are included in the remit of the Food Advisory Committee of the FDA, whereas in the UK, there is a specially dedicated committee to deal with them: the Advisory Committee on Novel Foods and Processes (ACNFP) (www.food.gov.uk/science/novel). In South Africa, such matters are dealt with in

the Department of Agriculture Forestry and Fisheries (see www.daff.gov.za/daffweb3/Branches/Agricultural-Production-Health-Food-Safety/Food-Safety-Quality-Assurance, last accessed 22 October 2017).

Chapter 2

1. Seattle Times staff (2005) *The Seattle Times,* 29 December.

2. London, Bianca (2012) *MailOnline,* 19 November. Available at: www.dailymail.co.uk/femail/article–2235161/Families-manage-sit-dinner-twice-week-10-NEVER-eating-together.html#ixzz4QMBh3NSl (last accessed 10 January 2016).

3. Wilson, Lauren (2014) *news.com.au*, 23 June. Available at: www.news.com.au/lifestyle/health/diet/research-shows-traditional-family-meal-is-rapidly-being-replaced-by-tv-dinners/news-story/72f291eac76449dea00de3011f5309e3 (last accessed 17 November 2016).

4. Thompson, Jonathan (2006) *The Independent on Sunday,* 30 July.

5. See, eg, www.businessnewsdaily.com/3808-families-mealtime-top-priority.html (last accessed 18 November 2016).

6. See www.centeronaddiction.org/addiction-research/reports/importance-of-family-dinners-2007 (last accessed 3 January 2009).

7. (2005) Hanover, New Hampshire: Steerforth Press.

8. He paid each family for his food expenses and took each family out to dinner.

9. See www.oecd.org/social/soc/47571423.pdf (last accessed 18 November 2016).

10. See www.census.gov/content/dam/Census/library/publications/2017/demo/p20-579.pdf (last accessed 4 January 2018).

11. Exceptions are those noticing gendered differences or those with a public health interest in nutritional quality, in which case dietary intake becomes the outcome measure.

12. See www.telegraph.co.uk/women/family/the-new-oxo-family-would-have-lynda-bellingham-turning-in-her-gr/ 2016-new OXO family advert. See also, www.campaignlive.co.uk/article/history-advertising–25-oxo-family/1100698 (last accessed 1 December 2017).

Chapter 3

1. Wallace, Hannah (2016) *Oregon Business,* 23 September. Available at: www.oregonbusiness.com/article/item/17213-generation-diner-why-everyone-you-know-is-eating-out, (last accessed 17 April 2017).

2. Shandwick, Weber (2014) *Food Industry: Asia's leading magazine for the food and beverage industry*, June. Available at: www.apfoodonline.com/index.php/bnf/item/348-weber-shandwick-shares-singaporeans-eating-habits, (last accessed 17 April 2017).

3. Tait, Morgan (2014) *New Zealand Herald*, 19 June.

4. See www.bha.org.uk/wordpress/wp-content/uploads/2015/09/Economic-contribution-of-the-UK-hospitality-industry.pdf (last accessed 3 May 2017).

5. See www.latimes.com/business/la-fi-restaurants-boom-20160217-story.html (last accessed 3 May 2017).

6. See www.food.gov.uk/research/food-and-you/food-and-you-wave-four (last accessed 24 December 2017).

7. See www.ava.gov.sg/docs/default-source/default-document-library/media-release-on-food-wastage-reduction-programme7e327b1875296bf09fdaff00009b1e7c.pdf (last accessed 2 May 2017).

8. Colloquial English for a certain type of British 'café', also known as a 'greasy spoon'. Usually opening early, often closing by the end of the afternoon, these are dedicated to providing filling platefuls of food accompanied by large mugfuls of tea, for those (typically men) doing heavy manual work, driving lorries (trucks) and similar occupations considered to generate a large appetite.

9. Although the literature on restaurants is growing (e.g. Beriss and Sutton 2007).

10. The acceptability of upper- and middle-class women eating in restaurants develops only slowly from the mid-nineteenth century emerging over the century and a half – see Williams 1991.

11. Invaluable discussions of the history of the restaurant in Europe, and, indeed its very definition, are found in Mennell 1985, Spang 2000 which are very different from origins elsewhere e.g. for China, see Yan (2000).

12. This is not always the case: restaurants now have private dining rooms for hire and in nineteenth- and early twentieth-century Paris, *cabinets particuliers* closed off from the restaurant's main dining room, were the 'perfect place for any sort of vaguely sneaky endeavour . . . most intimately associated with tales of seductive food and seducible women' (Spang 2000; 210).

13. See www.theguardian.com/lifeandstyle/2018/jan/15/the-new-rules-of-dining-out-resist-table-hogging-tip-in-cash-dont-moan-about-cakeage?CMP=share_btn_link (last accessed 15 January 2018).

14. To be pernickety, the exercise could take account of where the food is prepared – dwellings without cooking facilities, places of employment with no canteen, schools with no kitchens – meaning that either the person must find the food or the food has to be moved in.

15. The reverse is also being discussed in the UK – whether the break from school, and with it the provision of school meals, leads to children from disadvantaged homes going hungry during the school holidays. See www.bbc.co.uk/news/uk-scotland-40642594 (last accessed 13 September 2017).

16. The name given throughout North America to open air public feasting and drinking associated with a sports event (Bradford and Sherry 2016).

17. For the plight of the urban homeless in poorer nations see, e.g., Flynn 1999.

Chapter 4

1. Mailonline reporter (2014). Available at: www.dailymail.co.uk/news/article-2863508/Prisoners-eat-better-food-Students-slam-Michelle-Obama-pictures-disgusting-lunches-served-schools-America.html, 6 December (last accessed 5 July 2017).

See www.dailymail.co.uk/news/article-2863508/Prisoners-eat-better-food-Students-slam-Michelle-Obama-pictures-disgusting-lunches-served-schools-America.html; see also www.news.com.au/national/public-hospital-food-is-sickening-say-patients/news-story/910903f99f6d8589bbd5cd4415037e90 (both accessed 5 July 2017); see also http://news.bbc.co.uk/1/hi/england/south_yorkshire/5349392.stm (last accessed 11 October 2017); see also www.nzherald.co.nz/nz/news/article.cfm?c_id=1&objectid=2847047 (last accessed 5 July 2017).

2. Jones, Grant (2013) *news.com.au* Available at: www.news.com.au/national/public-hospital-food-is-sickening-say-patients/news-story/910903f99f6d8589bbd5cd4415037e90 (last accessed 5 July 2017).

3. Anon (2006) *BBC News,* 15 September. Available at: http://news.bbc.co.uk/1/hi/england/south_yorkshire/5349392.stm (last accessed 11 October 2017).

4. Macleod, Scott (2002) *New Zealand Herald* 13 September.

5. Known as 'buy ups' in Australia (Williams, Walton and Hannan-Jones 2009). In England, see also Valentine and Longstaff (1998).

6. The ingredients for this highly processed food are provided in a new report when the school lunch suppliers removed it from the menu. Available at: www.theguardian.com/society/2005/mar/06/schoolmeals (last accessed 18 February 2017).

7. Note that what Slocum et al do not do, incidentally, is analyse JOFR as a television programme. They completely by-pass dissecting it as a commercial enterprise put together by those who cannot afford to ignore having an eye either on viewing figures or future opportunities to continue in business – either for Oliver himself or the company making the programme. Instead, they come close to castigating Oliver and the programme makers for not being good social scientists. Despite this, here, however, is a discussion which conveniently summarizes an additional approach geared to understanding why children do not always like school food and why nutritionists are critical of its quality.

Chapter 5

1. Ferdman, Roberto A. (2015) *The Washington Post* 5 March.

2. Fort, Matthew (2003) *The Guardian* 10 May.

3. Hall, Carmen (2015) *Bay of Plenty Times.* Available at: www.nzherald.co.nz/bay-of-plenty-times/news/article.cfm?c_id=1503343&objectid=11494125 (last accessed 17 October 2017).

4. Daily Mail reporter (2015) *Mailonline* 19 October. Available at: www.dailymail.co.uk/tvshowbiz/article-3280032/Women-lost-cooking-skills-says-Michel-Roux-Jnr-MasterChef-says-mothers-don-t-pass-more.html#ixzz4vlDo472a (last accessed 17 October 2017).

5. See www.dailymail.co.uk/news/article-3707947/Only-stuck-senorita-sneer-dollop-Hellmann-s-Miriam-Clegg-hits-Sam-Cam-serving-mayo-jar-QUENTIN-LETTS-explains-s-fan.html (last accessed 9 December 2017).

6. See www.theguardian.com/uk/2008/feb/23/books.news (last accessed 9 December 2017). Did critics know Delia Smith's 1971 *How to Cheat at Cooking*? That book is described on the back as showing 'you how to escape long hours of kitchen drudgery by a little clever "cheating"' based on recipes using 'quick convenience foods – canned, frozen, dehydrated and pre-cooked' at a time when the disadvantage of using convenience food is its being 'dull and tasteless' rather than signalling laziness.

7. See www.todayonline.com/lifestyle/food/singaporeans-cant-cook; www.straitstimes.com/singapore/the-decline-of-home-cooking; www.asiaone.com/singapore/cook-home-its-hassle-many (last accessed 17 October 2017).

8. More anecdotally, but just as telling are autobiographical commentaries by those finding themselves in a strange country, yearning for a 'taste of home' who ask for family recipes: the actor Madhur Jaffrey recounts how her homesickness for familiar dishes started her parallel career as a cookery book writer and TV chef (BBC World Service 'The Food Chain'. Available at: www.bbc.co.uk/programmes/w3csv0pl (last accessed 9 October 2017) and a different route

for Singaporean chef Violet Oon. See www.channelnewsasia.com/news/singapore/mental-block-against-singapore-food-impossible-to-overcome-viole-8085446 (last accessed 9 October 2017).

9. See www.fooddive.com/news/convenience-food-sales-growth-2016/433092/ (last accessed 4 January 2017); Mintel 'Attitudes towards Ready Meals and Ready-to-Cook Foods – UK' June 2017. Available at: http://reports.mintel.com/display/793303/?__cc=1 (last accessed 12 July 2017).

Chapter 6

1. Clayton, Rachel (2017) *BusinessDay* 4 July. Available at: www.stuff.co.nz/business/94359166/my-food-bag-criticised-by-customers-for-unnecessary-packaging (last accessed 26 August 2017).

2. Law, James S (2015) *news.com.au* 14 March. Available at: www.news.com.au/finance/business/retail/customers-up-in-arms-about-excessive-packaging/news-story/21863691c4bf979489bdafd3d32a2d21 (last accessed 26 August 2016).

3. Ridler, James (2016) *Food Manufacture* 26 August. Available at: www.foodmanufacture.co.uk/Packaging/Top-chefs-call-for-polystyrene-packaging-ban/?utm_source=newsletter_daily&utm_medium=email&utm_campaign=26-Aug-2016&c=OsRJqH88G%2FMiQhN5gUKyihQCC%2FBSwSxC&p2 (last accessed 26 August 2016).

4. Easily followed online.

5. These are notoriously commercially fragile; several are closed, others reinvent themselves.

6. See www.incpen.org/displayarticle.asp?a=2491&c=6 (last accessed 7 September 2017).

7. See www.confectionerynews.com/Article/2018/02/15/Don-t-ditch-the-plastic-just-yet/?utm_source=Newsletter_Subject&utm_medium=email&utm_campaign=Newsletter%2BSubject&c=4cnkg3NAKh8PkBVuItXjQeqnQmP4M%2FrD (last accessed 20 February 2018).

8. I am indebted to Marion Familton for introducing me to this example.

9. Note that in asking what is food packaging, one answer illuminates a porous boundary between containers for storage as well as transport together with those also used as receptacles in which foods are cooked.

10. Polyethylene terephthalate.

11. As a schoolboy he helped both parents (his father in his brickyard and his mother in the garden) later helping to sell surplus preserves of homegrown foods – a routine task of running an early nineteenth-century household.

Chapter 7

1. Fisher, Marla Jo (2014) *The Orange County Register* 25 December. Available at: www.ocregister.com/2014/12/25/how-did-chinese-become-americas-favorite-ethnic-cuisine (last accessed 3 July 2017).

2. Hartman, Lauren R. (2016) *Food Processing* 29 January. Available at: www.foodprocessing.com/articles/2016/fl-fi-ethnic-foods (last accessed 3 July 2017).

3. Walsh, Dave (2012) *Weekend Notes* 31 August. Available at: www.weekendnotes.com/which-is-your-favourite-ethnic-food; (last accessed 3 July 2017).

4. Ibid.

5. At the time a restaurateur/food writer, later a sociologist.

6. I am indebted to Peter Jackson for reminding me of Heldke's book.

7. The literature on ethnic foods infrequently includes the cuisines of the majority – often the subject of separate enquiries (e.g. for the US Mintz 2013).

8. 'Ethnic Foods Shaping the UK Market' 2013 Available at: www.foodmanufacture.co.uk/Ingredients/Ethnic-foods-shaping-UK-market#Authenticity (last accessed 4 July 2017).

9. Butetown Archives, Cardiff; oral history collection interview with Selma Salaman, 31 July 1989.

10. An investigation worth repeating now to follow up impressions that there are geographic concentrations of certain types of 'ethnic' restaurants in particular cities.

11. *The Forsyte Saga.*

12. It is important not to forget that both corporations and food writers have commercial interests, even if the latter are also keen to promote whatever is their view of good eating.

13. 'Stigma' is the ancient Greek word for the mark made on the skin of slaves etc.

Chapter 8

1. Liebelson, Dana (2013) *MotherJones* 13 December. Available at: www.motherjones.com/environment/2013/12/restaurant-food-poisoning-bacteria (last accessed, 9 January 2017).

2. Parry, Lizzie and Hodgekiss, Anna (2014) *Mailonline* 1 August. Available at: www.dailymail.co.uk/health/article-2713388/Only-12-people-eat-washing-hands-despite-germier-park-bench-escalator-rail.html#ixzz4VG9KUN00 (last accessed, 9 January 2017).

3. Morgan, Roy (2015) *RoyMorgan* 7 January. Available at: www.roymorgan.com/findings/6003-most-of-us-dont-eat-enough-fruit-veg-201501062212 (last accessed, 9 January 2017).

4. Chandler, Victoria (2017) *Good Housekeeping* 6 July. Available at: www.goodhousekeeping.co.uk/lifestyle/declutter-your-home/fridge-storage-tips (last accessed 10 January 2018).

5. Anon (2016) *KingdomFM* 15 October Available at: www.kingdomfm.co.uk/news/local-news/most-scots-ignoring-healthy-eating-tips/ (last accessed, 9 January 2017).

6. See www.who.int/mediacentre/news/releases/2017/lack-investment-breastfeeding/en/ (last accessed 30 August 2017).

7. What Biltekoff reminds her readers is dubbed 'nutritionism' by Gyorgy Scrinis to refer to thinking of food's goodness solely in terms of nutrients, that 'eclipses other modes of understanding and assessing the value of food, such as level of processing, means of agricultural production, sensual properties and cultural or historical significance' (2013: 33).

Chapter 9

1. Petaling, Jaya (2016) *TheStaronline* 31 May. Available at: www.thestar.com.my/news/nation/2016/05/31/food-and-money-down-the-drain-research-shows-malaysians-waste-enough-to-feed-millions-daily/ (last accessed 3 March 2017).

2. Ahituv, Netta (2013) *Haaret.com* 7 February. Available at: www.haaretz.com/israel-news/why-do-israelis-throw-away-half-the-food-they-buy.premium-1.502075 (last accessed 3 March 2017).

3. Wee, Heesun (2016) *CNBC.com* 4 March. Available at: www.cnbc.com/2016/03/04/how-to-stop-american-waste-of-food.html (last accessed 3 March 2017).

4. Note that not all that is thrown away is easily deemed edible (e.g. banana peel, walnut shells), also that what is considered food waste is often formally distinguishable from post-harvest losses on the farm, with further losses during transport, storage, processing, manufacture etc.

5. See www.pret.co.uk/en-gb/pret-charity-run (last accessed 19 March 2017). See also www.foodshare.org.nz/ (last accessed 23 January 2016); www.theguardian.com/lifeandstyle/2016/sep/18/real-junk-food-project-revolutionising-how-we-tackle-food-waste?CMP=share_btn_link (last accessed 29 October 2016).

6. Note that the 2013 'scandal' after horse DNA was discovered in manufactured meat products in Europe was not that it was unsafe, but that, by law, labels must declare all the contents.

7. With the generous permission of my co-authors, this section draws extensively on this publication.

8. *Agri*-Food Studies in Australasia and the UK.

Chapter 10

1. A sugary cocoa flavoured cereal manufactured by Kelloggs on sale on several continents, sometimes under different trade names.

2. Guest Blogger (2014) *Oxfam America* 18 November. Available at: https://politicsofpoverty.oxfamamerica.org/2014/11/us-working-families-dependent-food-banks/ (last accessed 8 December 2014).

3. Bulman, May (2017) *Independent* 26 April. Available at: www.independent.co.uk/news/uk/home-news/food-bank-use-uk-rise-continue-poverty-family-children-income-benefits-cuts-report-a7703451.html (last accessed 27 April 2017).

4. Roberts, Gareth (2014) *Mirror* 8 December Available at: www.mirror.co.uk/news/uk-news/tory-baroness-slammed-saying-poor-4767987 (last accessed 8 December 2014).

5. See https://foodpovertyinquiry.files.wordpress.com/2014/12/food-poverty-feeding-britain-final.pdf (last accessed 24 December 2014).

6. See www.theguardian.com/society/2014/dec/08/poor-cannot-cook-peer-eats-words (last accessed 8 December 2014).

7. See www.urban75.net/forums/threads/baroness-jenkin-claims-food-banks-are-used-by-the-poor-as-they-dont-know-how-to-cook.329935/page-4 (last accessed 8 December 2014).

8. 'We heard how some landlords may offer tenants only a microwave or one ring on a cooker while calling these facilities a kitchen for rent purposes' (2014: 30). Available at: https://foodpovertyinquiry.files.wordpress.com/2014/12/food-poverty-feeding-britain-final.pdf (last accessed 24 December 2014).

9. This is not to claim that the increase is remotely comparable to the far wider scale, persistent hunger in less wealthy countries (Pottier 1999).

10. See www.newstatesman.com/politics/2014/12/food-banks-why-cant-people-afford-eat-worlds-sixth-richest-country *New Statesman* 8 December 2014 (last accessed 8 December 2014). See also *Hungry Holidays*. Available at: https://feedingbritain.files.wordpress.com/2015/02/hungry-holidays.pdf (last accessed 14 December 2017).

11. This chapter anachronistically refers to 'food poverty' as if it were a standard, neutral term, even though it is relatively new. Note there have been several shifts in relevant terminology e.g. the use of 'food security' is dated towards the end of the 1980 (Midgley 2013).

12. These records are kept for consecutive weeks (one kept for a single week, most for three and one for as many as 90 weeks).

13. Very roughly, today the pension provided by the UK state for one old person is £150 a week.

14. Glazed waterproof cotton cloth.

Chapter 11

1. Andersen, Charlotte Hilton (2012) *The Huffington Post* 6 October. Available at: www.huffingtonpost.com/charlotte-hilton-andersen/food-labels_b_1965889.html (last accessed 14 February 2018).

2. Sinnerton, Jackie (2017) *news.com.au* 30 March. Available at: www.news.com.au/lifestyle/health/diet/public-opposed-to-nannystate-approach-in-battle-of-obesity-study-finds/news-story/36abf8d651bacd03419d3c17cb555a3b (last accessed 14 February 2018).

3. Anon (2012) *The Economist* 15 December.

4. See www.fooddive.com/news/romaine-linked-e-coli-outbreak-continues-to-spread-but-its-origins-remain/523305/ (last accessed 11 May 2018).

5. BBC Radio 4 *Sunday* 7 August 2017. Some would argue that it is the responsibility of the state rather than simply of governments.

6. See www.fdf.org.uk/news.aspx?article=7182 (last accessed 18 November 2017).

7. c.f. The major events of Soviet history 'cannot be fully understood without reference to the presence or the threat of food shortages' (Borrero 2002: 258).

8. See, respectively: www.fda.gov/AboutFDA/Transparency/Basics/ucm194877.htm; www.foodstandards.gov.au/about/whatwedo/Pages/default.aspx; www.foodstandards.gov.scot/about-us (all accessed 14 August 2017).

9. See de Swaan 1988.

10. Ian Wright Director General of the Food & Drink Federation, interviewed on the *Today* programme BBC Radio 4, 24 August 2017.

11. Parliamentarians and civil servants are required publicly to declare receipt of gifts, hospitality etc.—e.g. in the US see www.citizen.org/sites/default/files/gift-rules-for-congress.pdf (last accessed 23 August 2017).

12. See www.gov.uk/government/news/next-stage-of-world-leading-childhood-obesity-plan-announced (last accessed 18 August 2017).

13. Where it seems to be used as a relatively routine term to refer generally to the broad area of study of human dietary behaviour as well as more specifically to refer to the range of activities associated with the foods that people report makes up their diet.

14. Seven managers of various supermarkets, talking to section managers at a trade show, studying business sections of newspapers, information from trade associations, the contents of many trade publications such as *Progressive Grocer* and *Supermarket News* – readers can follow parallel content in the UK publication *Food Manufacture* freely available online at www.foodmanufacture.co.uk/.

REFERENCES

Abbots, E. (2013) 'Negotiating Foreign Bodies: Migration, Trust and the Risky Business of Eating in Highland Ecuador' *in* Abbots, E.J. and Lavis, A. (eds) *Why we Eat, How we Eat* Aldershot: Ashgate.

Abbots, E. (2014). 'The Fast and the Fusion: Class, Colonialism and the Remaking of *Comida Típica* in Highland Ecuador' *in* J. A. Klein and A. Murcott, (eds) *Food Consumption in Global Perspective* London: Palgrave Macmillan.

Adelman, J. and Haushofer, L. (2018). 'Introduction: Food as Medicine, Medicine as Food' *Journal of the History of Medicine and Allied Sciences* 73(2): 127–134.

Adjrah, Y. et al (2013) 'Socio-economic Profile of Street Food Vendors and Microbiological Quality of Ready-to-Eat Salads in Lomé' *International Food Research Journal* 20(1): 65–70.

Aiko, P. (1989) 'The Changing Role of Reindeer in the Life of the Sámi' *in* Clutton-Brock, J. (ed.) *The Walking Larder* London: Unwin Hyman.

Alexander, C. and Smaje, C. (2008) 'Surplus Retail Food Redistribution' *Resources, Conservation and Recycling* 52(11): 1290–1298.

Alexander, J. (1993) *In Defense of Garbage* Westport, CT: Praeger.

Allen, P. and Sachs, C. (2007) 'Women and Food Chains: The Gendered Politics of Food' *International Journal of Sociology of Agriculture and Food* 15(1): 1–23.

Andersen, B. and Hedegaard, L. (2015). '"Reflection": Fighting Five Food Myths about the "Good Old Days"' *Food and Foodways*, 23(4): 286–294.

Anderson, A. (1995) 'Historical and Archaeological Aspects of Muttonbirding in New Zealand' *New Zealand Journal of Archaeology* 17: 35–55.

Anderson, W. (1971) 'Identifying the Convenience-Oriented Consumer' *Journal of Marketing Research* 8(2): 179–183.

Appadurai, A. (1988) 'How to Make a National Cuisine: Cookbooks in Contemporary India' *Comparative Studies in Society and History* 30(1) 3–24.

Aron, J. (1975) *The Art of Eating in France* London: Peter Owen.

Aron, J. (1979) 'The Art of Using Leftovers: Paris, 1850–1900' *in* Forster, E. and Ranum, O. (eds) *Food and Drink in History* Baltimore: Johns Hopkins University Press.

Åsebø, K. et al (2007) 'Farmer and Consumer Attitudes at Farmers' Markets in Norway' *Journal of Sustainable Agriculture* 30(4); 67–93.

Ashis, N. (2004) 'The Changing Popular Culture of Indian Food' *South Asia Research* 24(1): 9–19.

Atkins, P.J. (1991) 'Sophistication Detected: or, The Adulteration of the Milk Supply, 1850–1914' *Social History* 16(3): 317–339.

Atkins, P. (ed.) (2012) *Animal Cities; Beastly Urban Histories* London: Routledge.

Atkinson, P. (2017) *Thinking Ethnographically* London: Sage.

Autio, M. and Heinonen, V. (2007) 'Representation of Consumerism in the Finnish Consumer Policy Programmes 1983–2007' *in Proceedings of the Nordic Consumer Policy Research Conference* Helsinki, 3–5 October.

Avieli, N. (2011) 'Dog Meat Politics in a Vietnamese Town' *Ethnology* 50(1): 59–78.

Backett, Kathryn (1992) 'Taboos and Excesses: Lay Health Moralities in Middle Class Families' *Sociology of Health & Illness* 14(2): 255–274.

References

Bahr, P.R. (2007) 'Race and Nutrition: An Investigation of Black–White Differences in Health-Related Nutritional Behaviours' *Sociology of Health & Illness* 29(6): 831–856.

Ball, R.A and Lilly, J.R. (1982) 'The Menace of Margarine: The Rise and Fall of a Social Problem' *Social Problems* 29(5): 488–498.

Banton, M. (2015) *What we Now Know about Race and Ethnicity* New York: Berghahn.

Barton, K. L., Wrieden, W.L. and Anderson A. S. (2011) 'Validity and Reliability of a Short Questionnaire for Assessing the Impact of Cooking Skills Interventions' *Journal of Human Nutrition and Dietetics* 24(6): 588–595.

Beard, M. (2016) *SPQR: A History of Ancient Rome* London: Profile Books.

Beck, M.E. (2007) 'Dinner Preparation in the Modern United States' *British Food Journal* 109(7): 531–547.

Becker, H. S. (1963) *Outsiders: Studies in the Sociology of Deviance*. New York: The Free Press.

Becker, H. and Geer, B. (1957a) 'Participant Observation and Interviewing: A Comparison' *Human Organisation* 16: 28–32 [reprinted in Filstead, W.J. (ed.) (1970) *Qualitative Methodology* Chicago: Markham.]

Becker, H. and Geer, B. (1957b) 'Participant observation and interviewing: A rejoinder' *Human Organisation* 16: 39–40.

Beecher, C.E. (1874) *Miss Beecher's Housekeeper and Healthkeeper: Containing Five Hundred Recipes for Economical and Healthful Cooking; Also, Many Directions for Securing Health and Happiness* New York: Harper and Brothers.

Bender, A.E. (1975) *Dictionary of Nutrition and Food Technology*, London: Butterworths (4th edn).

Bennett, J.W. (1943) 'Food and Social Status in a Rural Society' *American Sociological Review* 8(5): 561–569.

Bennett, J.W., Smith, H.L. and Passin, H. (1942) 'Food and Culture in Southern Illinois – A Preliminary Report' *American Sociological Review* 7(5): 645–660.

Bentley, A. (2001) 'Martha's Food: Whiteness of a Certain Kind' *American Studies*, 42(2): 89–100.

Bentley, A. (2002) 'Inventing Baby Food: Gerber and the Discourse of Infancy in the United States' *in* Belasco, W. and Scraton, P. (eds) (2014) *Food Nations: Selling Taste in Consumer Societies* London: Routledge.

Bergeaud-Blackler, F. (2004) 'Social Definitions of Halal Quality: The Case of Maghrebi Muslims in France' *in* Harvey, M., McMeekin, A. and Warde, A. (eds) *Qualities of Food: Alternative Theories and Empirical Approaches,* Manchester: Manchester University Press.

Bergflødt, S., Amilien, V. and Skuland, S.E., 2012. 'Nordic Food Culture(s)-Thoughts and Perspectives By Way of Introduction' *Anthropology of Food,* S7. Available at: www.researchgate.net/profile/Virginie_Amilien/publication/277119678_Nordic_Food_Cultures_-_Thoughts_and_perspectives_by_way_of_introduction/links/5630d62408ae3de9381cb99e/Nordic-Food-Cultures-Thoughts-and-perspectives-by-way-of-introduction.pdf (last accessed January 2017).

Berris, D. and Sutton, D. (eds) (2007) *The Restaurant Book: Ethnographies of Where We Eat* Oxford: Berg.

Bezerra, I. N. and Sichieri, R. (2009) 'Eating Out of Home and Obesity: A Brazilian Nationwide Survey' *Public Health Nutrition* 12(11), 2037–2043.

Biggerstaff, M., Morris, P. and Nichols-Casebolt, A. (2002) 'Living on the Edge: Examination of People Attending Food Pantries and Soup Kitchens,' *Social Work*, 47(3): 267–277.

Biltekoff, C. (2013). *Eating Right in America: The Cultural Politics of Food and Health* Durham, NC: Duke University Press.

Bishop, L. (2007) 'A Reflexive Account of Reusing Qualitative Data: Beyond Primary/Secondary Dualism' *Sociological Research Online* 12(3): 1–14.

Bittman, M. (2011) 'A Food Manifesto for the Future' *New York Times Magazine* February.

Black, R., (2007) 'Eating Garbage: Socially Marginal Food Provisioning Practices' *in* MacClancy, J., Henry, J. and Macbeth, H. (eds) *Consuming the Inedible: Neglected Dimensions of Food Choice* New York: Berghahn Books.

Bloch, M. (1999) 'Commensality and Poisoning' *Social Research* 66(1) 133–149.

Bloom, J. (2010) *American Wasteland: How America Throws Away Nearly Half of its Food (and What We Can Do about It)* Boston: Da Capo Lifelong Books.

Bloomfield, S. (2001) 'Gastrointestinal Disease in the Domestic Setting: What are the Issues?' *Journal of Infection* 43(1): 23–29.

Blumer, H. (1971) 'Social Problems as Collective Behavior' *Social Problems* 18(3): 298–306.

Bolton-Smith, C., Smith, W.C.S., Woodward, M. and Tunstall-Pedoe, H. (1991) 'Nutrient Intakes of Different Social-class Groups: Results from the Scottish Heart Health Study' *British Journal of Nutrition* 65(3): 321–335.

Borrero, M. (2002) 'Food and the Politics of Scarcity in Urban Soviet Russia, 1917–1941' *in* Belasco, W.J. and Scranton, P. (eds) *Food Nations* New York: Routledge.

Bose, Christine (1979) 'Technology and Changes in the Division of Labor in the American Home' *Women's Studies International Quarterly* 2(3): 295–304.

Botonaki, A. and Konstadinos, M. (2010) 'Revealing the Values behind Convenience Food Consumption' *Appetite* 55(3): 629–638.

Bourdieu, P. (1977) *Outline of a Theory of Practice* Cambridge: Cambridge University Press.

Bourdieu, P. (1984) *Distinction: A Social Critique of Taste* Cambridge, MA: Harvard University Press.

Bourne, G. (1984 [1912]) *Change in the Village* Harmondsworth: Penguin.

Bowen, S., Elliott, S. and Brenton, J. (2014) 'The Joy of Cooking?' *Contexts* 13(3): 20–25.

Bradby, Hannah (2003) 'Describing Ethnicity in Health Research,' *Ethnicity & Health*, 8(1): 5–13.

Bradford, T.W. and Sherry Jr, J.F. (2016) 'Grooving in the Ludic Foodscape: Bridled Revelry in Collegiate Tailgating' *Journal of Consumer Culture* 17(3): 774–793.

Brannen, J., O'Connell, R. and Mooney, A. (2013) 'Families, Meals and Synchronicity: Eating Together in British Dual Earner Families' *Community, Work & Family* 16(4): 417–434.

Brannen, J., Dodd, K., Oakley, A. and Storey, P. (1994) *Young People, Health and Family Life* Buckingham: Open University Press.

Branscum, P., Kaye, G., Succop, P., Sharma, M. (2010) 'An Evaluation of Holiday Weight Gain Among Elementary-aged Children' *Journal of Clinical Medicine Research* 2(4): 167–171.

Braveman, P.A., Cubbin, C., Egerter, S., Williams, D.R. and Pamuk, E. (2010) 'Socioeconomic Disparities in Health in the United States: What the Patterns Tell Us' *American Journal of Public Health* 100(S1): S186–S196.

Brembeck, H. (2005) 'Home to McDonald's. The Domestication of McDonald's in Sweden' *in* Ekström, K.M. and Brembeck, H. (eds) *E – European Advances in Consumer Research, Vol 7* Goteborg: Association for Consumer Research.

Brinkly, C. and Vitiello, D. (2014) 'From Farm to Nuisance: Animal Agriculture and the Rise of Planning Regulation' *Journal of Planning History* 13(2): 113–135.

Brown, N. and Michael, M. (2003) 'A Sociology of Expectations: Retrospecting Prospects and Prospecting Retrospects' *Technology Analysis & Strategic Management* 15(1) 3–18.

Bruhn, C.M. and Schutz, H.G. (1999) 'Consumer Food Safety Knowledge and Practices' *Journal of Food Safety* 19(1): 73–87.

Bryant, A., Bush, L. and Wilk, R. (2013) 'The History of Globalization and the Food Supply' *in* Murcott, A. et al (ed.) *The Handbook of Food Research* London: Bloomsbury Academic.

Buckley, M., Cowan, C. and McCarthy, M. (2007) 'The Convenience Food Market in Great Britain: Convenience Food Lifestyle (CFL) Segments' *Appetite* 49(3): 600–617.

Bugge, A.B. and Almås, R. (2006) 'Domestic Dinner: Representations and Practices of a Proper Meal Among Young Suburban Mothers' *Journal of Consumer Culture* 6(2): 203–228.

189

References

Burgess, R.G. and Morrison, M. (1998) 'Ethnographies of Eating in an Urban Primary School' *in* Murcott, A (ed.) *The Nation's Diet: The Social Science of Food Choice* London: Longman.

Burnett, J. (1963) 'The Baking Industry in the Nineteenth Century' *Business History* 5(2): 98–108.

Burnett, J. (1989) *Plenty and Want: A Social History of Food in England from 1815 to the Present* London: Routledge.

Burnett, J. (2016) *England Eats Out: A Social History of Eating Out in England from 1830 to the Present* London: Routledge.

Burnett, K. (2014) 'Commodifying Poverty: Gentrification and Consumption in Vancouver's Downtown Eastside' *Urban Geography* 35(2): 157–176.

Burnett, K. and Murphy, S. (2014) 'What Place for International Trade in Food Sovereignty?' *The Journal of Peasant Studies* 41(6): 1065–1084.

Busch, L. (2004) 'Grades and Standards in the Social Construction of Food' *in* Lien, M.E. and Nerlich, B. (eds) *The Politics of Food* Oxford: Berg.

Caldwell, M.L. (2004) 'Domesticating the French Fry: McDonald's and Consumerism in Moscow' *Journal of Consumer Culture* 4(1): 5–26.

Cameron, D. (2007) *The Myth of Mars and Venus* Oxford: Oxford University Press.

Campbell, H., Evans, D. and Murcott, A., (2017) 'Measurability, Austerity and Edibility: Introducing Waste into Food Regime Theory' *Journal of Rural Studies* (51): 168–177.

Caner, C. and Pascall, M.A. (2010) 'Consumer Complaints and Accidents Related to Food Packaging' *Packaging Technology and Science* 23(7): 413–422.

Cappellini, B, Marshall, D. and Parsons, E. (eds) (2016) *The Practice of the Meal: Food, Families and the Market Place* London: Routledge.

Caraher, M. and Lang, T. (1999) 'Can't Cook, Won't Cook: A Review of Cooking Skills and their Relevance to Health Promotion' *International Journal of Health Promotion and Education* 37(3): 89–100.

Carolan, M. (2016) *The Sociology of Food and Agriculture* London: Routledge.

Carrington, C. (1999) *No Place Like Home* Chicago: Chicago University Press.

Carsten, J. (1995) 'The Substance of Kinship and the Heat of the Hearth: Feeding, Personhood, and Relatedness among Malays in Pulau Langkawi' *American Ethnologist* 22(2): 223–241.

Castellion, G. and Markham, S.K. (2013) 'Perspective: New Product Failure Rates: Influence of *Argumentum ad Populum* and Self-Interest' *Journal of Product Innovation Management* 30(5): 976–979.

Cathcart, E.P. and Murray, A.M.T. (1939) 'A Note on the Percentage Loss of Calories as Waste on Ordinary Mixed Diets' *Journal of Hygiene* 39(01): 45–50.

Chang J. and Hsieh, A. (2006) 'Leisure Motives of Eating Out in Night Markets' *Journal of Business Research* 59(12): 1276–1278.

Charles, N. and Kerr, M. (1988) *Women, Food and Families*, Manchester: Manchester University Press.

Cheng, S., Olsen, W., Southerton, D. and Warde, A. (2007) 'The Changing Practice Of Eating: Evidence from UK Time Diaries, 1975 and 2000' *British Journal of Sociology* 58(1): 39–36.

Chivers, T.S. (1973) 'The Proletarianisation of a Service Worker' *The Sociological Review* 21(4): 633–656.

Chukuezi, C.O. (2010) 'Food Safety and Hygienic Practices of Street Food Vendors in Owerri, Nigeria' *Studies in Sociology of Science* 1(1): 50–57.

Chung, S., Popkin, B.M., Domino, M.E., Stearns, S.C. (2007) 'Effect of Retirement on Eating Out and Weight Change: An Analysis of Gender Differences' *Obesity* 15:4: 1053–1060.

Cinotto, S. (2006) '"Everyone Would Be Around the Table": American Family Mealtimes in Historical Perspective, 1850–1960' *New Directions for Child and Adolescent Development* 111: 17–34.

Coates, K. and Silburn, R. (1970) *Poverty: The Forgotten Englishman* London: Penguin.

Cochoy, F. (2004) 'Is the Modern Consumer a Buridan's Donkey? Product Packaging and Consumer Choice' in Brembeck, H. and Ekström, K.M. (eds) *Elusive Consumption* Oxford: Berg.

Cochoy, F. (2007) 'A Sociology of Market-things: On Tending the Garden of Choices in Mass Retailing' *The Sociological Review* 55(s2): 109–129.

Cochoy, F. (2015) *On the Origins of Self-service* London: Routledge.

Cochoy, F. and Crandclément-Chaffy, C. (2005) 'Publicizing Goldilocks' Choice at the Supermarket: The Political Work of Shopping Packs, Carts and Talk' in Latour, B. and Weibel, P. (eds) *Making Things Public: Atmospheres of Democracy* Cambridge, MA: MIT Press.

Cohen, E. and Avieli, N. (2004) 'Food in Tourism: Attraction and Impediment' *Annals of Tourism Research* 31(4): 755–778.

Cohen, K.M. et al (2002) 'Food management practices used by people with limited resources to maintain food sufficiency as reported by nutrition educators' *Journal of the American Dietetic Association* 102(12): 1795–1799

Cohen, S. (1972) *Folk Devils and Moral Panics* London: MacGibbon and Kee.

Cohen, Y., Krumer-Nevo, M. and Avieli, N. (2017) 'Bread of Shame: Mechanisms of Othering in Soup Kitchens' *Social Problems*, 64(3): 1–16.

Coles, R. (2003) 'Introduction' in Coles, R., McDowell, D. and Kirwan, M. J. (eds) *Food Packaging Technology* Oxford: Blackwell.

Coles, R. (2012) 'Packaging for a Sustainable Future – the Need to Cost Effectively Design for the End User and the Environment' *Sustainable Innovation 2012: Resource Efficiency, Innovation and Lifestyles* 67–75.

Collingham, L. (2006) *Curry: A Tale of Cooks and Conquerors* Oxford: Oxford University Press.

Collingham, L. (2011) *Taste of War: World War II and the Battle for Food* London: Penguin.

Comfort, Megan L. (2002) '"Papa's house", The Prison as Domestic and Social Satellite' *Ethnography* 3(4): 467–499.

Connell, P.M. and Miller, E.G. (2012) 'Encouraging Healthier Food Consumption: The Role of Product Package Cues' *ACR North American Advances*.

Connor, M. and Armitage, C. J. (2002) *The Social Psychology of Food* Buckingham: Open University Press.

Cook, I. (2004) 'Follow the Thing: Papaya' *Antipode* 36(4): 642–664.

Cook, I. and Crang, P. (1996) 'The World on a Plate: Culinary Culture, Displacement and Geographical Knowledges' *Journal of Material Culture* 1(2): 131–153.

Cook, I., Crang, P. and Thorpe, M. (1998) 'Biographies and Geographies: Consumer Understandings of the Origins of Foods' *British Food Journal* 100(3): 162–167.

Coontz, S. (1992) *The Way We Never Were* New York: Basic Books.

Coveney, J. (2000) 'Food Security and Sustainability: Are we Selling Ourselves Short?' *Asia Pacific Journal of Clinical Nutrition* 9(S1): 97–100.

Coveney J. (2006) *Food, Morals and Meaning* London: Routledge.

Cowan, R. S. (1989) *More Work for Mother: The Ironies of Household Technology from the Open Hearth to the Microwave* London: Free Association Books.

Coxon, T. (1983) 'Men in the Kitchen: Notes from a Cookery Class' in Murcott, A. (ed.) *The Sociology of Food and Eating* Aldershot: Gower.

Crang, P. (1994) 'It's Showtime; On the Workplace Geographies of Display in a Restaurant in Southeast England' *Environment and Planning D: Society and Space* 12(6): 675–704.

Crockett, A.W.B. (1985) 'Injuries from Tin Cans in Patients Presenting to an Accident and Emergency Department' *British Medical Journal* 291(6511): 1767–1768.

Csiszárik-Kocsir, A., Fodor, M. and Varga, E. (2008) 'International and National Trends in the Market of Eating Out' 6th International Conference on Management, Enterprise and Benchmarking: 345–354. Available at: kgk.uni-obuda.hu/sites/default/files/28_Csiszarik.pdf, last accessed 1 May 2017.

References

Cullingford, C. (1985) 'The Idea of the School: The Expectations of Parents, Teachers and Children' *in* C. Cullingford (ed.) *Parents, Teachers and Schools* London: Robert Royce.

Dachner, N. and Tarasuk, V. (2002) 'Homeless "Squeegee Kids"' *Social Science & Medicine* 54(7): 1039–1049.

Dahlin, E.C. (2014) 'The Sociology of Innovation: Organizational, Environmental, and Relative Perspectives' *Sociology Compass* 8(6): 671–687.

Daniel, L.J. and Dawson, P. (2011) 'The Sociology of Innovation and New Biotechnologies' *New Technology, Work and Employment* 26(1): 1–16.

Daniel, P. and Gustafsson, U. (2010) 'School Lunches: Children's Services or Children's Spaces?' *Children's Geographies* 8(3): 265–274.

de Graaf, K. and Kilty, J.M. (2016) 'You are What you Eat' *Punishment & Society* 18(1): 27–46.

de Swaan, A. (1988) *In Care of the State* Cambridge: Polity.

Delva, J., O'Malley, P.M. and Johnston, L.D. (2006) 'Racial/ethnic and Socioeconomic Status Differences in Overweight and Health-related Behaviors among American Students: National Trends 1986–2003' *Journal of Adolescent Health* 39(4): 536–545.

DeSoucey, M. (2016) *Contested Tastes* Princeton: Princeton University Press.

Deutsch, T. (2010) *Building a Housewife's Paradise* Chapel Hill: University of North Carolina Press.

DeVault, M. L. (1991) *Feeding the Family* Chicago: University of Chicago Press.

DeVault, M. L. (1999) 'Comfort and Struggle' *The Annals of the American Academy of Political and Social Science* 561(1): 52–63.

DeVault, M.L. (2006) 'Introduction: What is Institutional Ethnography' *Social Problems*, 53(3): 294.

DeVault, M. L. and McCoy, L. (2002) 'Institutional Ethnography' *in* Gubrium, J. and Holstein, J. (eds) *Handbook of Interview Research* Thousand Oaks, CA: Sage Publications.

Devereux, E. (2013) *Understanding the Media* London: Sage.

Di Domenico, M. and Phillips, N. (2009) 'Sustaining the Ivory Tower: Oxbridge Formal Dining as Organizational Ritual' *Journal of Management Inquiry* 18(4): 326–343.

Di Vita, G., De Salvo, G., Bracco, S., Gulisano, G. and D'Amico, M. (2016) 'Future Market of Pizza' *AGRIS On-line Papers in Economics and Informatics* 8(4): 59–71.

Dixon, J. (2007) 'Supermarkets as New Food Authorities' *in* Burch, D. and Lawrence, G. (eds) *Supermarkets and Agri-food Supply Chains* Cheltenham: Edward Elgar.

Dixon, J. and Banwell, C. (2004) 'Heading the Table: Parenting and the Junior Consumer' *British Food Journal* 106(3): 181–193.

Dobson, B., Beardsworth, A., Keil, T. and Walker, R. (1994) *Diet, Choice and Poverty* London: Family Policy Studies Centre.

Domhoff, G.W. (2007) 'C. Wright Mills, Floyd Hunter, and 50 years of Power Structure Research' *Michigan Sociological Review* 21(Fall):1–54.

Domosh, M. (2003) 'Pickles and Purity: Discourses of Food, Empire and Work in Turn-of-the-Century USA' *Social & Cultural Geography* 4(1): 7–26.

Douglas, M. (1972) 'Deciphering a Meal' *Daedalus* 101(1): 61–81.

Douglas, M. and Nicod, M. (1974) 'Taking the biscuit' *New Society* 19: 744–747.

Downes, D. M. and Rock, P. E. (1982) *Understanding Deviance* Oxford: Clarendon Press.

Driver, C. (1983) *The British at Table: 1940–1980* London: Chatto and Windus.

du Gay, P. (2004) 'Self-Service' *Consumption Markets & Culture* 7(2):149–163.

Duizer, L.M., Robertson, T. and Han, J. (2009) 'Requirements for Packaging from an Ageing Consumer's Perspective' *Packaging Technology and Science* 22(4): 87–197.

Earle, R. (2010) 'If You Eat Their Food . . .' *The American Historical Review* 115(3): 688–713.

Edwards, F., and Mercer, D. (2012) 'Food Waste in Australia: The Freegan Response' *The Sociological Review* 60(2): 174–191.

Eisenberg, M. E., Olson, R. E., Neumark-Sztainer, D., Story, M., and Bearinger, L. H. (2004) 'Correlations Between Family Meals and Psychosocial Well-being Among Adolescents' *Archives of Pediatric and Adolescent Medicine* 158(8): 792–796.

Ekström, K. M. and Brembeck, H. (2005) 'Elusive Consumption in Retrospect' *Report From the Conference* CFK-Rapport 2005.

Ekström, M.P. and Jonsson, I.M. (2005) Family meals: competence, cooking and company. *Food in Contemporary Society*. Available at: www.theses.xlibx.info/t1-economy/983533-1-family-meals-competence-cooking (last accessed 3 June 2010).

Elias, N. (1969) *The Civilising Process* Oxford: Blackwell

Elliott, C.D. (2009) 'Healthy Food Looks Serious: How Children Interpret Packaged Food Products' *Canadian Journal of Communication*, 34(3): 359.

Engels, F. (1969 [1845]) *The Condition of the Working Class in England* London: Panther.

Engler-Stringer, R., and Berenbaum, S. (2007) 'Exploring Food Security with Collective Kitchens Participants in Three Canadian Cities' *Qualitative Health Research* 17(1): 75–84

Erickson, K.A. (2007) 'Tight Spaces and Salsa-stained Aprons: Bodies at Work in American Restaurants' in Berris, D. and Sutton, D. (eds) *The Restaurant Book: Ethnographies of Where We Eat* Oxford: Berg.

Evans, D. (2011) 'Blaming the Consumer–Once Again: The Social and Material Contexts of Everyday Food Waste Practices in some English Households' *Critical Public Health* 21(4): 429–440.

Evans, D. (2014) *Food Waste: Home Consumption, Material Culture and Everyday Life* London: Bloomsbury Publishing.

Evans, D., Campbell, H. and Murcott, A. (2013) *Waste Matters: New Perspectives of Food and Society* Hoboken: Wiley-Blackwell.

Farb, P. and Armelagos, G. (1980) *Consuming Passions* Boston: Houghton Mifflin.

Feldman-Savelsberg, P. (1995) 'Cooking Inside: Kinship and Gender in Bangangté Idioms of Marriage and Procreation' *American Ethnologist* 22(3): 483–501.

Ferrero, S. (2002) 'Comida sin par: Consumption of Mexican Food in Los Angeles: Foodscapes in a Transnational Consumer Society' in Belasco, W. and Scranton, P. (eds) 2014. *Food Nations: Selling Taste in Consumer Societies* Abingdon: Routledge.

Fine, G. A. (1996) 'Justifying Work: Occupational Rhetorics as Resources in Restaurant Kitchens' *Administrative Science Quarterly* 41(1): 90–115.

Finkelstein, J. (1989) *Dining Out: A Sociology of Modern Manners* Cambridge: Polity Press.

Finkelstein, J. (2014) *Fashioning Appetite: Restaurants and the Making of Modern Identity* London: I.B Tauris.

Firth, R. (1973) 'Food Symbolism in a Pre-industrial Society' in Firth, R. *Symbols, Public and Private* London: Allen and Unwin.

Fischler, C. (1980) 'Food Habits, Social Change and the Nature/Culture Dilemma' *Social Science Information* 19(6): 937–953.

Fischler, C. (1988) 'Food, Self and Identity' *Social Science Information* 27(2): 275–292.

Fisher, P. (1987) 'History of School Meals in Great Britain' *Nutrition and Health* 4(4): 189–194.

Flandrin, J-L. (1996) 'Mealtimes in France Before the Nineteenth Century' *Food and Foodways* 6(3–4): 261–282.

Flynn. K. C. (1999) 'Food, Gender, and Survival among Street Adults in Mwanza, Tanzania' *Food and Foodways* 8(3): 175–201.

Foley, W., Spurr, S., Lenoy, L., De Jong, M. and Fichera, R. (2011) 'Cooking Skills are Important Competencies for Promoting Healthy Eating in an Urban Indigenous Health Service' *Nutrition & Dietetics* 68(4): 291–296.

Food Standards Agency (FSA) (2016) *Our Food Future* London Available at: www.food.gov.uk/sites/default/files/media/document/our-food-future-full-report.pdf (last accessed January 2017).

Foreman, S. (1989) *Loaves and Fishes: An Illustrated History of the Ministry of Agriculture, Fisheries and Food, 1889–1989* London: HMSO.

Fortes, M. and Fortes, S. L. (1936) 'Food in the Domestic Economy of the Tallensi' *Africa: Journal of the International African Institute* 9(2): 237–276.

References

Fox, R. (2007) 'Reinventing the Gastronomic Identity of Croatian Tourist Destinations' *Hospitality Management* 26(3): 546–559.

Fox, N. J. et al (2018) 'The Micropolitics of Obesity: Materialism, Markets and Food Sovereignty' *Sociology* 53(1): 111–127.

Frank, D.J., Hironaka, A. and Schofer, E. (2000) 'Environmentalism as a Global Institution: Reply to Buttel' *American Sociological Review* 65(1): 122–127.

Frankenberg, R. (1993) *The Social Construction of Whiteness: White Women, Race Matters* London: Routledge.

Freidberg, S. (2004) *French Beans and Food Scares: Culture and Commerce in an Anxious Age* Oxford: Oxford University Press.

Freidberg, S. (2005) 'French Beans for the Masses' Watson, J.L. and Caldwell, M.L., eds *The Cultural Politics of Food and Eating: A Reader* Hoboken, NJ: Blackwell Publishing.

Freidberg, S. (2009) *Fresh* Cambridge, MA: Harvard University Press.

Friedman, H. and McMichael, P. (1989) 'Agriculture and the State System: The Rise and Decline of National Agricultures, 1870 to the Present' *Sociologia Ruralis* 29(2): 93–117.

Friel, S. et al (2003) 'Social Diversity of Irish Adults, Nutritional Intake' *European Journal of Clinical Nutrition* 57: 865–875.

Frohlich, X. (2016) 'The Informational Turn in Food Politics: The US FDA's Nutrition Label as Information Infrastructure' *Social Studies of Science* 47(2): 145–171.

Fuentes, M. and Brembeck, H. (2017) 'Best for Baby? Framing Weaning Practice and Motherhood in Web-mediated Marketing' *Consumption Markets & Culture* 20(2): 153–175.

Fumey, G., Jackson, P.A. and Raffard, P. (2016) 'Interview with Peter Scholliers, Amy Trubek and Richard Wilk'. *Anthropology of Food* 11. Available at: https://pdfs.semanticscholar.org/c045/87 12b337a053256f2222d8130c7f165a6d99.pdf

Gabaccia, D. R. (1998) *We Are What We Eat: Ethnic Food and the Making of Americans* Cambridge, MA: Harvard University Press.

Gabriel, Y. (1988) *Working Lives in Catering* London: Routledge & Keegan Paul

Garfinkel, H. (1997) *Studies in Ethnomethodology* Englewood Cliffs, NJ: Prentice Hall.

Garthwaite, K.A., Collins, P.J. and Bambra, C. (2015) 'Food for Thought: An Ethnographic Study of Negotiating Ill-health and Food Insecurity in a UK Foodbank' *Social Science & Medicine* 132: 38–44.

Gatley, A. (2016) 'The Significance of Culinary Cultures to Diet' *British Food Journal* 118(1): 40–59.

Geertz, C. (1973) 'Notes on the Balinese Cockfight' in Geertz, C. *The Interpretation of Cultures* New York: Basic Books.

Giddens, A. (2006) *Sociology* Cambridge: Polity Press.

Giddens, A. and Sutton, P.W. (2014) *Essential Concepts in Sociology* Cambridge: Polity Press.

Gilbert, B. B. (1965) 'Health and Politics: The British Physical Deterioration Report of 1904' *Bulletin of the History of Medicine* 39(2): 143–153.

Glasser, I. (1988) *More Than Bread: Ethnography of a Soup Kitchen* Tuscaloosa, AL: University of Alabama Press.

Godderis, R. (2006) 'Dining In: The Symbolic Power of Food in Prison' *The Howard Journal of Crime and Justice* 45(3): 255–267.

Goffman, E. (1956) *The Presentation of Self in Everyday Life* Edinburgh: University of Edinburgh, Monograph No. 2.

Goffman, E. (1961) *Asylums* New York: Doubleday Anchor.

Goffman, E. (1963) *Stigma* London: Penguin.

Goode, J. (2012) 'Feeding the Family When the Wolf's at the Door: The Impact of Over-Indebtedness on Contemporary Foodways in Low-Income Families in the UK' *Food and Foodways* 20(1): 8–30.

Goodman, D. (2001) 'Ontology Matters: The Relational Materiality of Nature and Agro-food Studies' *Sociologia Ruralis* 41(2): 182–200.

Goodman, S. (2018) 'Unpalatable Truths: Food and Drink as Medicine in Colonial British India' *Journal of the History of Medicine and Allied Sciences* 73(2): 205–222.

Goody, J. (1982) *Cooking, Cuisine and Class* Cambridge: Cambridge University Press.

Graf, Katherina (2018) Personal communication.

Greenfield, T.K., Midanik, L.T. and Rogers, J.D. (2000) 'Effects of Telephone versus Face-to-Face Interview Modes on Reports of Alcohol Consumption' *Addiction* 95(2): 277–284.

Griffith, C. and Redmond, E. (2001) 'Evaluating Hygiene Behaviour in the Domestic Setting and the Impact of Hygiene Education' *Journal of Infection* 43(1): 70–74.

Grignon, C. (1996) 'Rule, Fashion, Work: The Social Genesis of the Contemporary French Pattern of Meals' *Food and Foodways* 6(3–4): 205–41.

Grignon, C. (2001) 'Commensality and Social Morphology: An Essay of Typology' in Schollers, P. (2001) *Food, Drink and Identity: Cooking, Eating and Drinking in Europe since the Middle Ages* Oxford: Berg.

Gronow, J. and Holm, L. (forthcoming) *Everyday Eating. A Comparative Study of Meal Patterns 1997–2012 in Denmark, Finland, Norway and Sweden* London: Bloomsbury.

Gronow, J. and Warde, A. (eds) (2001) *Ordinary Consumption* London: Routledge.

Gubrium, J. F. (1975) *Living and Dying at Murray Manor* London: St James Press.

Gullberg, E. (2006) 'Food for Future Citizens: School Meal Culture in Sweden' *Food, Culture & Society* 9(3): 337–343.

Guthman, J. (2003) 'Fast Food/Organic Food: Reflexive Tastes and the Making of "Yuppie Chow"' *Social & Cultural Geography* 4(1): 45–58.

Guthman, J. (2008) '"If They only Knew": Color Blindness and Universalism in California Alternative Food Institutions' *The Professional Geographer* 60(3): 387–397.

Guthman, J. (2011) *Weighing in: Obesity, Food Justice, and the Limits of Capitalism* Berkeley, CA: University of California Press.

Gvion, L. (2012) *Beyond Hummus and Falafel* Berkeley: University of California Press.

Haines, P.S., Hama, M.Y., Guilkey, D.K. and Popkin, B.M. (2003) 'Weekend Eating in the United States is Linked with Greater Energy, Fat, and Alcohol Intake' *Obesity* 11(8): 945–949.

Halkier, B. et al (2007) 'Trusting, Complex, Quality Conscious or Unprotected? Constructing the Food Consumer in Different European National Contexts' *Journal of Consumer Culture* 7(3): 379–402.

Halloran, A. et al (2014) 'Addressing Food Waste Reduction in Denmark' *Food Policy*, 49(1): 294–301.

Hallsworth, A.G. (2013) 'Food Retailing' *in* Murcott, A., Belasco, W. and Jackson, P. (eds) *The Handbook of Food Research* Oxford: Berg.

Halsey, A. H. (2004) *A History of Sociology in Britain* Oxford: Oxford University Press.

Hammersley, M. and Atkinson, P. (2007) *Ethnography: Principles and Practice* London: Taylor & Francis (3rd edn).

Hartwell, H.J., Edwards, J.S. and Beavis, J. (2007) 'Plate Versus Bulk Trolley Food Service in a Hospital: Comparison of Patients' Satisfaction' *Nutrition* 23(3): 211–218.

Harty, C. (2005) 'Innovation in Construction: A Sociology of Technology Approach' *Building Research & Information* 33(6): 512–522.

Harvey, A. (1945) 'Food Preservation in Australian Tribes' *The Australian Journal of Anthropology* 3(7): 191.

Haukanes, H. (2007) 'Sharing Food, Sharing Taste? Consumption Practices, Gender Relations and Individuality in Czech Families' *Anthropology of food* [Online] S3. Available at: aof.revues.org/1912.

Hawkins, G. (2006) *The Ethics of Waste: How we Relate to Rubbish* Lanham, MD: Rowman & Littlefield.

Hawkins, G. (2013) 'The Performativity of Food Packaging: Market Devices, Waste Crisis and Recycling' *in* Evans, D., Campbell, H. and Murcott, A. (eds) *Waste Matters* Oxford: Wiley.

References

Hayden, D. (1978) 'Two Utopian Feminists and Their Campaigns for Kitchenless Houses' *Signs* 4(2): 274–290.

Heaven, B., Bamford, C., May, C. and Moynihan, P. (2013) 'Food Work and Feeding Assistance on Hospital Wards' *Sociology of Health & Illness* 35(4): 628–642.

Heimtun, B. (2010) 'The Holiday Meal: Eating Out Alone and Mobile Emotional Geographies' *Leisure Studies* 29(2) 175–192.

Heldke, L. (2003) *Exotic Appetites* London: Routledge.

Henderson, J., Coveney, J. and Ward, P. (2010) 'Who Regulates Food? Australians' Perceptions of Responsibility for Food Safety' *Australian Journal of Primary Health* 16(4): 344–351.

Hendley, A. (2016) 'Seeking Self-Verification: Motives for Private and Personal Chefs' Boundary Work' *Cultural Sociology* 10(4): 466–482.

Herbert, J. et al (2014) 'Wider Impacts of a 10-week Community Cooking Skills Program – Jamie's Ministry of Food, Australia' *BMC Public Health* 14: 1161.

Heredia-Blonval, K. et al (2014) 'The Salt Content of Products from Popular Fast-Food Chains in Costa Rica' *Appetite* 83: 173–177.

Heritage, John (1987) 'Ethnomethodology' *in* Giddens A. and Turner, J. (eds) *Social Theory Today* Cambridge: Polity Press.

Hess, A. (2007) 'The Social Bonds of Cooking: Gastronomic Societies in the Basque Country' *Cultural Sociology* 1(3): 383–407.

Hierholzer, V. (2007) 'Searching for the Best Standard: Different Strategies of Food Regulation during German Industrialization' *Food and History* 5(2): 295–318.

Hine, T. (1995) *The Total Package: The Secret History and Hidden Meaning of Boxes, Bottles, Cans, and other Persuasive Containers* New York: Little, Brown, and Company.

Hochschild, A. R. (2003) *The Managed Heart: Commercialization of Human Feeling* Berkeley: University of California Press.

Holm, L. (2010) 'Blaming the Consumer: On the Free Choice of Consumers and the Decline in Food Quality in Denmark' *Critical Public Health* 13(2): 139–154.

Holm, L. and Møhl, M. (2000) 'The Role of Meat in Everyday Food Culture: An Analysis of an Interview Study in Copenhagen' *Appetite*, 34(3): 277–283.

Horning, M. L. et al (2016) 'Associations between Nine Family Dinner Frequency Measures and Child Weight, Dietary and Psychosocial Outcomes' *Journal of the Academy of Nutrition and Dietetics* 116(6): 991–999.

Houthakker, H.S. (1957) 'An International Comparison of Household Expenditure Patterns, Commemorating the Centenary of Engel's Law' *Econometrica, Journal of the Econometric Society*, 25(4): 532–551.

Hsu, C. L. (2005) 'A Taste of "Modernity": Working in a Western Restaurant in Market Socialist China' *Ethnography* 6(4): 543–565.

Hughes, D. and Griffiths, L. (1999) 'On Penalties and the *Patient's Charter*: Centralism v de-centralised Governance in the NHS' *Sociology of Health & Illness* 21(1): 71–94.

Hull, E. (2016) 'Supermarket Expansion, Informal Retail and Food Acquisition Strategies: An Example from Rural South Africa' in Klein, J. and Watson, J. L. (eds) *The Handbook of Food and Anthropology* London: Bloomsbury.

Hutchinson, S. (1992) '"Dangerous to Eat": Rethinking Pollution States among the Nuer of Sudan' *Africa* 62(4): 490–504.

Inter-Departmental Committee on Physical Deterioration (1904) *Report of the Inter-Departmental Committee on Physical Deterioration* London: HMSO.

Iversen, V and Raghavendra P.S. (2006) 'What the Signboard Hides: Food, Caste and Employability in Small South Indian Eating Places' *Contributions to Indian Sociology* 40(3): 311–341.

Jabs, J. and Devine, C.M. (2006) 'Time Scarcity and Food Choices: An Overview' *Appetite*, 47(2): 196–204.

Jackson, P. (1998) 'Constructions of "whiteness" in the geographical imagination'. *Area* 30(2): 99–106.

Jackson, P. (2009) *Changing Families, Changing Food* London: Palgrave Macmillan.

Jackson, P. (2015) *Anxious Appetites: Food and Consumer Culture* London: Bloomsbury.

Jackson, P. and Viehoff, V. (2016) 'Reframing Convenience Food' *Appetite* 98: 1–11.

Jackson, P., Olive, S., and Smith, G. (2009) 'Myths of the Family Meal: Re-Reading Edwardian Life Histories' *in* Jackson, P. (ed.) *Changing Families, Changing Food* Basingstoke: Palgrave-Macmillan.

Jackson, P, Ward, N. and Russell, P. (2010) 'Manufacturing Meaning Along the Chicken Supply Chain: Consumer Anxiety and the Spaces of Production' *in* Goodman, D., Goodman M., and Redclift, M. (eds) *Consuming Space: Placing Consumption in Perspective* Aldershot: Ashgate.

Jackson, P., Watson, M. and Piper, N. (2010) 'Locating Anxiety in the Social' *European Journal of Cultural Studies* 16(1): 24–42.

Jackson, P., Evans, D. N., Truninger, M., Meah, A. and Baptista, J. A. (2018) 'The Multiple Ontologies of Freshness in the UK an Portuguese Agrifood Sectors' Transactions of the Institute of British Geographers. Published online. doi: 10017H/tran.12260.

Jackson, P. et al. (2018) *Reframing Convenience Food* London: Palgrave.

Jaffe, J. and Gertler, M. (2006) 'Victual Vicissitudes: Consumer Deskilling and the (Gendered) Transformation of Food Systems' *Agriculture and Human Values* 23(2): 143–162.

Jahoda, M., Lazarsfeld, P.F. and Zeisel, H. (1974 [1972]) *Marienthal: The Sociography of an Unemployed Community* London: Tavistock.

Jakobsen, E. (2015) 'The Future of the Shop and Shopping' *in* Strandbakken, P. and Gronow, J. (eds) *The Consumer in Society* Oslo: Abstrakt Forlag A S.

Jambeck J.R. et al (2015) 'Plastic Waste Inputs from Land into the Ocean' *Science* 347(6223): 768–771.

Janowski, M. and Kerlogue, F. (2007) *Kinship and Food in South East Asia* Copenhagen: NIAS Press.

Jarosz, L. (2011) 'Defining World Hunger: Scale and Neoliberal Ideology in International Food Security Policy Discourse' *Food, Culture and Society* 14(1): 117–136.

Jellil, A., Woolley, E., and Rahimifard, S. (2018) 'Towards Integrating Production and Consumption to Reduce Consumer Food Waste in Developed Countries' *International Journal of Sustainable Engineering*. doi: 10.1080/19397038.2018.1428834. Online 21 January 2018.

Johnston, J. and Baumann S. (2007) 'Democracy versus Distinction: A Study of Omnivorousness in Gourmet Food Writing' *American Journal of Sociology* 113(1): 165–204.

Johnston, J., and Baumann. S. (2015) *Foodies: Democracy and Distinction in the Gourmet Foodscape.* (2nd edn) London: Routledge.

Julier, A. P. (2013) *Eating Together: Food, Friendship and Inequality* Champaign, IL: University of Illinois Press.

Kahn, B. E. and McAllister, L. (1997) *Grocery Revolution. The New Focus on the Consumer* Reading, M A: Addison-Wesley.

Keay, J. (2006) *Spice Route* Berkeley: University of California Press.

Kemmer, D., Anderson, A. S. and Marshall, D.W. (1998) 'The Marriage Menu' *in* Murcott, A. (ed.) *The Nation's Diet* London: Longman

Kim, Y.G., Eves, A. and Scarles, C. (2009) 'Building a model of local food consumption on trips and holidays: a grounded theory approach' *International Journal of Hospitality Management,* 28(3): 423–431

Kirwan, J. (2004) 'Alternative strategies in the UK agro-food system: interrogating the alterity of farmers' markets' *Sociologia Ruralis* 44(4): 395–415

Kjærnes, U. (2001) (ed.) *Eating Patterns: A Day in the Lives of Nordic Peoples* Oslo: National Institute for Consumer Research

References

Kjærnes, U. (2012) 'Ethics and Action' *Journal of Agricultural and Environmental Ethics* 25(2): 145–162.

Klein, J. A. (2017) Personal Communication.

Kling, W. (1943) 'Food waste in distribution and use' *Journal of Farm Economics* 25(4): 848–859.

Kniazeva, M. and Belk, R.W. (2007) 'Packaging as Vehicle for Mythologizing the Brand' *Consumption Markets & Culture* 10(1): 51–69.

Koch, S. (2012) *A Theory of Grocery Shopping* London: Berg.

Koch, S. (2017) 'Trends in Food Retail' *in* Lebesco, K. and Naccarato, P. (eds) *The Bloomsbury Handbook of Food and Popular Culture* London: Bloomsbury.

Koehn, N. F. (1999) 'Henry Heinz and Brand Creation in the Late Nineteenth Century: Making Markets for Processed Food' *The Business History Review* 73(3); 349–393.

Kopytoff, I. (1986) 'The Cultural Biography of Things' *in* Appadurai, A. (ed.) *The Social Life of Things* Cambridge: Cambridge University Press.

Korczynski, M. and Ott, U. (2006) 'The Menu in Society: Mediating Structures of Power and Enchanting Myths of Individual Sovereignty *Sociology*' 40(5): 911–928.

Kyle, R. (1999) *Middle Class Men's Conceptualisations of Food: A Sociological Investigation* Doctoral dissertation: London South Bank University.

Lachat, C. et al (2012) 'Eating Out of Home and Its Association with Dietary Intake: A Systematic Review of the Evidence' *Obesity Reviews* 13(4): 329–346.

Lambie-Mumford, H. (2015) 'Addressing Food Poverty in the UK: Charity, Rights and Welfare'. *SPERI Paper* (18) University of Sheffield.

Lambie-Mumford, H. et al (2014) 'Household Food Security in the UK: A Review of Food Aid, Final Report' Food Ethics Council & University of Warwick.

Lanfranchi, M. et al (2016) 'Household Food Waste and Eating Behaviour: Empirical Survey' *British Food Journal* 118(12): 3059–3072.

Laudan, R. (2016) 'Slow Food: The French Terroir Strategy, and Culinary Modernism' *Food, Culture & Society* 19(3): 133–144.

Laura, J. and Brace-Govan, J. (2014) 'Maternal Visibility at the Commodity Frontier: Weaving Love into Birthday Party Consumption' *Journal of Consumer Culture* 14(1): 88–112.

Laurier, E. and Wiggins, S. (2011) 'Finishing the Family Meal. The Interactional Organisation of Satiety' *Appetite* 56(1): 53–64.

Lavelle, F. et al (2016) 'Learning Cooking Skills at Different Ages: A Cross-sectional Study' *International Journal of Behavioral Nutrition and Physical Activity* 13: 119.

Levenstein, H. (1993) *Paradox of Plenty* Oxford: Oxford University Press.

Levenstein, H. (1998) *Revolution at the Table: The Transformation of the American Diet* Oxford: Oxford University Press.

Levine, S. (2010) *School Lunch Politics: The Surprising History of America's Favorite Welfare Program* Princeton: Princeton University Press.

Lévi-Strauss, C. (1966) 'The Culinary Triangle' *New Society* 8(221): 937–940.

Lewis, H. (2008) 'Eco-design of Food Packaging Materials' *in* Chiellini, E. (ed.) *Environmentally Compatible Food Packaging* Cambridge: Woodhead Publishing Limited.

Lhuissier, A. (2014) 'Anything to Declare? Questionnaires and What they Tell Us' *Anthropology of Food* [Online] S10 aof.revues.org/7625.

Littlejohn, J. (1963) *Westrigg: The Sociology of a Cheviot Village* London: Routledge.

Liu, H. and Lin, L. (2009) 'Food, Culinary Identity, and Transnational Culture: Chinese Restaurant Business in Southern California' *Journal of Asian American Studies*, 12(2): 135–162.

Lockie, S. et al (2002) 'Eating "Green": Motivations Behind Organic Food Consumption in Australia' *Sociologia ruralis* 42(1): 23–40.

López-Azpiazu, I. et al (1999) 'Perceived Barriers of, and Benefits to, Healthy Eating Reported by a Spanish National Sample' *Public Health Nutrition* 2(2): 209–215.

Lu, S. and Fine, G.A. (1995) 'The Presentation of Ethnic Authenticity: Chinese Food as a Social Accomplishment' *The Sociological Quarterly* 36(3): 535–553.

Lugosi, P. (2011) 'Review Essay' *Hospitality & Society* 1(1): 85–89.

Lumey, L.H. (1998) 'Reproductive Outcomes in Women Prenatally Exposed to Undernutrition: A Review of Findings from the Dutch Famine Birth Cohort' *Proceedings of the Nutrition Society* 57(1): 129–135.

Lupton, D. (2000) 'The Heart of the Meal: Food Preferences and Habits Among Rural Australian Couples' *Sociology of Health & Illness*. 22(1): 94–109.

Lynd, R.S. and Lynd, H.M. (1929) *Middletown; A Study in Contemporary American Culture*. Oxford: Harcourt, Brace.

Lysons, D. (1976) 'Market Gardens in London', in *The Environs of London: Volume 4, Counties of Herts, Essex and Kent*. 573–576. *British History Online*. Available at: www.british-history.ac.uk/london-environs/vol4/573–576 (last accessed 4 December 2016).

Ma, H. et al (2006) 'Getting Rich and Eating Out: Consumption of Food Away from Home in Urban China' *Canadian Journal of Agricultural Economics* 54(1): 101–119.

MacClancy, J., Macbeth, H., and Henry, J. (2007) 'Introduction: Considering the Inedible, Consuming the Ineffable' *in* MacClancy, J., Macbeth, H. and Henry, J. (eds) *Consuming the Inedible: Neglected Dimensions of Food Choice* Oxford: Berghahn Books.

Mackenzie, M. (1993) 'Is the Family Meal Disappearing?' *Journal of Gastronomy*, 7(1): 36–37.

Maes, E. et al (2017) 'A Vehicle of Punishment? Prison Diets in Belgium Circa 1900' *Food, Culture and Society* 20(1) 77–100

Mäkelä, J. (2000) 'Cultural Definitions of the Meal' in Meiselman, H. L. (ed.) *Dimensions of the Meal: The Science, Culture, Business and Art of Eating* New York: Aspen Publishers.

Mäkelä, J., Kjærnes, U. and Ekström, M.P (2001) 'What Did They Eat' *in* Kjærnes, U (ed.) *Eating Patterns: A Day in the Lives of Nordic Peoples* Oslo: National Institute for Consumer Research.

Mao, A.A. and Odyuo, N. (2007) 'Traditional Fermented Foods of the Naga Tribes of Northeastern India' *Indian Journal of Traditional Knowledge* 6(1): 37–41.

Markham, T. (2017) *Media and Everyday Life: A Textbook*. Basingstoke: Palgrave Macmillan.

Marra, F. (2014) 'Fighting Food Loss and Food Waste in Japan' *Innovative Research in Japanese Studies* 1(1): 50–88.

Mars, G. and Nicod, M. (1984) *The World of Waiters* London: Allen & Unwin.

Mars, L. (1997) 'Food and Disharmony: Commensality among Jews' *Food and Foodways* 7(3): 189–202.

Marshall, D., Pettinger, C. and Meiselman, H.L. (2009) 'Revisiting British Meals' *in* Meiselman, H.L. (ed.) *Meals in Science and Practice: Interdisciplinary Research and Business Applications* Oxford: Woodhead Publishing Limited.

Martin, K. et al (2004) 'Social Capital is Associated with Decreased Risk of Hunger' *Social Science and Medicine*, 58(12): 2645–2654.

Martin-Biggers, J. et al (2014) 'Come and Get It! A Discussion of Family Mealtime Literature and Factors Affecting Obesity Risk' *Advances in Nutrition* 5(3): 235–247.

Mason, J. (1987) 'A Bed of Roses? Women, Marriage and Inequality in Later Life' *in* Allatt, P. et al (eds) *Women and the Life Cycle* London: Macmillan.

Matalas, A.L. and Grivetti, L.E. (2007) 'Non-Food During the Famine: the Athens Famine Survivor Project' *in* MacClancy, J., Henry, J. and Macbeth, H. (eds) (2009) *Consuming the Inedible: Neglected Dimensions of Food Choice* Oxford: Berghahn.

Maye-Banbury, A. and Casey, R. (2016) 'The Sensuous Secrets of Shelter: How Recollections of Food Stimulate Irish Men's Reconstructions of their Early Formative Residential Experiences in Leicester, Sheffield and Manchester' *Irish Journal of Sociology* 24(3): 272–292.

McClancy, J., Henry, J. and Macbeth, H. (2007) *Eating the Inedible* Oxford: Berghan Books.

McIntosh, W.A. (2010) 'Mothers and Meals. The Effects of Mothers' Meal Planning and Shopping Motivations on Children's Participation in Family Meals' *Appetite* 55(3): 623–628.

References

McIntyre, L. (2003). 'Food Security: More than a Determinant of Health' *Policy Options*: 46–51.

McKenzie, L. (2015) *Getting By* Bristol: Policy Press.

McKeown, T. (1976b) *The Role of Medicine: Dream, Mirage or Nemesis* London: Nuffield Provincial Hospitals Trust.

McKinlay, J.B. and McKinlay, S.M. (1977) 'The Questionable Contribution of Medical Measures to the Decline of Mortality in the United States in the Twentieth Century' *The Milbank Memorial Fund Quarterly. Health and Society* 55(3): 405–428

McMichael, P. (2009) 'A Food Regime Analysis of the "World Food Crisis"' *Agriculture and Human Values* 26(4): 281–295.

Meah, A. (2014) 'Still Blaming the Consumer? Geographies of Responsibility in Domestic Food Safety Practices' *Critical Public Health* 24(1): 88–103.

Meah, A. and Jackson, P. (2013) 'Crowded Kitchens: The "Democratization" of Domesticity' *Gender, Place & Culture*, 20(5): 578–596.

Meah, A. and Jackson, P. (2017) 'Convenience as Care: Culinary Antinomies in Practice' *Environment and Planning A*, 49(9): 2065–2081.

Meah, A. and Watson, M. (2011) 'Saints and Slackers: Challenging Discourses About the Decline of Domestic Cooking' *Sociological Research Online* 16(2):6 Available at: www.socresonline.org.uk/16/2/6.html.

Meier, A. and Musick, K. (2014) 'Variation in Associations between Family Dinners and Adolescent Well-being' *Journal of Marriage and the Family* 76(1): 13–23.

Melosi, M.V. (1981) 'Waste Management: The Cleaning of America' *Environment: Science and Policy for Sustainable Development* 23(8): 6–44.

Mennell, S. (1985) *All Manners of Food. Eating and Taste in England and France from the Middle Ages to the Present* Chicago: University of Illinois Press.

Mennell, S., Murcott, A. and van Otterloo. A. H. (1992) 'The Sociology of Food, Eating, Diet and Culture' London: Sage.

Merton, R.K. (1987) 'The Focused Interview and Focus Groups: Continuities and Discontinuities' *The Public Opinion Quarterly* 51(4): 550–566.

Mestdag, I. (2005) 'Disappearance of the Traditional Meal: Temporal, Social and Spatial Destructuration' *Appetite* 45(1): 62–74.

Mestdag, I. and Glorieux, I. (2009) 'Change and Stability in Commensality Patterns: A Comparative Analysis of Belgian Time-use Data from 1966, 1999 and 2004' *The Sociological Review* 57(4): 703–726.

Mestdag, I. and Vandeweyer, J. (2005) 'Where Has the Family Time Gone? In Search of Joint Family Activities and the Role of the Family Meal in 1966 and 1999' *Journal of Family History* 30(3): 304–323.

Midgley, J. L. (2013) 'Food (In)Security in the Global "North" and "South"' *in* Murcott, A., Belasco, W. and Jackson, P. (eds) *The Handbook of Food Research* London: Bloomsbury.

Miller, D. (1998) *A Theory of Shopping* Cambridge: Polity Press.

Miller, D. and Harkins, C. (2010) 'Corporate Strategy, Corporate Capture: Food and Alcohol Industry Lobbying and Public Health' *Critical Social Policy* 30(4): 564–589.

Miller, D.P., Waldfogel, J. and Wen-Jui, H. (2012) 'Family Meals and Child Academic and Behavioral Outcomes' *Child Development* 83(6): 2104–2120.

Mills, C.W. (1959) *The Sociological Imagination.* New York: Oxford University Press.

Mintz, S.W. (1985) *Sweetness and Power: The Place of Sugar in Modern History* London: Penguin.

Mintz, S. W. (2008) 'Afterword' *Ethnology* 47(2/3): 129–135.

Mintz, S.W. (2013) 'Eating American' *in* Counihan, C. (ed.) *Food in the USA* New York: Routledge.

Moisio, R., Arnould, E. J. and Price, L.L. (2004) 'Between Mothers and Markets: Constructing Family Identity through Homemade Food' *Journal of Consumer Culture* 4(3): 361–384.

Monaghan, L. (2008) *Men and the War on Obesity* London: Routledge.

Morgan, D.H.G. (2011) 'Locating "Family Practices"' *Sociological Research Online*, 16(4): 14. Available at: journals.sagepub.com/doi/abs/10.5153/sro.2535.

Morgan, K. (2006) 'School Food and the Public Domain: The Politics of the Public Plate' *The Political Quarterly*, 77(3): 379–387.

Morgan, K. and Sonnino, R. (2006) 'Empowering Consumers: The Creative Procurement of School Meals in Italy and the UK' *International Journal of Consumer Studies*, 31(1): 19–25.

Morgan, K., Marsden, T. and Murdoch, J. (2006) 'Networks, Conventions and Regions: Theorizing "Worlds of Food"' *Place, Power and Provenance in the Food Chain*. Oxford: Oxford University Press.

Muniesa, F., Millo, Y. and Callon, M. (2007) An Introduction to Market Devices. *The Sociological Review*, 55(s2): 1–12.

Muñoz, C. L. and Wood, N. T. (2009) 'A Recipe for Success: Understanding Regional Perceptions of Authenticity in Themed Restaurants' *International Journal of Culture, Tourism and Hospitality Research* 3(3): 269–280.

Murcott, Anne (1982) 'On the Social Significance of the "Cooked Dinner" in South Wales' *Social Science Information* 21(4/5): 677–695.

Murcott, Anne (1983a) (ed.) *The Sociology of Food and Eating: Essays on the Sociological Significance of Food* Aldershot, Hants: Gower.

Murcott, Anne (1983b) 'It's a pleasure to cook for him . . .': Food, Mealtimes and Gender in some South Wales Households' *in* Gamarnikow, E., Morgan, D., Purvis, J., and Taylorson, D. (eds) *The Public and the Private* London: Heinemann.

Murcott, Anne (1983c) 'Women's Place: Cookbooks' Images of Technique and Technology in the British Kitchen' *Women's Studies International Forum* 6(2): 33–39.

Murcott, Anne (1983d) 'Cooking and the Cooked' *in* Anne Murcott (ed.) *The Sociology of Food and Eating* London: Gower.

Murcott, Anne (1986) 'Opening the "Black Box": Food, Eating and Household Relationships' *Sosioaaliliaaketieteellinen Aikakauslehti* Vuosikerta 23(2): 85–92.

Murcott, Anne (1988a) 'Sociological and Social Anthropological Approaches to Food and Eating' *World Review of Nutrition and Dietetics* 55: 1–40.

Murcott, Anne (1988b) 'On the Altered Appetites of Pregnancy' *The Sociological Review* 36(4): 733–64.

Murcott, Anne (1993) 'Talking of Good Food: An Empirical Study of Women's Conceptualisations' *Food and Foodways* 5: 305–318.

Murcott, Anne (1994) 'Food and Nutrition in Post-war Britain' *in* Jim Obelkevich and Peter Caterall (eds) *Understanding Post-War British Society* London: Routledge.

Murcott, Anne (1996) 'Food as an Expression of National Identity' *in* Sverker Gustavsson and Leif Lewin (eds) *The Future of the Nation State: Essays on Cultural Pluralism and Political Integration* Stockholm, Sweden: Nerenius & Santérus.

Murcott, Anne (1997) 'Family Meals: A Thing of the Past?' *in* Caplan, P. (ed.) *Food, Health and Identity* London: Routledge.

Murcott, Anne (1999a) '"Not science but PR": GM Food and the Makings of a Considered Sociology' *Sociological ResearchOnline* 4(3) September. Available at: www.socresonline.org.uk/socresonline/–1999/1/murcott.html.

Murcott, Anne (1999b) '"The Nation's Diet" and the Policy Contexts' *in* John Germov and Lauren Williams (eds) *The Social Appetite: An Introduction to the Sociology of Food & Nutrition* Sydney: Oxford University Press.

Murcott, Anne (2001) 'Public Beliefs about GM Foods: More on the Makings of a Considered Sociology' *Medical Anthropology Quarterly* March 15(1): 1–11.

Murcott, Anne (2002) 'Nutrition and Inequalities: A Note on Sociological Approaches' *European Journal of Public Health* 12(3): 203–7.

References

Murcott, Anne (2011) 'Family Meal' *in* Southerton, Dale (ed.) *Encyclopedia of Consumer Culture* New York: Sage. pp 576–578.

Murcott, Anne (2012a) 'Lamenting the 'Decline of the Family Meal' as a Moral Panic?: Methodological Reflections' *Recherches sociologiques et anthropologiques* 43(1): 97–118 special issue on Moral Panics (ed Jean Michel Chaumont).

Murcott, A. (2012b) 'Book Review: Douglas Harper and Patrizia Faccioli, *The Italian Way: Food and Social Life*' *Sociology* 46(2): 379–380

Murcott, A. (2013a) 'A Burgeoning Field: Introduction to *The Handbook of Food Research*' *in* Murcott, A., Belasco, W. and Jackson, P. (eds) *The Handbook of Food Research* London: Bloomsbury.

Murcott, A. (2013b) 'Interlude: Reflections on the Elusiveness of Eating' *in* Abbots, E.-J. and Lavis, A. (eds) *Why We Eat, How We Eat: Contemporary Encounters between Food and Bodies* Farnham, Surrey: Ashgate.

Murcott, A. (2013c) 'Models of Food and Eating in the United Kingdom' *Gastronomica* 13(3): 32–41.

Murcott, A. (2018) 'Redressing the Balance: Towards Reintroducing Materiality, the Case of Food Packaging' Keynote address. Tours: Fourth International Convention on Food History and Food Studies, June.

Murphy, E. (1999) '"Breast is Best": Infant Feeding Decisions and Maternal Deviance' *Sociology of Health & Illness* 21(2): 187–208.

Murphy, E. (2000) 'Risk, Responsibility, and Rhetoric in Infant Feeding' *Journal of Contemporary Ethnography* 29(3) 291–325.

Murphy, E. (2003) 'Expertise and Forms of Knowledge in the Government of Families' *The Sociological Review* 51(4): 433–462

Murphy, E. (2004) Anticipatory Accounts *Symbolic Interaction* 27(2): 129–154.

Musick, K. and Meier, A. (2012) 'Assessing Causality and Persistence in Associations between Family Dinners and Adolescent Well-being' *Journal of Marriage and the Family* 74(3): 476–493.

Nestle, M. (2002) *Food Politics* Berkeley, CA: University of California Press.

Neuman, N., Gottzén, L. and Fjellström, C. (2016) 'Masculinity and the Sociality of Cooking in Men's Everyday Lives' *The Sociological Review* 65(4) 816–831.

Neumark-Sztainer D. et al (2010) 'Family Meals and Adolescents: What Have we Learned from Project EAT (Eating Among Teens)?' *Public Health Nutrition* 13: 1113–1121.

O'Brien, M. (2008) *A Crisis of Waste?* Abingdon: Routledge.

O'Connell, R. and Brannen, J. (2016) *Food, Families and Work* London: Bloomsbury.

Ochs, E., Pontecorvo, C. and Fasulo, A. (1995) 'Socializing Taste' *Ethnos* 60(3–4): 7–36.

Oddy, D.J. (2003) *From Plain Fare to Fusion Food: British Diet from the 1890s to the 1990s* Suffolk: Boydell Press.

Oddy, D.J. (2007) 'Food Quality in London and the Rise of the Public Analyst 1870–1939' *in* Atkins, P.J, Lummel, P. and Oddy D.J. (eds) *Food and the City in Europe since 1800* Aldershot, Hants: Ashgate.

Orr, J.B. (1966) *As I recall: the 1880's to the 1960's* London: MacGibbon and Kee.

Oswoski, C.P., Göranzon, H. & Fjellström, C. (2010) 'Perceptions and Memories of the Free School Meal in Sweden' *Food Culture & Society* 13(4): 555–572.

Pacyga, D.A. (2015) *Slaughterhouse: Chicago's Union Stock Yard and the World it Made* Chicago: University of Chicago Press.

Paddock, J., Warde, A. and Whillans, J. (2017) 'The Changing Meaning of Eating Out in Three English Cities 1995-2015' *Appetite* 119: 5–13.

Padel, S. and Foster, D. (2005) 'Exploring the Gap between Attitudes and Behaviour: Understanding why Consumers Buy or Do Not Buy Organic Food' *British Food Journal* 107(8): 606–625.

Panayi, P. (2008) *Spicing up Britain: The Multicultural History of British Food*. London: Reaktion Books.

Park, C. (2004) 'Efficient or Enjoyable? Consumer Values of Eating-out and Fast Food Restaurant Consumption in Korea' *Hospitality Management* 23(1) 87–94.

Park, J. (1991) *Ladies a Plate: Change and Continuity in the Lives of New Zealand Women* Auckland: Auckland University Press.

Parratt, C.M. (2001) *More Than Mere Amusement: Working-class Women's Leisure in England, 1750–1914* Boston: Northeastern University Press.

Parsons, J.M. (2015a) '"Good" Food as Family Medicine: Problems of Dualist and Absolutist Approaches to "Healthy" Family Foodways' *Food Studies: An Interdisciplinary Journal* 4(2): 1–13.

Parsons, J.M. (2015b) *Gender, Class and Food: Families, Bodies and Health* Basingstoke: Palgrave Macmillan.

Parsons, J.M. (2016) 'When Convenience is Inconvenient: "Healthy" Family Foodways and the Persistent Intersectionalities of Gender and Class' *Journal of Gender Studies*, 25(4): 382–397.

Patel, R. and McMichael, P. (2014) 'A Political Economy of the Food Riot' *in* Pritchard, D. and Pakes. F. (eds) *Riot, Unrest and Protest on the Global Stage* Basingstoke: Palgrave Macmillan.

Paules, G.F. (1991) *Dishing it Out: Power and Resistance among Waitresses in a New Jersey Restaurant* Philadelphia: Temple University Press.

Paulson-Box, E. and Williamson, P. (1990) 'The Development of the Ethnic Food Market in the UK' *British Food Journal* 92(2): 10–15.

Pember Reeves, M. (1979 [1913]) *Round About a Pound a Week* London: Virago.

Pennell, S. (2016) *The Birth of the English Kitchen, 1600–1850* London: Bloomsbury Publishing.

Perks, R. and Thomson, A. (eds) (2016) *The Oral History Reader*. London: Routledge (3rd edn).

Petrick, G. M. (2011) '"Purity as Life"': H.J. Heinz, Religious Sentiment, and the Beginning of the Industrial Diet' *History and Technology* 27(1): 37–64.

Petrini, C. (2001) *Slow Food: Collected Thoughts on Taste, Tradition and the Honest Pleasures of Food* Chelsea, VT: Chelsea Green Publishing.

Physician Task Force on Hunger in America (1985) *Hunger in America: The Growing Epidemic* Middletown, CT: Wesleyan University Press.

Pinch, T.J. and Bijker, W.E. (1987) 'The Social Construction of Facts and Artifacts: Or how the Sociology of Science and the Sociology of Technology Might Benefit Each Other' *in* Bijker, W.E., Hughes, T.P. and Pinch, T.J. (eds) *The Social Constructions of Technological Systems: New Directions in the Sociology and History of Technology* Cambridge, MA: The MIT Press.

Poe, T.N. (2001) 'The Labour and Leisure of Food Production as a Mode of Ethnic Identity Building Among Italians in Chicago, 1890–1940' *Rethinking History* 5(1): 131–148.

Pollan, F. and Fisher, M. (2014) 'Why Behavioural Health Promotion Endures Despite its Failure to Reduce Health Inequities' *Sociology of Health & Illness* 36(2): 213–225.

Pollan, M. (2009) 'Out of the Kitchen, Onto the Couch' *New York Times* Magazine. Available at: www.nytimes.com/2009/08/02/magazine/02cooking-t.html (last accessed 17 November 2017).

Poppendieck, J.E. (1985) 'Policy, Advocacy, and Justice: The Case of Food Assistance Reform' *Toward Social and Economic Justice* 101–131.

Poppendieck, J.E. (1998) *Sweet Charity? Emergency Food and the End of Entitlement* New York City: Viking.

Poppendieck, J. (2010) *Free for All: Fixing School Food in America* Berkeley, CA: University of California Press.

Ponte, S. (2009) 'Quality Conventions and Governance in the Wine Trade: A Global Value Chain Approach' in Inglis, D. and Gimlin, D. (eds) *The Globalization of Food* Oxford: Berg.

Poti, J.M. and Popkin B.M. (2011) 'Trends in Energy Intake among US Children by Eating Location and Food Source, 1977–2006' *Journal of the American Dietetic Association* 111(8): 1156–1164.

References

Pottier, J. (1999) *Anthropology of Food: The Social Dynamics of Food Security* Cambridge: Polity.

Poulain J.P. (2002) 'The Contemporary Diet in France: "De-structuration" or from Commensalism to "Vagabond Feeding"' *Appetite* 39(1): 43–55.

Pratt, J. (1999) 'Norbert Elias and the Civilized Prison' *The British Journal of Sociology* 50(2): 271–296.

Pritchard, B. (2013) 'Food Chains' *in* Murcott, A. Belasco, W. and Jackson, P. (eds) *The Handbook of Food Research* London: Bloomsbury.

Purdam, K., Garratt, E.A. and Esmail, A. (2016) 'Hungry? Food Insecurity, Social Stigma and Embarrassment in the UK' *Sociology*, 50(6): 1072–1088.

Rathje, W. and Murphy, C. (1992) *Rubbish! The Archaeology of Garbage* New York: HarperCollins.

Ray, K. (2004) *The Migrants' Table: Meals and Memories in Bengali-American Households* Philadelphia: Temple University Press.

Ray, K. (2013) 'Food and identity' *in* Murcott, A. Belasco, W. and Jackson, P. (eds) *The Handbook of Food Research* London: Bloomsbury Publishing.

Ray, K. (2016) *The Ethnic Restaurateur*. London: Bloomsbury Publishing.

Redclift, M. (2004) *Chewing Gum: The Fortunes of Taste* London: Routledge.

Renne, E.P. (2007) 'Mass Producing Food Traditions for West Africans Abroad' *American Anthropologist* 109(4): 616–625.

Richards, A.I. and Land, L. (1939) *Diet in Northern Rhodesia. An Economic Study of the Bemba Tribe* Oxford: Oxford University Press.

Richards, G. (2002) 'Gastronomy: An Essential Ingredient in Tourism Production and Consumption?' *in* Richards, G. and Hjalager, A. (eds) *Tourism and Gastronomy* London: Routledge.

Roberts, G.H. (2014) 'Message on a Bottle: Packaging the Great Russian Past' *Consumption Markets & Culture* 17(3): 295–313.

Roberts, R. (1971) *The Classic Slum: Salford Life in the First Quarter of the Century* Manchester: Manchester University Press.

Robertson, G.L. (2005) *Food Packaging: Principles and Practice* Boca Raton, FL: CRC Press.

Roe, E.J. (2006) 'Things Becoming Food and the Embodied, Material Practices of an Organic Food Consumer' *Sociologia Ruralis* 46(2): 104–121.

Rogers, D. (2005) 'Moonshine, Money, and the Politics of Liquidity in Rural Russia' *American Ethnologist* 32(1): 63–81.

Roos, E. et al (1998) 'Gender, Socioeconomic Status and Family Status as Determinants of Food Behaviour' *Social Science & Medicine* 46(12): 1519–1529.

Roos, G. et al (2001) 'Disparities in Vegetable and Fruit Consumption: European Cases from the North to the South' *Public Health Nutrition* 4(1): 35–43.

Rose, G. (2001) 'Sick Individuals and Sick Populations' *International Journal of Epidemiology* 30(3): 427–432.

Rotenberg, R. (1981) 'The Impact of Industrialization on Meal Patterns in Vienna, Austria' *Ecology of Food and Nutrition* 11(1): 25–35.

Rowntree, B.S. (1901) *Poverty: A Study of Town Life* London: Macmillan.

Rozin, P. et al (2006) 'Attitudes Towards Large Numbers of Choices in the Food Domain: A Cross-cultural Study of Five Countries in Europe and the USA' *Appetite* 46(3): 304–308.

Rundh, B. (2013) 'Linking Packaging to Marketing: How Packaging is Influencing the Marketing Strategy' *British Food Journal* 115(11): 1547–1563.

Saarikangas, K. (2006) 'Displays of the Everyday. Relations between Gender and the Visibility of Domestic Work in the Modern Finnish Kitchen from the 1930s to the 1950s' *Gender, Place and Culture* 13(2): 161–172.

Sachs, C. et al (2014) 'Front and Back of the House: Socio-spatial Inequalities in Food Work' *Agriculture and Human Values* 31(1): 3–17.

Sampson, H. (2005) 'Left High and Dry? The Lives of Women Married to Seafarers in Goa and Mumbai' *Ethnography* 6(1): 61–85.

Sandgren, F. (2009) 'From "Peculiar Stores" to "a New Way of Thinking": Discussions on Self-service in Swedish Trade Journals 1935–1955' *Business History* 51(5): 734–753.

Saumarez-Smith, C. (2000) *The Rise of Design: Design and Domestic Interior in Eighteenth-Century England* London: Pimlico.

Schanes, K., Dobernig, K., and Gözet, B. (2018) 'Food Waste Matters – A Systematic Review of Household Food Waste Practices and their Policy Implications' *Journal of Cleaner Production* 182: 978–991.

Schermuly, A.C. and Forbes-Mewett, H. (2016) 'Food, Identity and Belonging: A Case Study of South African-Australians' *British Food Journal* 118(10): 2434–2443.

Schmidt, J. (2007) 'How to Feed Three Million Inhabitants: Berlin in the First Years after the Second World War, 1945–1948' *in* Atkins, P.J., Lummel, P. and Oddy, D.J. (eds) *Food and the City in Europe since 1800* Aldershot: Ashgate.

Scholliers, P. (2007) 'Novelty and Tradition. The New Landscape for Gastronomy' *in* Freedman, P. (ed.) *Food. The History of Taste* Berkeley: University of California Press.

Scholliers, P. (2014) 'Constructing New Expertise: Private and Public Initiatives for Safe Food' *Medical History* 58(4): 546–563.

Scholliers, P. (2015) 'Convenience Foods. What, Why, and When' *Appetite* 94: 2–6.

Scola, R. (1992) *Feeding the Victorian City: The Food Supply of Manchester, 1770–1870* Manchester: Manchester University Press.

Shahaduz, Z., Nasima, S. and Joarder, T. (2013) 'McDonaldization without a McDonald's' *Food Culture & Society* 16(4): 551–568.

Shapiro, L. (1986) *Perfection Salad: Women and Cooking at the Turn of the Century* Berkeley: University of California Press.

Shapiro, L. (2004) *Something from the Oven* New York: Penguin Books.

Sheely, M. (2008) 'Global Adoption of Convenience Foods' *American Journal of Agricultural Economics* 90(5): 1356–1365.

Short, F. (2006) *Kitchen Secrets: The Meaning of Cooking in Everyday Life* Oxford: Berg.

Shove, E. (2010) 'Beyond the ABC: Climate Change Policy and Theories of Social Change' *Environment and Planning A*, 42(6), 1273–1285.

Sidenvall, B., Nydahl, M. and Fjellström, C. (2000) 'The Meal as a Gift – The Meaning of Cooking among Retired Women' *Journal of Applied Gerontology* 19(4): 405–423.

Silva, E.B. (2000) *The Politics of Consumption at Home: Practices and Dispositions in the Uses of Technologies* Pavis Centre for Social and Cultural Research.

Silva, E.B. (2002) 'Time and Emotion in Studies of Household Technologies' *Work, Employment and Society* 16(2): 329–340.

Simpson, T. (2008) 'The Commercialization of Macau's Cafés' *Ethnography* 9(2): 197–234.

Sims, R. (2009) 'Food, Place and Authenticity: Local Food and the Sustainable Tourism Experience' *Journal of Sustainable Tourism* 17(3): 321–336.

Skafida, V. (2013) 'The Family Meal Panacea: Exploring How Different Aspects of Family Meal Occurrence, Meal Habits And Meal Enjoyment Relate to Young Children's Diets' *Sociology of Health & Illness* 35(6) 906–923.

Slater, J.M. (ed.) (1991) *Fifty Years of the National Food Survey 1940–1990* London: HMSO.

Slocum, R. (2006) 'Anti-racist Practice and the Work of Community Food Organizations' *Antipode*, 38(2): 327–349.

Slocum, R. et al (2011) '"Properly, with Love, from Scratch" Jamie Oliver's Food Revolution' *Radical History Review* 110: 178–191.

Smith, D.E. (2005) *Institutional Ethnography: A Sociology for People* Lanham, MD: Rowman Altamira.

Smith, F.B. (1979) *The People's Health 1830–1910* New York: Holmes and Meier.

Smith, G.D., Bartley, M. and Blane, D. (1990) 'The Black Report on Socioeconomic Inequalities in Health 10 Years on' *British Medical Journal* 301(6748): 373–377.

References

Smith, G.D. et al (2002) 'Health Inequalities in Britain: Continuing Increases up to the End of the 20th Century' *Journal of Epidemiology & Community Health* 56(6): 434–435.

Smith, J. and Jehlička, P. (2007) 'Stories Around Food, Politics and Change in Poland and the Czech Republic' *Transactions of the Institute of British Geographers* 32(3): 395–410.

Smith-Howard, K. (2014) *Pure and Modern Milk* Oxford: Oxford University Press.

Smoyer, A.B. and Blankenship, K.M. (2014) 'Dealing Food: Female Drug Users' Narratives about Food in a Prison Place and Implications for their Health' *International Journal of Drug Policy* 25(3): 562–568.

Sobal, J. (2000) 'Sociability and Meals: Facilitation, Commensality, and Interaction' *in* Meiselman, H.L. (ed.) (2000) *Dimensions of the Meal: The Science, Culture, Business and Art of Eating* New York: Aspen Publishers.

Spang, R.L. (2001) *The Invention of the Restaurant: Paris and Modern Gastronomic Culture* London: Harvard University Press.

Spencer, C. (2004) *British Food – An Extraordinary Thousand Years of History* London: Grub Street.

Staples, James (2018) Personal communication.

Stephen, J.L., Comar, D. and Govenlock, D. L. (1999a) 'A National Australian Food Safety Telephone Survey' *Journal of Food Protection* 62(8): 921–928.

Stephen, J.L., Comar, D. and Govenlock, D. L. (1999b) 'A Video Study of Australian Domestic Food-Handling Practices' *Journal of Food Protection* 62(11): 1243–1357.

Stobart, J. (2012) *Sugar and Spice: Grocers and Groceries in Provincial England, 1650–1830* Oxford: Oxford University Press.

Stock, P.V., Phillips, C., Campbell, H. and Murcott, A. (2016) 'Eating the Unthinkable: The Case of ENTO, Eating Insects and Bioeconomic Experimentation' *in* Le Heron et al (eds) *Biological Economies: Experimentation and the Politics of Agrifood Frontiers* London: Routledge/Taylor & Francis.

Strasser, S. (1989) *Satisfaction Guaranteed: The Making of the American Mass Market* New York City: Pantheon Books.

Stuart, T. (2009) *Waste: Uncovering the Global Food Scandal* New York City: W W Norton & Company.

Sudbury-Riley, L. (2014) 'Unwrapping Senior Consumers' Packaging Experiences' *Journal of Marketing Intelligence & Planning*, 32(6): 666–686.

Sutton, D.E. (2014) *Secrets from the Greek Kitchen: Cooking, Skill, and Everyday Life on an Aegean Island* Oakland, CA: University of California Press.

Symons, M. (1984) *One Continuous Picnic: A History of Eating in Australia* Victoria, Aus: Penguin Books.

Symons, M. (1994) 'Simmel's Gastronomic Sociology: An Overlooked Essay' *Food and Foodways* 5(4): 333–351.

Szabo, M. (2011) 'The Challenges of "Re-engaging with Food"' Connecting Employment, Household Patterns and Gender Relations to Convenience Food Consumption in North America' *Food, Culture and Society* 14(4): 547–566.

Szreter, S. (2004) 'Health, Economy, State and Society in Modern Britain: The Long-run Perspective' *Hygiea Internationalis*, 4(1): 205–227.

Testart, A. et al (1982) 'The Significance of Food Storage Among Hunter-gatherers: Residence Patterns, Population Densities, and Social Inequalities [and Comments and Reply]' *Current Anthropology* 23(5): 523–537.

Thane, P. (2011) *Happy Families? History and Family Policy* London: The British Academy.

Thompson, C. et al (2016) 'Contrasting Approaches to "Doing" Family Meals: A Qualitative Study of How Parents Frame Children's Food Preferences' *Critical Public Health* 26(3): 322–332.

Thompson, E.P. (1971) 'The Moral Economy of the English Crowd in the Eighteenth Century' *Past & Present* (50): 76–136.

Thongcheen, K. and Jarupan, L. (2014) Optimal Practicable Environmental Model for Canned Tuna Products. *in Proceedings of the 9th International Conference on Life Cycle Assessment in the Agri-Food Sector (LCA Food 2014), San Francisco, California, USA, 8–10 October, 2014* American Center for Life Cycle Assessment: 1315–1321.

Thorne, S. (1986) *The History of Food Preservation* Totowa, NJ: Barnes & Noble Books.

Todd, S. (2014) *The People: The Rise and Fall of the Working Class, 1910–2010* London: Hachette.

Townsend, P. (1979) *Poverty in the United Kingdom: A Survey of Household Resources and Standards of Living* London: Allen Lane.

Trabsky, M. (2014) 'Institutionalising the Public Abattoir in Nineteenth Century Colonial Society' *Australian Feminist Law Journal* 40: 169–184.

Travers, K.D. (1997) 'Nutrition Education for Social Change: Critical Perspective' *Journal of Nutrition Education and Behavior* 29(2): 57–62.

Tregear, A. (2003) 'From Stilton to Vimto: Using Food History to Re-think Typical Products in Rural Development' *Sociologia Ruralis* 43(2): 91–107.

Trentmann, F. (2006) 'The Modern Genealogy of the Consumer: Meanings, Identities and Political Synapses' *in* Brewer, J. and Trentmann, F. *Consuming Cultures, Global Perspectives: Historical Trajectories, Transnational Exchanges* London: Bloomsbury

Trow, M. (1957) 'Comment on "Participant observation and interviewing: a comparison"' *Human Organisation* 16: 33–35.

Tuomainen, H. (2014) 'Eating Alone or Together? Commensality among Ghanaians in London' *Anthropology of Food* (S10). Available at: https://journals.openedition.org/aof/7718.

Turgeon, L. and Pastinelli, M. (2002) '"Eat the World": Postcolonial Encounters in Quebec City's Ethnic Restaurants' *Journal of American Folklore*, 115(456): 247–268.

Turnbull, C. (1972) *Mountain People* London: Jonathan Cape.

Turner, K.L. (2014) *How the Other Half Ate* Berkeley: University of California Press.

Ugelvik, T. (2011) 'The Hidden Food: Mealtime Resistance and Identity Work in a Norwegian Prison' *Punishment & Society* 13(1): 47–63.

Uttley, S. (1997) 'Hunger in New Zealand: A Question of Rights?' *in* Riches, G. (ed.) *First World Hunger* London: Palgrave Macmillan.

Valentine, G. and Longstaff, B. (1998) 'Doing Porridge: Food and Social Relations in a Male Prison' *Journal of Material Culture* 3(2): 131–152.

Van Caudenberg, A. and Heynen, H. (2004) 'The Rational Kitchen in the Interwar Period in Belgium: Discourses and Realities' *Home Cultures* 1(1):23–49.

Van den Berghe, P.L. (1984) 'Ethnic Cuisine: Culture in Nature' *Ethnic and Racial Studies* 7(3): 387–397.

van der Horst, H., Pascucci, S. and Bol, W. (2014) 'The "Dark Side" of Food Banks? Exploring Emotional Responses of Food Bank Receivers in the Netherlands' *British Food Journal* 116(9): 1506–1520.

van Huis, Arnold et al (2013) *Edible Insects: Future Prospects for Food and Feed Security* Rome: Food and Agriculture Organization of the United Nations. Available at: www.fao.org/docrep/018/i3253e/i3253e.pdf (last accessed 11 November 2016).

Vanhouche, A-S. (2015) 'Acceptance or Refusal of Convenience Food in Present-Day Prison' *Appetite* 94: 47–53.

Vernon, J. (2007) *Hunger, A Modern History* Cambridge MA: Harvard University Press.

Verriet, J. (2015) 'Convenience and the Hierarchy of Meal Preparation. Cooking and Domestic Education in the Netherlands 1910–1930' *Appetite* 94 7–12.

Vialles, N. (1994) *Animal to Edible* Cambridge: Cambridge University Press.

Videon, T.M. and Manning, C.K. (2003) 'Influences on Adolescent Eating Patterns: The Importance of Family Meals' *Journal of Adolescent Health* 32(5): 365–373.

Vijayan, G. et al (2014) 'Sustainability in Food Retail Industry Through Reverse Logistics' *International Journal of Supply Chain Management*, 3(2): 11–23.

References

Vuorisalo, T. (2004) '"It's War and Everyone Can Do as They Please!": An Environmental History of a Finnish City in Wartime' *Environmental History*, 9(4): 679–700.

Waddington, K. (2013) '"We Don't Want Any German Sausages Here!" Food, Fear, and the German Nation in Victorian and Edwardian Britain' *Journal of British Studies* 52(4): 1017–1042.

Wagner, D.R., Larson, J.N. and Wengreen, H. (2012) 'Weight and Body Composition Change over a Six-week Holiday Period' *Eating and Weight Disorders* 17(1): 54–6.

Wahlen, S. (2009) 'The Consumer Stuck Between a Rock of Victimhood and A Hard Place Called Responsibility: Political Discourses on the "Consumer" in Finnish and German Governmental Policy Documents' *International Journal of Consumer Studies* 33(4): 361–368.

Wahlen, S., van der Horst, H. and Pothoff, R. (2016) 'How Convenient!? Adolescents' Vistas on Food Competences in a Convenience Context' *British Food Journal* 118(11): 2828–2838.

Walton, J.K. (1992) *Fish and Chips, and the British Working Class, 1870–1940* London: Leicester University Press.

Wandel, M. et al (2008) 'Changes in Food Habits after Migration among South Asians Settled in Oslo' *Appetite* 50(2–3) 376–385.

Warde, A. (1997) *Consumption, Food and Taste* London: Sage.

Warde, A. (1999) 'Convenience Food: Space and Timing' *British Food Journal*, 101(7): 518–527

Warde, A. (2009) 'Imagining British Cuisine: Representations of Culinary Identity in the *Good Food Guide, 1951–2007*' *Food, Culture & Society*, 12(2): 151–171.

Warde, A. (2012) 'Eating' *in* Trentmann, F. (ed.) *The History of Consumption* Oxford: Oxford University Press.

Warde, A. (2014) 'After Taste: Culture, Consumption and Theories of Practice' *Journal of Consumer Culture* 14(3): 279–303.

Warde, A. (2016) *The Practice of Eating* Cambridge: Polity Press.

Warde, A. and Hetherington, K. (1994) 'English Households and Routine Food Practices: A Research Note' *The Sociological Review*, 42(4): 758–778.

Warde, A. and Martens, L. (2000) *Eating Out: Social Differentiation, Consumption and Pleasure* Cambridge: Cambridge University Press.

Warde, A. et al (2007) 'Changes in the Practice of Eating: A Comparative Analysis of Time-Use' *Acta Sociologica* 50(4): 363–385.

Watson, J.L. (2006) *Golden Arches East: McDonald's in East Asia* Stanford: Stanford University Press.

Watson, J.L. and Caldwell, M.L. (eds) (2005) 'Introduction' *in The Cultural Politics of Food and Eating: A Reader* Oxford: Blackwell.

Watson, M. and Meah, A. (2013) 'Food, Waste and Safety' *in* Evans, D., Campbell, H. and Murcott, A. (eds) *Waste Matters* Oxford: Wiley.

Weatherell, C., Tregear, A. and Allinson, J. (2003) 'In Search of the Concerned Consumer: UK Public Perceptions of Food, Farming, and Buying Local' *Journal of Rural Studies* 19(2): 233–244.

Weinreb, A. (2017) *Modern Hungers: Food and Power in Twentieth-century Germany*. Oxford: Oxford University Press.

Wessel, G. (2012) 'From Place to Nonplace: A Case Study of Social Media and Contemporary Food Trucks' *Journal of Urban Design* 17(4): 511–531.

Whiteford, M. (2010) 'Hot Tea, Dry Toast and the Responsibilisation of Homeless People' *Social Policy & Society* 9(2): 193–205.

Whyte, W.F., (1949) 'The Social Structure of the Restaurant' *American Journal of Sociology*, 54(4): 302–310.

Whyte, W.F. (1963) 'Human Relations in the Restaurant Industry' *Cornell Hotel and Restaurant Administration Quarterly* 4(3): 2–8.

Wiggins, S. (2004) 'Good for "You": Generic and Individual Healthy Eating Advice in Family Mealtimes' *Journal of Health Psychology* 9(4): 535–548.

Wiggins, S. 'Family Mealtimes, Yuckiness and the Socialization of Disgust Responses by Preschool Children' *in* Szatrowski, P.E. (ed.) *Language and Food: Verbal and Nonverbal Experiences* Philadelphia: John Benjamins Publishing Company.

Wilk, R.R. (1999) '"Real Belizean Food": Building Local Identity in the Transnational Caribbean' *American Anthropologist* 101(2): 244–255.

Wilk, R. (2006) 'Bottled Water: The Pure Commodity in the Age of Branding' *Journal of Consumer Culture* 6(3): 303–325.

Wilk, R., (2009) 'Anchovy Sauce and Pickled Tripe: Exporting Civilised Food in the Colonial Atlantic World' *in* Belasco, W. and Horowitz, R. (eds) *Food Chains: From Farmyard to Shopping Cart* Philadelphia: University of Pennsylvania Press.

Wilk, R. (2010) 'Power at the Table: Food Fights and Happy Meals' *Cultural Studies' Critical Methodologies* 10(6): 428–36.

Wilkins, J.L. (2005) 'Eating Right Here: Moving from Consumer to Food Citizen' *Agriculture and Human Values* 22(3): 269–273.

Willetts, A. (1997) 'Meat-eating and Vegetarianism in South-East London' *in* Caplan, P. (ed.) *Food, Health, and Identity* London: Routledge.

Williams, A. (1991) 'Historical Attitudes to Women Eating in Restaurants' *in Public Eating: Proceedings of the Oxford Symposium on Food and Cookery 1991*: 311–14.

Williams, J. (1997) 'We Never Eat Like This at Home: Food on Holiday' *in* Caplan, P (ed.) *Food, Health and Identity* London: Routledge

Williams, R. (2014) *Keywords: A Vocabulary of Culture and Society* Oxford: Oxford University Press.

Wills, A.B. (2003) 'Pilgrims and Progress: How Magazines Made Thanksgiving' *Church History* 72(1): 138–158.

Wills, W.J., Danesib, G. and Kapetanaki, A.B. (2016) 'Lunchtime Food and Drink Purchasing: Young People's Practices, Preferences and Power Within and Beyond the School Gate' *Cambridge Journal of Education* 46(2): 195–210.

Wills, W.J, Meah, A., Dickinson, A. and Short, F. (2013) 'Domestic Kitchen Practices: Findings from the "Kitchen Life" Study' London: Social Science Research Unit: Food Standards Agency.

Wills, W.J., Meah, A., Dickinson, A.M. and Short, F. (2015) '"I don't think I ever had food poisoning" A Practice-based Approach to Understanding Foodborne Disease that Originates in the Home' *Appetite* 85: 118–125.

Wood, R.C. (1995) *The Sociology of the Meal* Edinburgh: Edinburgh University Press.

Woronoff, D. (2015) *Histoire de l'emballage en France du XVIIIe siècle à nos jours.* Valenciennes: Presses Universitaires de Valenciennes.

Worsley, P. M. (1961) 'The Utilization of Natural Food Resources by an Australian Aboriginal Tribe' *Acta Ethnographica* 10: 153–190.

Wurgaft, B.A. (2006) 'Incensed: Food Smells and Ethnic Tension' *Gastronomica* 6(2): 57–60.

Wynne, B. (1995) 'Public Understanding of Science' *in* Jasanoff, S. et al (eds) *Handbook of Science and Technology Studies* London: Sage Publications.

Xun, Z. (2012) *Forgotten Voices of Mao's Great Famine, 1958–1962: An Oral History* New Haven: Yale University Press.

Yale, L. and Venkatesh, A. (1986) 'Toward the Construct of Convenience in Consumer Research' *Advances in Consumer Research* 13: 403–408.

Yan, Y. (2000) 'Of Hamburger and Social Space' *in* Davis, D. (ed.) *The Consumer Revolution in Urban China* Berkeley: University of California Press.

Zaman, S., Selim, N., and Joarder, T. (2013) 'McDonaldization without a McDonald's: Globalisation and Food Culture as Social Determinants of Health in Urban Bangladesh' *Food, Culture and Society* 16(4): 551–568.

Zdrodowski, D. (1996) 'Eating Out: The Experience of Eating in Public for the "Overweight" Woman' *Women's Studies International Forum* 19(6): 655–664.

References

Zelinsky, W. (1985) 'The Roving Palate: North America's Ethnic Restaurant Cuisines' *Geoforum* 16(1): 51–72.

Zimmet, P.Z. and James, W.P.T. (2006). 'The Unstoppable Australian Obesity and Diabetes Juggernaut. What Should Politicians Do?' *Medical Journal of Australia* 185(4): 187–188.

Zubaida, S. (2014) 'Drink, Meals and Social Boundaries' *in* Klein, J. A., and Murcott, A. (eds) *Food Consumption in Global Perspective: Essays in the Anthropology of Food in Honour of Jack Goody* Basingstoke: Palgrave Macmillan.

NAME INDEX

Name Index

Freidberg, S. 23
Friedmann, H. 142–143

Gabaccia, D.R. 78–79, 86, 109, 110–111, 121, 138
Garfinkel, H. 124–125, 175
Geertz, C. 24
Giddens, A. 13, 25, 115–116
Glasser, I. 153
Godderis, R. 72
Goffman, E. 57, 58, 69, 80, 120, 154
Goode, J. 153
Goody, J. 21–22
Graf, K. 167–168
Grignon, C. 47–48
Gubrium, J.F. 71, 73
Guthman, J. 12, 87, 119, 135, 165
Gvion, L. 118, 121

Halkier, B. 165
Halsey, A.H. 155
Hammersley, M. 40
Haukanes, H. 43
Hawkins, G. 105–107
Hayden, D. 61
Heaven, B. 73–74
Heldke, L. 111–112
Henderson, J. 159
Herbert, J. 83
Hierholzer, V. 161
Hine, T. 98, 104
Hochschild, A.R. 58
Holm, L. 18
Hull, E. 168

Inter-Departmental Committee on Physical
    Deterioration (1904) 77
Iversen, V. 47

Jackson, P. 33, 37–38, 85, 86, 91, 100, 127,
    177 n.6
Jahoda, M. 153, 154
Jakobsen, E. 169
Jellil, A. 147–148
Johnston, J. 13, 86, 109, 113, 114
Julier, A.P. 44, 46, 54, 56, 63

Kjaernes, U. 165–166
Kniazeva, M. 102–103
Koch, S. 166, 167, 168, 169–170
Koehn, N.F. 6, 104
Kopytoff, I. 105

Lanfranchi, M. 145
Laudan, R. 11–12
Levenstein, H. 11, 60, 86, 94
Levine, S. 76–77, 78

Lévi-Strauss, C. 21, 23
Lhuissier, A. 53
Littlejohn, J. 39–41
Liu, H. 113, 114, 117
Long, L. 17
Lópes-Azpiazu, I. 131–133
Lu, S. 120
Lynd, R.S. 38

Maes, E. 70–71
Mars, L. 34
Mason, J. 42
Matalas, A.L. 144
Maye-Banbury, A. 63–64, 73
Mayhew, H. 60
McIntosh, W.A. 46
McKenzie, L. 153
Mead, G.H. 120
Meah, A. 82, 88, 93
Melosi, M.V. 144
Mennell, S. 42, 113
Merton, R.K. 89
Midgley, J.L. 185 n.11
Miller, D. 136, 163
Mills, C.W. 13, 15, 86, 137, 173, 174
Mintz, S.W. 10, 22–23, 55, 117, 143, 167
Moisio, R. 48–49
Morgan, K. 76, 77, 78, 79, 162
Morrison, M. 72–73
Muniesa, F. 105
Murcott, A. 25, 35, 39, 41, 45, 98, 114, 130, 174
Murphy, E. 128–130, 135

National Center on Addiction and Substance
    Abuse (CASA) 30–32
Nestle, M. 163
Nicod, M. 21

O'Brien, M. 138
O'Connell, R. 46
Oddy, D.J. 10, 160
Orr, J.B. 77

Pacyga, D.A. 7
Paddock, J. 54–56
Panayi, P. 109, 119
Park, C. 53, 61
Park, J. 63
Parratt, C.M. 87
Parsons, J.M. 88, 135
Pember Reeves, M. 152, 154
Pennell, S. 90
Perks, R. 37
Petrini, C. 11, 83, 141
Physician Task Force on Hunger in America
    154

212

SUBJECT INDEX

Headings in italics are artworks, books or magazines. Page numbers followed by n. refer to notes.

Subject Index